Girlhood, Schools, and Media

This book explores the circulation and reception of popular discourses of achieving girlhood, and the ways in which girls themselves participate in such circulation. It examines the figure of the achieving girl within wider discourses of neoliberal self-management and post-feminist possibility, considering the tensions involved in being both successful and successfully feminine and the strategies and negotiations girls undertake to manage these tensions.

The work is grounded in an understanding of media, educational and peer contexts for the production of the successful girl. It traces narratives from school, television and online in texts produced for and by girls, drawing on interviews with girls in schools, online forum participation (within the purpose-built site www.smartgirls.tv) and girls' discussions of a range of teen dramas.

Michele Paule works as a Senior Lecturer in media, culture and education at Oxford Brookes University, UK. Her research interests focus on youth and gender in popular and educational contexts. She has published work on gendered learning myths and on girls and religion in media settings; as a former secondary school teacher she also published a range of work for teachers and for pupils. She is currently engaged in researching youth and the gendering of leadership in different European contexts.

Routledge Research in Cultural and Media Studies

For a full list of titles in this series, please visit www.routledge.com.

Girlhood, Schools, and Media
Popular Discourses of the Achieving Girl

Michele Paule

Routledge
Taylor & Francis Group

LONDON AND NEW YORK

First published 2017
by Routledge

2 Park Square, Milton Park, Abingdon, Oxfordshire OX14 4RN
52 Vanderbilt Avenue, New York, NY 10017

Routledge is an imprint of the Taylor & Francis Group, an informa business

First issued in paperback 2019

Library of Congress Cataloging-in-Publication Data

Names: Paule, Michele, author.
Title: Girlhood, schools, and media: popular discourses of the achieving
girl / by Michele Paule.
Description: New York: Routledge, 2016. | Series: Routledge research in
cultural and media studies; 93 | Includes bibliographical references and
index.
Identifiers: LCCN 2016016188
97813157330743 (ebk.)
Subjects: LCSH: Mass media and girls. | Girls in mass media. | Girls in
popular culture. | Sex differences in education.
Classification: LCC P94.5.G57 P38 2016 | DDC 305.23082—dc23
LC record available at https://lccn.loc.gov/2016016188

ISBN: 978-1-138-84006-5 (hbk)
ISBN: 978-0-367-87177-2 (pbk)

Typeset in Sabon
by codeMantra

To my mother Pauline Chennells, a smart woman whom I still miss every day, and also to my father Terence Allen-Miles whom I have just begun to miss.

Contents

Acknowledgements

Someone once told me that we generally end up researching who we are; as a former council-estate pupil at a selective school the experiences of my own girlhood and education were a constant presence to me throughout this work. The particular seed however was planted by a conversation with a teenage pupil when I was myself a secondary school teacher running an after-school film club; my first thanks therefore go to Lauren, who introduced me to some great teen TV shows and websites and told me what they meant to her. The ideas fermented for a while and some years later formed the basis of my PhD Thesis at Oxford Brookes University and I owe a great debt of thanks to friends and colleagues there, foremost to Professor Beverley Clack, for her unfailing support, guidance and generosity. The late Dee Amy-Chinn gave me early encouragement, especially to develop the website forum and Tom Tyler shared not only his insights into Foucault but his web design skills, while former student Kevin Carmody provided PHP expertise in customising the forum. I was exceptionally fortunate in my external examiners Pamela-Sue Anderson and Heather Mendick, both of whom continue to provide inspiration. Other colleagues deserve thanks including Linet Arthur, Chris Beck, Martin Groves, Juliet Henderson, Cyrus Mower, Jane Potter and Anne Price. The late Shameem Akhtar was an administrative mainstay and a dear friend, both to me and to the project.

I am deeply grateful to the staff and the girls at the participating schools and to the smartgirls.tv forum members for taking part in the research, for their time and enthusiasm and for the insights and stories they shared with me, and also to all those who helped promote the website. Their participation made this work possible. I should also express my gratitude to Leonie Miles, Holly Miles, Harriet Miles, Sophie Miles, Milly Bell, Katie Buntic and Iona Adair for their advice on the website design from a teenaged girl perspective; their input was invaluable in creating a space that other girls wanted to use. Laura Davison deserves particular appreciation for sitting through many hours of teen television with me.

My family tolerated my virtual disappearance during stages of this project but were always supportive, especially my sister Julia Miles and my aunts Janette Miles, June Shepherd and Valerie Thacker. My beloved father Terence Allen-Miles died just a week after I submitted the final MS; his pride and encouragement never failed even while his health did. Friends Juliette Adair, Sue Bell, Clare Buntic, Susan Crozier, Wendy Frost, Frances Hall and Denise Margetts all offered kindness and encouragement along the way. Finally, especial thanks go to Claire Mulgan for caring for the redoubtable Morris when I could not

Introduction

Something of a perfect storm of contingencies has created the conditions for the rise of the achieving girl in the popular imaginary. I began this study as a wave of interest in the 'smart girl' was building. What first attracted my attention was the ubiquitous alpha girl heroine of teen TV, juxtaposed with press celebration and simultaneous hand-wringing over girls' school success. As I began to look further, I found a myriad of parental guidebooks, girls' websites, policy documents and teacher advice exploring, advocating for, cautioning, selling to and attempting to ascribe meaning to the achieving girl. Even against a background of austerity politics and increasing precariousness in the West, her popular visibility is sustained as her manifestations become yet more widely distributed via celebrity advocacy, development economics, emerging online feminisms, 'YA' fiction and comic books.

McRobbie (2009, 26) argues that the conceptual 'girl' has come to occupy a culturally central position because she has been created as the focus of political and market forces which both map her path to success and regulate the means by and boundaries within which she can be or must be both 'successful' and 'successfully girl'. The conditions to which girls are apparently so well adapted to succeed are those of the wider social changes under late modernity and neoliberalism as described by Giddens (1991) and Beck (1992, 2002). Here it may be useful to include a brief and necessarily simplified definition of neoliberalism. I find Hall's (2011) justification of the continuing use of the term as an umbrella convincing, despite its inadequacy to render its complexities and geopolitical reach, as a political necessity to focus criticality and resistance. I therefore employ the term 'neoliberalism' to encompass both the theories and the economic practices that cast individual and entrepreneurial freedoms within unrestrained markets as the best route to socio-economic well-being. The role of the neoliberal state is only to ensure the proper freedom for markets to function, and to create markets in previously state-run institutions such as health and education (Harvey 2005). Neoliberalism casts the welfare state and its institutions' role as one of interference in the operation of free markets and as eroding the personal responsibility of individuals and the moral fibre of society (Hall 2011). Neoliberalism as both a specific approach to economics and an idea permeates every aspect of young women's lives, from the funding it provides (or not) for their educational, social and physical well-being, to the stories it spins for them of equal opportunities to thrive.

In these conditions, the certainties and structures provided by industrialised society in terms of class, employment and ascribed life courses have been replaced by new conditions of possibility and agency in which traditional barriers are dissolved and individuals themselves are responsible for their destinies. Such conditions are seen as contributing to a 'feminisation' of culture, in which qualities of flexibility, self-awareness, communication and diligence are valued (Adkins 2002). As conditions and discourses of austerity overtake those of economic optimism, the figure of the successful self-reflexive individual has paradoxically appeared more strongly entrenched; a pervasive 'rhetoric of blame' (McDowell 2012, 585) has become attached to disadvantage, and even while women and girls bear the brunt of the downturn, an investment in the can-do discourse of self-betterment persists among young women (Allen 2015; Mendick, Allen, and Harvey 2015).

In the neoliberal orthodoxy, with the lessening of formerly limiting determinants such as class and gender, identities and lives become personal projects constructed and consumed into being by the individual. Education is central to this process in its apparent ability to neutralise differences created by disadvantage and to reward merit in the aspiring individual (Goldthorpe and Jackson 2008). In the policies and practices of 'gifted' education in particular, discourses of meritocracy and aspiration take on particular vigour and produce some individuals as specifically gifted subjects. However, the unequal distribution of such identities draws attention to their production within wider structures of power and processes of social reproduction. Virtually unheard of terms in UK schools before 1999, 'gifted' and 'talented' provision, developed as a means of promoting social mobility and appealing to middle-class parents in state sector schools (Tomlinson 2008), formed a cornerstone of Tony Blair's New Labour government from 1997 onward (DfEE 1999), thus coinciding with the years in which girls began to overtake boys in national school tests. This study takes place in an era in which the vocabularies, practices and policies associated with gifted education have become embedded in UK schools, and have prompted interest among scholars seeking to understand the complex ways in which the discourses are enacted and achieving identities are managed in school settings.

At the same time, within the media we have seen the rise of what Gill (2007a) describes as a 'post-feminist sensibility'. One of the key features of this sensibility is the development of girls as the subjects rather than just the objects of popular texts, as their increased economic power brings them into the focus of the consumer media address. Gill argues that post-feminist media texts are characterised by 'an emphasis upon self-surveillance, monitoring and self-discipline; a focus on individualism, choice and empowerment; the dominance of a makeover paradigm; and a resurgence of ideas about natural sexual difference' (149). Here we see a close alignment with neoliberal and educational discourses of the aspiring, self-reflexive subject;

in fact, Gill suggests that neoliberalism is already gendered as female in the subjectivities it creates. This post-feminist media sensibility has developed in the context of deregulation of media industries and, within television, the growth in number of commercial channels chasing the most valuable niche audiences (Wee 2008). Accounts of the gendering of political economies of broadcasting find that girls – or girls with spending power – form a highly desirable audience category (Schofield Clarke 2003; Meehan 2002; Ross and Stein 2008). A proliferation of texts in which they are constructed as hyperfeminised consumers has contributed to the creation of new modes of highly visible girlhood. In these texts, new possibilities and freedoms available to girls are celebrated, while at the same time ideal forms of girlhood are represented in increasingly commoditised ways (Renold and Ringrose 2008; McRobbie 2009; Bullen 2015).

The rise of the successful girl has been closely observed by academics concerned to expose the limits of post-feminist optimism and neoliberal self-construction, and their promises of agency (Budgeon 2003; McRobbie 2009; Harris 2015). My study aligns with this purpose, and seeks to extend this body of work in the following ways: While distinct contemporary conditions have given rise to the achieving girl, they do not call forth entirely new forms of femininity. Newer discourses of choice and self-actualisation have not supplanted traditional femininities, but draw on and re-animate them. I am interested in the ways which contemporary accounts of gendered success rework historical restrictions, and in the resurfacing of anxieties associated with achieving girls and women. Such a tracing of historical patterns can illuminate ways in which current discourses arise from current contingencies (Adkins 2002). It enables the recognition of contemporary 'truths' as constructs, and of the processes by which such truths have come into general acceptance.

Further, I seek to understand not only the nature of prevailing institutional discourses of gender and achievement, but also how such discourses are taken up and recirculated by those identified or identifying as achieving or smart girls. I am particularly interested in the extent to which girls reproduce and rationalise structural inequalities and gendered restrictions, and in how institutional discourses provide tools for the expression of intelligibility for girls.

The Achieving Girl in the Discourse and the Discourse in the Achieving Girl

What do I mean by the 'achieving girl'? By this term I am not attempting to fix or universalise the category of 'achieving girl' in terms of age, biology or of any markers of 'ability', but to consider the discursive constructions of a particular kind of girlhood as rendered in diverse educational and media contexts. Whether on screen or off, the achieving girl is not a stable, unified category; as an object of knowledge and an experienced subjectivity she can be positioned variously along intersecting trajectories of age, class, ethnicity, sexuality and nationality. She is also differently produced in the different contexts of the study; in schools, the girls in the study are formally identified as 'gifted'. In UK schools this means that the student is considered to be in the top 5–10% of the school population academically. However, government and school policies and practices regarding the nature of the 'giftedness' present an ambiguous blend of innate, learned and developmental models underpinned by an assumption that ability is an inborn quality, evenly distributed if potentially masked by disadvantage, and realisable by good teaching and individual aspiration (Youdell 2004; Smithers and Robinson 2012); the girls further describe experiences of compliant behaviour ensuring placement on the register – or not. In the television and other media texts, the category encompasses those identified by the study's participants and by other scholars via a range of terms such as 'smart', 'achieving', 'alpha girls' and 'A1 girls', as well as the more marginal 'geek' girls. These TV girls are the product of the affluent West, mostly white and either privileged or aspiring to be so. I describe later (see Chapter 3) the relationship of the television 'successful girl' with heightened consumer femininities. 'Smart' was the preferred term of the participants both on- and offline, suggesting the international permeation of American discourses of success. The title of the website, www.smartgirls.tv, was suggested by the group of teenage girls I consulted in its construction. On the website, participants self-identified as smart girls and were drawn from a range of known contexts, such as UK schools and existing teen TV fan sites, and also some international and unknown contexts. Thus, the 'achieving girl' category of this study includes those produced by educational practices and media tropes and those who take up the subject position on the website forum.

A Multi-Site Enquiry

Educational and media sites are strongly associated with the production of discourses of gendered youth. This is hardly surprising given the key role of both in the reproduction of cultural values and ideologies, and in their centrality to the lives of young people (Hill 2006; Giroux 1994, 2009). Schools are popularly held to be sites of cultural feminisation as the diligence, compliance and aspiration they foster are seen to both typify and benefit girls (Jackson and Nyström 2015), frequently at the expense of the boys for whose failure their success is held responsible (Walkerdine 2003; Francis and Skelton 2005). Education is thus a key location for the production of girls as neoliberal subjects (Walkerdine 2003). Schools are also spaces in which identities connected with perceived ability are constructed, and also where broader cultural and popular gendered identities are enacted in local conditions.

Constructing a multi-site enquiry enables me to explore the ways in which educational discourses and subject positions circulate beyond school itself. Electronic and mass media are deeply implicated in the formation of adolescent subjectivities (Giroux 1994, 2009; Fisherkeller 1999, 2002; Buckingham 2008; Georgakopoulou 2014). Not only is television of particular importance in mediating teen identities heretofore rooted in traditional institutions and practices, but teen television genres need to be viewed 'in the context of contemporary culture's unresolved conflicts over teenage life in general' (Schofield Clarke 2003, 47).

Girls are an increasingly desirable target audience, but it is not just the proliferation of girl-focused texts that makes television a central site for enquiry. Television continues to occupy a central role in the lives and media engagements of young people, even while new conditions of consumption and audience practices emerge across digital platforms (Wartella and Robb 2008; Ofcom 2010, 2015). As Duits (2010, 245) points out, television does not stop when the viewing device is turned off. In fact, a range of online and offline practices extend the idea of 'audiencehood' into social realms; Thomas (2006, 126) observes that 'for children, there exists a seamlessness of life in, out and around technological spaces'. I focus on two particular audience contexts in this study: girls talking about their media experience in schools, and their discussion on a teen TV–focused web forum.

My rationale for building an online forum as well as conducting group interviews in schools is five-fold: As well as interviewing girls formally identified in school settings as achieving, I wanted to be able to access participants who self-identify as smart girls. Partly inspired by the proliferation and popularity of TV fan sites among teen girls, creating a website allows me to exploit conditions of media convergence and explore some methodological possibilities of digital platforms for qualitative research. The website also enables me to exploit the potential of the Internet for the expression of teen identities (Stern 2004a; Paechter 2013; Keller 2015). The creation of a space in which participants discuss similar questions to those in the school interviews invites consideration of the relationship between context and statements. Finally, I had an overt feminist purpose in that I wanted to provide one of those 'spaces for young women to critically and collectively examine changing discourses of femininity', which Gonick (2003, 15) advocates, without making the potentially damaging assumptions of vulnerability to which she is justly alert.

It is important to point out that this is not an examination of girls' online practices and identities per se, nor of public perceptions of such practices; that fast-changing and complex field is being fascinatingly documented elsewhere (see e.g. Ringrose et al. 2013; Dobson 2014; Busetta and Coladonato 2015; Keller 2015; Mascheroni et al. 2015). Rather, this study focuses on online and offline teen fan engagements as instances of successful girl discourses, and draws particularly on the more traditional medium of television, which still plays a central role in teen media consumption even while that consumption takes place in new platforms and contexts.

In her study on the ways in which girls grow up within television cultures, Fisherkeller (1999, 187) describes how adolescents 'have to start negotiating their sense of themselves as sexually reproductive beings and as workers in the economy – the core identities of adulthood'. The achieving girl carries the dual weight of these core gendered and classed identities; they are complex not only in themselves and in their relation to each other, but also in relation to other prevailing discourses. It is this complexity and interrelatedness that I seek to elucidate.

A Note on the Archaeology, Genealogy and Agency

Although I discuss Foucault's (1969) *The Archaeology of Knowledge* as an epistemological frame and research strategy in detail in Chapter 3, I would like to offer a brief rationale here for my choices in order to put the study in context.

In its blending of empirical enquiry and textual analysis, this interdisciplinary endeavour draws on work in the fields of education, cultural studies and audience studies. In considering girls as the 'audiences' of both the media and educational discourses by which they are interpellated (Althusser 1997), I am attempting to navigate between textual determinism, which assumes that texts are invariably read much as was intended by their makers, leaving little scope for either contradiction or variation among their interpreters, and 'active audience' models with their often optimistic assumptions of agency with regard to a text's hegemonic blandishments. I am interested in examining girls as both the subjects and the objects of knowledge produced by success discourses. To do this, I am constructing this enquiry upon the model of discourse analysis suggested by *The Archaeology of Knowledge* (Foucault 1969). This allows approach allows me to regard the statements and accounts produced by my research participants as texts in themselves rather than as truthful claims to lived experience (Hills 2005a). As such, they can be examined alongside popular, institutionally produced texts such as TV shows. This will enable an understanding not only of how knowledge of achieving girlhood may be produced and regulated by schools and by television, but also of how those occupying achieving girl subject positions participate in such regulation.

The *Archaeology* (Foucault 1969) involves new ways of looking at familiar notions – here of gender and achievement/ability – as part of a network forming a wider truth or system of knowledge, and questioning forms of knowledge that can be characterised as 'common sense'. It draws attention not only to their constructed nature and instability, but also to the wider relations of knowledge/power in which they are reproduced. For Foucault (1969), discourse determines what we perceive – by transforming familiar notions into discourse, we can begin to question the assumptions on which they are based, and look at them rather as the cultural products specific to a time and place. Foucault's terming of this approach as 'archaeology' is descriptive of its intent to create a history of the present through examining the objects which appear within a stratum of time, considering their nature and their relationship to each other and to what is known of their production. Discourses, however, do not spring into being fully formed to suit times and purposes. As Foucault (1969, 192) points out,

> The episteme is not a motionless figure that appeared one day with the mission of effacing all that preceded it: it is a constantly moving set of articulations, shifts, and coincidences that are established, only to give rise to others

I have therefore also drawn on Foucault's (1977) genealogical model in order to explore the historical bases of achieving girl discourses, and to illustrate how their assumptions and myths are reproduced in contemporary narratives. Foucault himself saw his archaeological and genealogical approaches as complementary (1981), with the archaeology involving the study of an 'historical slice' and the genealogy accounting for the 'historical process' of discourse (Kendall and Wickham 1999). A genealogical approach allows a consideration not just of the historical antecedents of contemporary discourses, but also of the contingencies for their emergence. In the *Archaeology of Knowledge*, Foucault advocates an exploration of discourses within such a specific historical moment in all its particularity (1969, 11).

For Foucault, subjectivity is produced within discursive relations of power. This involves a consideration of the subject's role in terms of her position in relation to dominant discourses, of the ways that they speak and are spoken by her, not as individualised responses but as positioned within a framework of culturally determined possibilities. It is such an exploration of the discursive production of a particular gendered object (that of achieving girl) within a specific historic moment (the early years of the twenty-first century) that forms the basis of this enquiry. This approach enables a challenge to the tenets of individual control and self-invention that are core to neoliberal vision, and provides tools for exposing the paradoxical and multi-layered nature of discursive limitation in the possibilities of girlhood.

The value of the archaeological approach then lies in its potential for realising the dispersal and reproduction of dominant discourses across diverse sites, as I demonstrate below. With its prescriptive view of the subject and limitation of agency, the *Archaeology of Knowledge* can provide a useful framework in key ways: I suggest that it can address concerns raised regarding the overcelebration of individual agency in the appropriation of meaning in mass-produced texts, which McRobbie (2009, 2) terms the 'vernacular features of resistance and opposition' and which has characterised much audience research of the previous two decades; it similarly avoids the 'reification' of media texts as sources of evidence (Jensen 2002a, 167). Further, it defines both discourse and approaches to its analysis as interdisciplinary, intertextual and distributed, thus offering possibilities for researching within contemporary convergence cultures of media proliferation, production and consumption (Jenkins 2006).

Gutting observes that the 'archaeology turns away from the subject and towards the conditions that define the discursive space in which speaking subjects exist' (1989, 244). The adoption of the archaeological epistemology may appear as an attempt to elide the issue of agency; such is not my intent. If, after Butler (1997), one conceives of agency as a property endowed by subjectification itself, then the achieving girl as constituted by the discourse must be allowed some power to recognise the conditions created for her and to manoeuvre within them. The discursive spaces for such manoeuvrings and the strategies employed by girls form a rich terrain for research, and have been the focus of significant studies of achieving girls (Archer 2005; Gonick 2005; Renold and Allan 2006; Skelton, Frances, and Read 2010; Allan 2010; Raby and Pomerantz 2015). However, in turning to the discourse itself, I aim to provide a different perspective and extend the scope of enquiry examining how educational and media discourses provide the structures for such subjectification, and the ways in which girls themselves participate in maintaining them.

1   The Future Girl's Problem Past

In his preface to the *Order of Things*, Foucault (1970) describes the need to examine not merely the contents of taxonomic categories, but also the boundaries which contain them, which determine their inclusion or exclusion and frame them in such a way as to make them intelligible. When embarking on this study, I began by considering the category of 'achieving girl' in this way. That is, it is not the empirical existence and properties of 'ability' or the highly achieving girl that are of interest, so much as the questions of how such a category exists, what kind of object becomes intelligible through such categorisation and what broader systems of knowledge/power are manifested through this taxonomisation.

One of my aims in undertaking this work was to gain a sense of where ideas about successful girlhood come from, and to provide an historical context for contemporary explorations of girlhood and schooling. Such a context extends critical consideration of the conditions in which ideas about contemporary girlhood are produced. It provides a platform for the challenging of 'novel' contemporary claims about gender through exposing their historical assumptions and cultural foundations. In this chapter, I aim to provide such a context through exploring ideas about gender and ability in the past across a range of fields of production – philosophic, artistic and scientific. I aim to demonstrate that the active categorisations and hierarchies of the present replicate those of the past. I employ Michèle Le Doeuff's (2003) heuristic of 'casting off' to identify which attributes are absorbed into masculine intellectual heritage and which cast off to women, and argue that similar categorisations are at work in the achieving girl discourse.

Foucault describes the purpose of genealogies as being to create a history of the present (1979, 30), and to oppose unitary discourses and 'the scientific hierarchisation of knowledge and its intrinsic power effects' (2003, 10). In undertaking such an operation. Le Doeuff (2003, 11) observes we are challenging the understanding of 'woman' as a stable and knowable object by turning our attention instead to the variable values and categories ascribed to gender. Le Doeuff is particularly concerned with the exclusion of women from philosophical and scientific endeavour, the privileging of masculinity as rational and the casting off to women of less valued intellectual attributes. She aims to uncover 'some aspects of a framework common to certain forms of institutionalised knowledge and everyday life', and recognises that this necessitates working with history to help 'to decipher the present'. This, she declares,

> demands scrutiny of the myths and images that regulate the relation-ships between the intellect and sex, between the sexes and the order of knowledges. Myths broadly diffused ensure the persistence of the sex question in the collective epistemic imaginary. They also show the link between social beliefs and beliefs current in institutions of learning. (2003, xv)

Her work has a particular relevance for education in its insistence on the relationship between institutional and social knowledge, and her deter-mination to challenge its gendered shibboleths. Whereas Battersby (1988) exposes the exclusionary and misogynist nature of the philosophical canon, Le Doeuff moves beyond texts to look at practices and institutions, drawing on popular examples and her own experience.

Le Doeuff claims that 'there is no intellectual activity that is not grounded in an imaginary' (2003, xvi). 'Imaginary' here refers to a shared, largely unexamined system of beliefs that shape our social world (Steger and James 2013, 23). However, this is not to say that the imaginary exists in tension with endorsed knowledge or scientific 'truths' – indeed these are key to its being. As Foucault observes,

> The imaginary is not formed in opposition to reality as its denial or compensation; it grows among signs, from book to book, in the inter-stice of repetitions and commentaries; it is born and takes shape in the interval between books. It is the phenomena of the library. (1964, 91)

Foucault (1977) conceives of an imaginary as formed in libraries, in reading, in texts, in repetition. Developing an historical sensibility to gendered learn-ing myths involves tracing not only their claims, but also their patterns and repetitions across different texts and contexts that derive authority from elite and scientific fields.

The enduring patterns Le Doeuff traces in the past can be identified in the present. Important among these is a process of categorisation that she terms 'casting off'. She describes it as a process by which

> everything that acquires value is absorbed into the heritage of those to whom the value is attributed, whereas everything that has low value is off-loaded onto those whose lot in life is to accept other people's hand-me-downs. (2003, 32)

In applying this simple heuristic of what is appropriated and what is cast off, Le Doeuff illuminates the historical masculinisation of rationality as male privilege and draws attention to the essentialising and subjugating tendencies in equal but different discourses of intellectual complementarity.

Discourses of learning, academic ability and intelligence as they are now understood are difficult to pursue prior to the growth of universal education in the newly industrialised West. Before this, it is in elite discourses – elite in the sense of concerning privileged, educated groups, as well as in the sense of pertaining to the highest orders of attainment and performance in artistic, philosophical and scientific fields – that we find ideas about potential, capacity and aptitudes, and how these are gendered. Discourses of genius provide particularly rich ground for examining the historical operations of privilege with regard to gender, knowledge and power. They are important to examine not only as sources of cultural authority in the past, but also as providing insight into gendering of what we now term 'abilities' in the present. They also have particular relevance in the context of the growing body of work on academic elites and high achievers in schools (e.g. Renold 2001; Renold and Allan 2006; Ringrose 2007; Allan 2010; Francis, Skelton, and Reid 2010; Skelton and Francis 2012; Jackson and Nyström 2015).

'Genius' is always explained according to the mythologies of a given age (Kivy 2001) and, as observed by Duchin (2004, 1), it 'has a politics, and in particular a sexual politics'. Exploring how categories of genius have worked historically to preserve masculine privilege and to contain and subjugate feminine achievement enables recognition of ways in which the same categorisations and exclusions continue to operate in gendered learning myths. Three broad types of genius emerge within the overarching elite discourse. These have dimensions that can provide us with a template for understanding the gendering of achievement and the elision of other forms of structural disadvantage in contemporary contexts. The categories are those of innate ability, of achievement through diligence and finally of collaborative attainment.

The Innate Genius and the Brilliant Boy

The dominance of the figure of the brilliant boy who achieves apparently effortlessly, and the greater value placed on such learning behaviour in classrooms, has been well documented (Cohen 1998; Benjamin et al. 2003; Francis and Skelton 2005; Epstein, Mendick, and Moreau 2010; Francis et al. 2010; Stables et al. 2014). Jackson and Nyström (2015) comment on the paradox of schools inciting students to work hard, yet lauding most highly those who seem to achieve with least effort.

Such an idea of natural brilliance has exercised a powerful hold over the Western imagination, within both educational settings and wider public discourse. A model of innate gifts with which individuals are randomly bestowed allows for differential educational treatment, because one is merely realising what is already there rather than creating the conditions for success. It also presents a determinist view in which biological accident replaces other forms of random privilege. Thus, it appeals to the conservative, 'common-sense' view of educational provision and lends a gloss of fairness to the unequal distribution of advantage. Jackson and Nyström (2015) argue that its role in upholding certain kinds of privilege is precisely what enables the 'effortless achievement' model to perpetuate. It also maintains a focus on identifying, measuring and nurturing the individual rather than examining the structural reproduction of advantage (Dyson et al. 2010). While this works to explain something of its persistence in education practice and policy, the function of innate genius discourses within wider patriarchal culture also merit some attention.

Innate genius is an ancient idea, closely associated with elite groups. The earliest accounts of genius as a 'divine gift' derive from classical Greek philosophy (Battersby 1988, 35; Plato, trans. Jowett 2008) – arguably the most elite of educational fields (Cookson and Persell 1985). The divinely gifted genius idea perpetuates through received Western history; it is found in early and medieval Christianity, and while later Renaissance notions shifted to take into account the importance of mastery and labour in the production of genius – as, for example, in Vasari's *Lives of the Artists* (1550 and 1558) – it remains nonetheless an innate gift rather than an achieved state (Battersby 1988, 36).

This early concept of genius finds its popular apotheosis in the highly influential Romantic model. Here, the Romantic genius is possessed by a creative force that approaches divinity (Kant 1790, trans. Goldthwait 2003); it is innate, spontaneous and irrepressible inspired by 'the god within'; it cannot be learned (Young 1759, 101). It is this model which perpetuates most identifiably in the contemporary popular imagination (Kivy 2001).

The Romantics' idea of innate genius also illustrates the workings of masculine privilege and appropriation described by Le Doeuff (2003). The most highly regarded talents have historically been constructed as specifically male entities, even where traditionally feminised qualities are also evoked. The Romantic genius poet or musician may be imbued with imagination and sensitivity, but these potentially feminising qualities have to be united with a specifically male vigour and vision. They create a persistent tension in which masculinity has to be consistently reaffirmed and femininity contained and subordinated, lest it overpower its male possessor (Battersby 1988; Elfenbein 1996; Stadler 1999).

While reflections on the nature of genius had been the preserve of the philosopher and the art historian, toward the end of the nineteenth century, they became the concern of the scientist, namely, the psychologist and the geneticist (Albert 1969). The notion of a measurable, hereditary form of innate genius can be seen as representative of development in the scientific thinking of the Victorian age in its technological innovation, but also as representative of its social conservatism. The forerunner of psychometrics, the work of Galton in particular forms a foundation for later models of testing for 'giftedness' in children as a predictor of adult genius (Terman

1926). Interested in predicting eminence in the young, Galton designed his measurements through examining the biographies of great men (Galton and Schuster 1906).

A move from aesthetic evaluation, with all its elite assumptions, to the scientific measurement of exceptionality might be expected to lead to a more inclusive and expanded model. However, the shift signalled by Galton's work also represents what Delap (2004, 102–103) has termed a 'closing down' of genius in its endorsement of gender and class restrictions through science. Since Galton's chief criterion was eminence in a narrow range of public fields, anyone who had not achieved eminence could not be considered a genius – and Galton maintained that 'genius will out' and no circumstances of birth or context could repress it. His method of drawing on retrospective biography is still supported by some psychologists late into the twentieth century – Eysenck (1995) uses it to come to the conclusion that there have been no women of genius. Such a method is still common too in the field of 'gifted' research.

Feminist scholars in diverse fields identify a legacy of gendered exclusion and appropriation in genius discourse persisting in the twentieth century: For example, Duchin's (2004, 3) study of genius narratives surrounding mathematicians finds that virility and power are stressed; male mathematicians are described as 'vigorous, alert' and 'keenly interested in manly things'. The rare female mathematician, on the other hand, inevitably finds that her gendered biological destiny exerts a stronger pull than her mathematical ability. In her study of gender and genius in Black music discourse, Rustin (2005) draws our attention to some ways in which musical instruments are gendered in twentieth-century jazz reviews to secure the masculine identities of male performers, and therefore have an exclusionary impact on women. A key legacy of the innate genius model is the need to reaffirm manhood; genius is masculinity enhanced, not effeminised.

It is possible to identify similar categorisations and anxieties in contemporary education contexts, in discourses of gendered learning and their relative valuation (Francis and Skelton 2005; Elwood 2010). Masculinised talent as innate and inevitably working its way out, rather than produced by effort, reappears in accounts of the erratic, inspired boy. Coursework – and the diligence and cooperation it fosters – is seen as a dilution of the more masculine vigour and rigour demanded by exams (Francis and Skelton 2005). They play out too in social and learning behaviours of pupils, in the compensatory efforts of some highly achieving boys to affirm their masculine identities in the face of academic success, and in the pressure they describe to achieve without the appearance of effort (Jackson 2006; Francis et al. 2010; Jackson and Nyström 2015).

It is possible to identify the similar categorisations, appropriations and anxieties in contemporary education contexts, for example, in discourses of gendered learning behaviours and their relative valuation (Francis and Skelton 2005; Elwood 2010). Here masculinised talent as innate and inevitably working its way out, rather than as produced by application, reappears in accounts of the erratic, inspired boy. Anxieties surrounding the need to reaffirm masculinity in intellectual endeavour re-emerge in fears regarding the feminisation of the curriculum and testing system, and in the belief that the cooperation and diligence fostered by coursework are girl-friendly and dominate at the expense of the more masculine vigour and rigour demanded by exams (Francis and Skelton 2005). They are also present in the compensatory efforts of some highly achieving boys to affirm their masculine identities in the face of academic success, and in the pressure they describe to achieve without the appearance of effort (Jackson 2006; Francis et al. 2010).

The Diligent Genius and the Hard-Working Girl

The concept of the hard-working genius has historically existed in a subjugated binary with that of the inspired genius (Kivy 2001), and this binary is inevitably gendered. In 1758 Rousseau writes that women

> can acquire a knowledge ... of anything through hard work. But the celestial fire that emblazons and ignites the soul, the inspiration that consumes and devours ... these sublime ecstasies that reside in the depths of the heart are always lacking in women. (Trans. Citron 1989, 225)

If the concept of innate brilliance illustrates the absorption of what is valued into the heritage of men, in the historical valuing of alternative models we can see the mirror process of casting off of the devalued to the heritage of women (Le Doeuff 2003).

Post-structuralist critical examination of genius mythologies has involved a re-appraisal of debased models of achievement, and of the ways in which these have been cast as feminised. Some scholarship in the humanities endorses the notion of the hard-working genius as a part of the larger project of deconstructing the 'great man' of liberal humanist individualism. For example, Stadler's (1999) study of Victorian women's writing finds evidence of a concept of genius which is the result of sustained application rather than the descent of the muse; Miller's (2000) revision of the mythology of the Brontë sisters argues that, contrary to the popular notion of the Brontës as socially isolated genii receiving inspiration from the wild Yorkshire landscape, in fact their writing skills were finely honed over years of practice, and through both peer and expert mentoring.

Despite such competing accounts, the hard-working genius continues to be seen not only as a debased form, but also as one which continues to characterise girls' achievement rather than boys' (Renold 2001; Skelton and Francis 2003, 2010; Mendick 2005). The contemporary productive, compliant, conscientious girl is positioned as the achieving 'other' to the mercurial, assertive boy (Walkerdine 1989; Archer 2005; Skelton and Francis 2005). This hard-working discourse is a means of taking girls' achievements into account and dismissing them, a casting off of both a learning behaviour and the results it produces.

Historically, the prospect of the female genius has provoked intense cultural anxieties: She is either at risk of unwomanliness or a threat to civilisation – or both (Battersby 1988). For example, Kant argues that it should never be attempted by a woman because it 'destroys the merits that are proper to her sex' (Kant 1790, trans. Goldthwait 2003, 78); Rousseau's ideal republic separates women from men because of the dangers femininity posed to masculine vigour (Rousseau 1758); intellectual activity in women, typified in the pejorative 'bluestocking' – a term originally describing male politicians but later cast off to women (Le Doeuff 2003) – was held as unnatural and as such threatening (Bodek 1976). In contemporary contexts we see the same patterns. The supposed diligence of girls is constructed as doubly problematic: Not only is it seen to mask their own lack of innate ability, but also the exam success produced by their diligence eclipses and renders invisible the superior, innate abilities of boys. This hard-working discourse is a means of taking girls' achievements into account and dismissing them, a casting off of both a learning behaviour and the results it produces. As with performance of effortlessness in boys, the culturally endorsed 'hard-working girl' identity is taken up by girls as a conscious strategy for balancing academic success and femininity through avoiding those achievement models associated with masculinity (Renold and Allan 2006; Allan 2010; Raby and Pomerantz 2015).

The 'diligent achiever' model also serves as an educational category for the classification of the achievements of some minority groups. Jackson and Nyström (2015) have drawn attention to the cultural specificity of the valuing of effortless achievement in the West, describing how in Asian countries hard work is seen as the basis of excellence and is valued accordingly. Just as the work produced by hard-working girls in UK classrooms is seen as the 'wrong' sort of achievement, so the success of some Chinese and British Muslim girls is seen as produced by passivity and undue pressure from families (Archer and Francis 2006). The possible relationships that raced, classed subjects may have to even the narrow definitions of success within schools are complex and multi-layered (Archer 2005). The 'hard-working achiever' category appears broad enough to hold in subordination a complex range of variables in terms of gender, ethnicity and class, while masking the difficulties for disadvantaged groups in attaining legitimated forms of success. As Archer (2005, 21) observes, 'even the "best" performances may still be judged as lacking in some way'.

The diligent achiever model is thus not only gendered as feminine, but also linked to other forms of structural privilege and disadvantage. In fact, it first appears in the West as a response to the perceived elitism of the inspired genius model as a part of a wider discourse of aspiration from a

newly wealthy middle class during the early industrial age. It expressed suspicion of aristocratic traditions of patronage and privilege, and through it
we begin to see the growth of the notion of intellect, rather than inspiration,
as central to genius as a new, virtuous and educated middle class argued
for 'intelligence and merit … as the basis of social distinction' (Hemingway
1992, 623). In this early association of the hard-working genius with social
aspiration, we can see a foreshadowing of contemporary ideas of educational meritocracy, particularly with regard to 'gifted and talented' agendas
with their unclear blend of heritability and just deserts (Youdell 2004). The
meritocratic ideal is extremely seductive; Tomlinson (2008, 69) describes it
as 'theodicy of privilege', meaning that the fact that some may be disadvantaged by it does not conflict with their conviction of its essential rightness.
Developing an historical sensibility to ways in which the 'hard-working'
category functions to define and contain the performances of subordinate
groups helps illuminate how they continue to be cast as failures within success, and to challenge such a casting.

The Collaborative Genius and the Caring, Sharing Girl

Running in direct opposition to narratives of the eminent individual and the
solitary visionary, the collaborative model of achievement is not so much
traditionally debased and as historically invisible. Its invisibility lies in its
association with marginalised and subordinate groups, and it owes its contemporary discursive presence to revisionist work which seeks to challenge
the basis of the great man model of history.

Le Doeuff (2003, 36) points out that the physical exclusion of women
from institutions and formal processes of learning has led to their being
hidden from history. Socialist, feminist and post-colonial revisionist works
identify intellectual, scientific and artistic production emerging from previously obscured sources, and challenge the locus of production and ownership in the individual (Western) man (Battersby 1988; Macherey 1978;
Schiebinger 1989; Lunsford and Ede 1990; Stadler 1999).

Inherent in the collaborative model are both appropriation and casting
off; the achievements and expertise of subjugated populations are appropriated, and the role of collective production hidden. This has been attributed
to the exploitations of early forms of capitalism: Zilsel (2003) argues that it
was capitalist activity that first brought together the educated classes with
the skilled craftsmen, thus uniting trained thinkers with practical exper-
imenters and expert artisans. From this encounter, the educated classes
emerged with the credit. It led to the establishment of scientific principle
which drew on artisanal skills, and it is these skills that Zilsel identifies as
the 'forerunners of the physical laws of modern science', rather than lone
scientists' individual inspirations (p. 14). Conner (2005) extends this thesis; he too challenges canonical conceptions of science and specifically the
cult of genius. Like Zilsel, Conner contends that the production of scientific

knowledge was not the work of a series of luminary greats. Furthermore, he asserts that knowledge creation is essentially a social activity and collective in nature, and he challenges the Euro/ethno-centric nature of scientific knowledge through exploring aspects of its Afro-Asiatic roots. Conner also draws attention to the exclusion of women from expert productive artisanship (except midwifery) and so from narratives of scientific eminence.

The importance of collaboration for women as a means of overcoming institutional and cultural exclusion from certain fields and kinds of learning emerges from revisionist work. Schiebinger (1989) traces the historical exclusion of women from institutions, cultures and practices of early modern science, including the ways in which their collaborative contributions were habitually diminished or ignored. Exploring genius discourses in mathematics, Duchin describes how the lone (male) genius model obscures 'the important community aspects of mathematics ... controlling who would even think to enter the field' (interviewed in Vanderkam 2008). Le Doeuff particularly recognises the value of collaborative work for women in ending their intellectual isolation, especially in research which 'involves going off the beaten track in search of items passed over by an establishing structuring of knowledge'. Engaged in feminist revision work and finding it difficult to track down a source, she describes a young colleague 'handing me bibliographic information across the back fence' (2003, 6), a knowingly domestic image to describe alternative routes for the transmission of feminist knowledge.

We can see evidence of the emergence of theories of collaborative production in the humanities as well as the sciences: Kelley (2008) highlights the collaborative nature of genius in what she terms 'self-reliant circles of practice' in (white) women's writing, and traces a line from nineteenth-century collaborative practices to contemporary scholarship as a collective enterprise; Royster (1989) similarly explores the history of collaboration in the development of Black women's writing. Brandels (2008) posits a model of genius as both collaborative and contextual, taking due account of the artisans and communities involved in the various stages and practices of production, for example, asserting that

> genius did not descend upon (Gertrude Stein) from the heavens as she sat working solitarily in her room of her own, but instead was a result of numerous influences and countless collaborations. (385)

The politics of collaboration as a challenge to both capitalist and patriarchal structures is highlighted Stollery's (2002) analysis of the gendering of genius in early modernist USSR film. He demonstrates Soviet reversal of the two key principles of an organising hierarchy of genius in the Western liberal tradition: the individual over the collective, and the association of the more debased form with female production. He shows how 1920s' Soviet Russia saw Western concepts of individual genius as 'self-regarding, dedicated to creation of individual biography' (as exemplified in the work of the male film-maker Sergei Eisenstein) and sought instead to promote collective principles and, in film-making, social truth over aesthetic effect (as exemplified in the work of the female archivist and film-maker Esfir Shub). Such revisionist work models a Foucauldian questioning of categories and the power structures they reflect and support.

The Philosophical Masculinisation of Rationality and the Gendering of School Subjects and Spaces

If imaginative and creative aspects of genius have historically been combined with a specifically masculine vigour to produce the male genius, in domains associated with the exercise of logic, analysis and rationality no such compensatory combination is necessary; these domains are already closely associated with masculinity. The association of rationality with masculinity is a cornerstone of Enlightenment philosophy (Battersby 1988; Walkerdine 1988); the gendered dichotomy it creates is not only fundamental to Western philosophy, but also forms the basis of the ways essential distinctions between female and male genders are conceived (Lloyd 1979). These distinctions still play out in the gendering of school subjects and in wider learning domains. Jay (1981, 54) suggests that such dichotomous models of thinking both work to sustain privilege and are particularly resistant to change because those who subscribe to them find it very hard to conceive of the possibility of alternatives, or 'third possibilities', positing that, within such thinking, the only alternative to the one order is 'disorder'. This may help explain the persistence of Cartesian dualism within gendered learning myths.

Early feminists had much to do to counter doubts about the very existence of the female intellect, let alone its capacity for excellence, and so tended to argue first and foremost for the understanding of woman as rational beings, capable of independent intellectual endeavour and deserving of the same education as men – most famously Mary Wollstonecraft's *A Vindication of the Rights of Woman* (1792). Le Doeuff argues that women's exclusion from the status of rational knowingness is associated with their exclusion from the physical institutions of learning. A denial of presence is also a denial of process – outside institutions of learning women did not develop familiarity with the 'exercise of logic and dialectic' (Lloyd 1989), the argument, the lecture and the seminar, all of which cultivate rationality (Le Doeuff 2003). As Le Doeuff states, 'Deprivation stems from prohibition' (36).

Although girls and women are no longer physically excluded from learning institutions, there is a wealth of evidence suggesting that they are both excluded and self-excluding from the classroom processes that cultivate 'rationality'. Walkerdine (1989, 46) argues that for girls, engaging in debate, especially with teachers and in a public arena, implies the assumption of a kind of masculinised power (46). While it can bestow a certain kind of enhanced status, the earning of teacher recognition through the rationalities of highly visible classroom discourse can mean girls have increased difficulty in negotiating feminised and social identities – as one participant describes it, 'You've kind of got to watch yourself and make sure you're not putting your hand up all the time'. Teachers can also reinforce the gendered dichotomy, demonstrating differing questioning styles and expectations when dealing with girls and boys, especially in 'rational' subjects such as mathematics (Benjamin et al. 2003).

Genius, Feminist Critique and the Achieving Girl

If the history of feminist thought is a history of recognising repression and exclusion, one can recognise within it a concern with genius as a concept which consistently serves to articulate binaries, to justify patriarchal elites and to make sense of exceptionality within overarching ideologies of gender (Battersby 1988). Moreover, the concept of such exceptionality itself is one which has presented and continues to present particular challenges to feminist critique in its encapsulation of some tensions between essentialism and constructionism, between elitism and egalitarianism.

The latter part of the twentieth century saw a burgeoning of feminist revisionist studies which addressed the exclusion and marginalisation of women from traditions of genius and explored contextual barriers to women achieving eminence (see e.g. Petersen and Wilson 1976; Collins 1978; Greer 1979; Broude and Garrard 1982; Sydie 1989; Hagaman 1990). These revisited notions of genius and exposed their masculine and exclusionary nature, offering new and inclusive models which not only draw attention to the works of individual women, but also propose female traditions of genius. The struggles that women creators, whether writers, artists, composers or scientists, experienced in establishing their credentials while maintaining their identity as women have been a rich field for feminist studies (see e.g. Moers 1976; Gilbert and Gubar 1979; Spender 1981; Showalter 1982; Spencer 1986). Such works aim to expose the difficulties faced by creative and inventive women, and expose the innate patriarchalism of the creation of canons through drawing attention to the historically excluded. Battersby's (1988) *Gender and Genius: Towards a Feminist Aesthetic* remains a key work on the exclusion of women not only from accounts, but also from the very concepts of genius or giftedness within Western philosophical and aesthetic traditions.

However, in attempting to establish an alternative tradition of women's achievement, such work runs the risk of upholding the grand narrative of individual genius itself. Toril Moi (1985, 54), while applauding the pioneering nature of feminist revisionist critique, alerts us to the problematic nature of 'greatness' for feminists given that the criteria 'militate heavily against the inclusion of women' and in themselves reproduce a patriarchal schematic.

Here a tension for the feminist scholar is revealed, for if, as Moi suggests, we collude in the death of the genius, we are, Battersby cautions, denying the possibility of women working within a specifically female tradition – a possibility identified by Alice Walker (1976) as essential to the development of women's creative achievement. While both explicatory frameworks for the subjugation of women on the basis of sex alone and patriarchal structures as narrative frameworks for female success should rightly be regarded with caution, it is also worth noting Hall's (1990) caution that recovery histories to some extent inevitably impose a narrative coherence on what is fractured.

Battersby (1988) is critical of the post-structuralist view, arguing that just as the Romantics appropriated qualities of mind previously associated with the feminine, so the 'otherness' and 'fragmentation' of femininity have been appropriated by 'post-patriarchal' culture. This tension between the risks of essentialism in 'female genius' traditions and the potential denial of specific oppression of women's talent in post-structuralist scholarship is illustrative of some larger tensions between progressive and post-structural feminisms, and also between competing discourses in education and 'gifted' education fields, which I discuss in more detail later.

Historically, the consideration of genius has presented feminists with further issues. Delap (2004) identifies Edwardian feminists' dilemma in reconciling discomfort with perceived elitism in the idea of the philosophical 'superwoman', and the location of their hopes for change in the 'exceptional' individual. These hopes can be seen to persist after the feminist gains after the Great War, for example, in Kopald's (1924) assertion that

> wise feminists today are concentrating their forces upon women geniuses. Women have won the right to an acknowledged mind; they want now the right to draw for genius and high talents in the 'curve of chance'. (619)

This anticipates contemporary concern surrounding the ways in which highly achieving girls have come to signify the success of the feminist project and school effectiveness. McRobbie (2010) describes feminism as having been

> made to fold into the new values of competition and excellence so that the high-achieving girl came to embody the improvements and changes in the educational system as a whole. (76)

Here it is important to highlight the discursive alignment of the achieving girl with discourses of competitiveness; the disassociation of feminism from ideas of solidarity also has discernible roots in earlier times. For Victorian feminists, Alaya (1977) finds, emerging models of scientific genius had profound repercussions in divorcing feminism itself from its philosophical roots in egalitarianism.

Complementarity as Biological Destiny

In acceding to the new sciences of intellectual difference, women accepted a remit which involved promoting a feminism that 'defined its role around the socialising genius of women's complementary sexuality', promoting their 'cultural mission' and 'co-operative destiny' (Alaya 1977, 277). This is, in effect, a 'new sexual contract' for the Victorian feminist constructed along lines similar to that described by McRobbie (2009), where women are allowed a certain presence and visibility within traditionally masculine preserves and spaces, but that presence is rendered non-threatening through its association with enhanced femininity.

It is not only in a gendered division of roles regarding family and professional life, and an acceptance of women's civilising influence in general, that such discourses promoted complementarity; it was also held to exist within the field of scientific enquiry itself (Alaya 1977; Schiebinger 1989). For example, Henry Thomas Buckle states in his lecture at the Royal Institution in 1858 that while women 'are capable of exercising and have actually exercised an enormous influence' over the progress of knowledge, an influence 'in fact, so great that it is hardly possible to assign limits to it', such influence lies in improving and refining the different and superior talents of men. In what he describes as a 'coalition, a union of different faculties', he expresses hopes that

> the imaginative and emotional minds of one sex will continue to accelerate the great progress, by acting upon and improving the colder and harder minds of the other sex. (1858, n.p.)

The acceptance of such complementarity not only strengthened a binary conception of gendered intelligence, but also vitiated the climate of feminist debate itself as women's demands for social and political equality became dependent on their capacity to demonstrate exceptionality (Alaya 1977). The suffrage movement reflected this shift in focus in its arguments that it was the most exceptional women who suffered the most under the tyranny of conventional femininity, and that the talents of such women were in danger of being lost to the world (Delap 2004). However, there was such scientific force in the argument that women's particular talents connected them with altruistic and sacrificial virtues that challenges to the proposed different but 'complementary roles' of the sexes made little headway; feminist argument was disarmed by the social and psychological uses to which the new biology was put (Alaya 1977).

Both Battersby and Alaya points out ways in which the science of gendered intellectual difference itself was flawed – in its empirical, apparently objective methods for measurement which fail to acknowledge their own cultural groundings and therefore (gendered) bias (Battersby 1988, 181), and in its persistent refusal to consider context and the impossibility of scientific control (Alaya 1977, 273). These criticisms are revived in contemporary feminist critique of 'neuorosexism' (Fine 2010).

The invocation of science to reify sexual difference and defend gendered inequalities takes on a disturbing renewed vigour and relevance in contemporary discourses of neuroscience. As with Victorian psychology, a range of essentialist claims permeate educational discourse and the wider imaginary, relating to 'abilities' and biologically ascribed gender. However uneasy these claims might make their audience, challenging them seems to require 'advanced, discipline-specific skills or knowledge' (Tinkler and Jackson 2014, 73), thus creating difficulties for the layperson, or indeed the social scientist, in countering them. The alacrity with which neuroscientific truths about gender become accepted educational norms is a disturbing reminder of the tenacity of gendered binaries. Jay (1981, 47) argues that 'taken for granted distinctions are dangerous' precisely because of their 'peculiar affinity with gender distinctions' and stresses the importance for feminist theory to be systematic in recognising them (47).

Countering the claims of such sciences is both particularly necessary and particularly difficult for the feminist scholar, as not only does the science appear to offer proofs of essential gendered distinctions, but feminist analysis itself is dismissed as political (Le Doeuff 2003; Fine 2010). Examining the uses to which sciences are put and questioning the categories they create or reinforce enables us to recognise the ways in which, despite their claims to novelty, 'they are often activated by longstanding tropes' (Pickersgill 2013).

Despite the infancy of neuroscience and the tentativeness and complexity of its early findings (Francis and Skelton 2005), works expounding theories of gendered cognitive and neuroscientific difference, such as the *Female Brain* (Brizendine 2008), have gained in popularity and become translated into educational practice, for example, in *Teaching the Female Brain* (James 2009). The circulation of science into popular domains and its use to support existing dogma are illuminated by Hasinoff (2009), who shows how the discourse of socio-biology has circulated in women's magazines since the 1990s, displacing other accounts of gendered difference, and supported by an invoking of scientific expertise. Examining the circulation of gendered neuromyths in contemporary conditions of digital media convergence, O'Connor and Joffe (2014) track the journey of a high-profile study of neurobiological sex differences through five media domains: the original scientific article, the press release, the traditional news platform, online comments on that platform, and blogs discussing the news item. They find that scientific 'proofs' are framed within gendered stereotypes at each stage. Their findings show that neuroscience is invoked by both experts and non-experts to support pre-existing notions of subordinated complementarity, even to the point of citing categories of learning behaviour which do not feature in the findings of the original experiment, such as women's ability to 'multi-task'.

Useful work is being undertaken to counter such mythologising; some of this deals directly with methodological flaws. Paechter (1998), for example, argues that the claims of neuroscience itself need to pay greater attention to the effect of socialised context on neural development, thus reversing the argument that different brains create different gendered behaviour, and calling for a focus on how nurturing different behaviours may shape brains differently. Chalfin, Murphy, and Karkazis (2008) call for the establishment of specific 'women's neuroethics' that continue to question issues of wider gendered categorisation in scientific enquiry. Fine (2010, 172) undertakes a detailed critique of the flawed method of keys studies. She observes how contemporary gender stereotypes are legitimated by 'pseudo-scientific explanations' invoking the brain with no regard for their validity. She also addresses neuroscientific explanations' neglect of context and cultural grounding, advancing critique similar to that of Battersby (1988) and Alaya (1977) in their consideration of Victorian scientific claims.

Foucault (2003, 9) asserts that 'genealogies are, quite specifically, anti-sciences'. By this, he does not mean a rejection of concepts, methods or knowledge that sciences produce, but rather a challenge to 'the power-effects that are bound up with the institutionalisation and workings of any scientific discourse' within wider society. In his *Archaeology* (1969), he identifies ideology as the way science legitimates particular aspects of knowledge. Claiming objectivity and rationality of method, scientific proofs of gendered learning difference have historically involved a turning away from philosophical and political questions of equality, yet the knowledge produced draws on and re-animates historical and taken-for-granted dichotomies circulating in the wider imaginary and coalescing in the figure of the achieving girl.

Tinkler and Jackson (2014) highlight the importance of developing 'historical sensibility' not only in understanding 'how history is (mis)used in discourse' (83), but also in questioning 'novelty claims' (73). In developing a critical, historical sensibility to the essentialising claims of 'new' sciences with regard to gender and learning, it is possible to reassert the centrality of the feminist political struggle which is too often dismissed as dogma itself when science is examined through its feminist lens (Le Doeuff 2003). Le Doeuff's model of concentrating on the social values and categories assigned to gender rather than on 'woman' as a knowable object, and her suggested heuristic of tracing the privileged and the 'cast-off' discourses enable a questioning of both the essentialism of gendered achievement and the deterministic claims made in the name of neuroscience through exposing their cultural foundation and historical function. Nonetheless, the alacrity with which neuroscientific truths become accepted educational norms is a disturbing reminder of the tenacity of gendered binaries. Le Doeuff (2003, x) observes that the problem of the persistence of such a myth as the gendering of intellect may be 'insoluble precisely because it is false'.

2 The Achieving Girl as the Ideal Subject

In this chapter, I consider the rise of academic interest in the achieving girl, as well as celebration and anxieties expressed in popular realms. Drawing on research exploring dominant discourses of girlhood and girls' subjectivities, I show how a contemporary questioning of claims to agency made with regard to girl audiences has resulted in an examination of feminism's legacy and aims in girlhood studies. I identify areas for investigation opened up in terms of the circulation of discourses of successful girlhood in particular, and identify possibilities for exploring subjectivities through the structure as well as the content of prevailing narratives.

The term 'girl' itself is a broad signifier; it is employed in a wide range of contexts and for diverse purposes. In recognising the discursively and culturally constructed nature of girlhood, scholars are united in resisting a conception of girls as a homogenised group, and in their commitment to exploring the power relations that frame diverse girls' experiences and identities. This is particularly with regard to inclusion, exclusion and intersectionality (Harris 2004; Gonick 2006; Bradford and Hey 2007; Nayak and Kehily 2008; Keller 2015). In social and cultural studies traditions, girlhood has historically been located within or subsumed by 'youth', itself a shifting term, and in which gender distinctions are collapsed and a male universality often assumed (Currie, Kelly, and Pomerantz 2009). This can be understood in terms not only of the relative invisibility of girls within youth subcultures historically, but also of the dominance of male models of development which research into youth behaviours and cultures drew on (Harris 2004; Currie et al. 2009). Feminist scholars also note the ways in which terms such as 'youth' and 'adolescence' elide cultural and economic differences such as class and ethnicity, as well as gender (Finders 1997; Schultz 1999; T. Skelton 2001).

During the twentieth century, the culturally produced category of 'youth' attracted increasing academic interest. Giroux (1994, 2005) argues that this is due to the emblematic status of youth both as the barometer for the success of the modernist project and as the locus of anxiety in an era of rapid change. In the fast-developing field of psychology, this interest led to the production of a range of theories of adolescence and identity formation; adolescence was defined as the process by which the realisation of adulthood – especially self-determining, moral adulthood – occurred. Adolescence became defined as a time of crisis and identity experimentation as the young person developed a sense of self which was autonomous, morally self-directing and relatively independent from family (Kohlberg 1963, 1973; Erikson 1968). The subordinate position of women and girls, and their conceptual exclusion from 'prevailing definitions of full personhood' (Gonick 2006, 4), ensured their preclusion from such studies; because they could not become fully self-determining adults, they could not meet the criteria of adolescence (Gilligan 1982; Walkerdine 1990; McRobbie 1991; Driscoll 2002; Aapola, Gonick, and Harris 2005).

In the late twentieth century, therefore, cultural research on girls, like educational research, tended to focus on issues of invisibility and exclusion. McRobbie and Garber's (1976) pioneering enquiry into 'girls and subcultures' prepared the ground for a growth of feminist research exploring the ways in which working-class girls were marginalised, existing on the edge of male teen worlds. Growing from research which characterised adolescence as a time of risk for girls, the 1990s also saw a proliferation of popular psychology texts on the issue of the 'silencing' and vulnerability of girls (Currie et al. 2009, 6). Exemplified by Pipher's (1994) *Reviving Ophelia*, these texts sought to rescue girls' sense of self in the face of the harmful effects of school and popular cultures. Baumgardner and Richards (2000, 179) describe this as a 'cottage industry' of vulnerable girl literature.

In terms of girls' relationship with popular culture, research into girlhood has followed the ethnographic turn in audience studies, moving from a focus on representation which seeks to expose the (harmful) hegemonic pedagogies of mass-produced texts of theorists such as Adorno (1991), toward reception studies models which draw on active audience theorists such as de Certeau (1984). These studies valorised the ways in which audiences take ownership of and make meaning from popular texts and discourses, with such meaning making constituting a form of dissenting agency performed alongside and with consciousness of the text's inscribed meaning as the authorised activity – as, de Certeau analogises, industrial wigmakers construct their own products from discarded scraps using company machinery in odd moments of unsupervised time between their paid labour (de Certeau 1984, 25). The optimism of such interpretations and the limitations of the agency they identify have since become a focus for contemporary feminists' concern (McRobbie 2009; Duits 2010).

In the very field of feminist studies, girlhood has been rendered as an incomplete state. Driscoll (2002) offers a genealogy of girlhood in which the development of the cultural girl is traced from the renaissance to the new millennium. She examines how the idea of girlhood works across a range of historical and contemporary sites, and argues that the subjugation and relegation she traces can also be found in feminist scholarship, and indeed are as central to the tenets of feminism as they are to those of the patriarchy. She finds that girlhood is characterised as unachieved subjectivity, and argues for a focus on girls' experience of the ways they are represented, and of the discursive world of girlhood.

The notional girl of scholarship then is a construct, but also a constructor of her identity and meaning(s). Historically, she exists at the edge of popular and educational discourses, without economic power or cultural significance, but nonetheless the claimer of secret spaces and maker of marginal meanings out of the mainstream narratives she consumes. In feminist scholarship in particular, the concerns of researchers have been not only to trace the conditions of marginalisation, but also to discover the green shoots of agency and resistance as girls turn debilitating cultural messages to their own ends. The possibilities of such agency are themselves now the object of feminist scrutiny under the onslaught of celebratory neoliberal and post-feminist discourses of the achieving girl.

The Twenty-First-Century Girl

The turn of the twentieth and twenty-first centuries saw an explosion of interest, both popular and scholarly, in girls and girlhood. McRobbie describes young women as having 'replaced youth as a metaphor for social change' (2000, 200). A contextualising rationale is given by Johnson (1993) in her account of the recognition of woman as self-determining subject; this, she argues, is not simply an outcome of the successful prosecution of the feminist agenda, but can be located within changes in global economies and technologies which created new demands for women as workers, and from women as consumers. Such recognition was, as Gonick (2006) argues, a necessary precursor to the rise of the girl as a focus for cultural concern and scholarship. The distinct conditions created by this recognition, which offers choice, individualism and self-realisation but does not entirely supplant traditional feminine discourses of cooperation and self-sacrifice, is a key focus of twenty-first-century scholarship (Budgeon 2003, 2011; Walkerdine 2003; Francis and Skelton 2005; Harris 2004; McRobbie 2000, 2003, 2009).

The power of a proliferation of media, institutional and academic texts lies in their ability to coalesce and cohere into social knowledge that appears to derive from inherent truths about girlhood itself (Currie et al. 2009, 15). Scholars of girlhood have worked both to undo the various discursive strands that go to make up the monolithic, essential girl, focusing on contrasting and marginal narratives (vulnerable girls, mean girls, urban girls, global girls, violent girls, 'riot grrls', phallic girls, super girls, digital girls), on diverse sites of production (magazines, television, film, music, schools, youth clubs, bedrooms, chat rooms, SMS and SNS), and to explore the ways in which discourses both compete and combine with one another, working together to 'define the boundaries of normalcy' for everyday girls (Currie et al. 2009, 48).

Most identifiable among newer discourses of female success is that of 'girl power'. Appearing in the 1990s, this discourse is broadly characterised by scholars as the media industries' appropriation of the alternative riot grrls movement to accommodate it within neoliberal consumerism (Aapola et al. 2005; Zaslow 2009; Currie et al. 2009), while Zaslow (2009, 13) offers a useful summation of four popular discourses converging to produce the girl power era: the proliferation of popular feminist psychosocial studies of girls, the conservative backlash against second-wave feminism, the emergence of third-wave feminism, and the riot grrl movement. One can now add to this the celebration and anxieties evoked by girls' outperforming boys in educational measures of success (Raby and Pomerantz 2015).

McRobbie (2009) argues that new discourses of female success should not be viewed as emancipatory, but as new 'technologies of the self' in that young women's subjectivities are now shaped by gendered regimes of consumption; the consumer and sexual freedoms available to young women are in fact the new markers of gendered subordination. As Gonick et al. (2010, 2) observe, 'While girl power emerged during the 1990s where girls could be active, in the 2000s they are now excepted/demanded to be fully self-actualised neo-liberal subjects'. A central concern of contemporary scholars of girlhood in the West is the relationship of the individual to pervading neoliberal discourses and the impact of their selective address, and their restrictions, promises and exclusions.

The Rise of the Achieving Girl in Schools

Feminist education researchers focusing on girls' achievement have historically been interested in the underperformance of girls in school contexts which favoured boys. Feminist scholars in education in the 1970s and 1980s therefore focused on what Spender (1981) calls the 'patriarchal paradigm' in education. This included gender-differentiated and patriarchal structures, curricula and language in schools (Mahoney 1985; Weiner and Arnot 1987). Dillabough (2001) describes the agenda of such scholars as drawing on wider concerns for and about women to address pragmatic problems of gender inequality and to engage in school reform.

If the feminist project was that of exposing the gendered nature of school curricula and reforming them (Bernstein 1978), in the popular imagination this has been more than successfully accomplished: on the cusp of the new century, public concern centred on the underperformance of girls shifted to their 'overachievement' as they overtook boys in public examination performance in every stage and almost every subject (Epstein et al. 1998; DfES 2007). In popular discourses, accounts of girls' success are oppositionally positioned in relation to the failure of boys. Such accounts are deeply anxious, with the superior performance of girls seen as leading to social calamity; female ambition and exceptionality are viewed with suspicion (Delamont 1999).

Popular explanations for the rise of the achieving girl in schools are varied. They are located in a range of perceived problems arising, from changing masculinities to current methods of assessment and pedagogy favouring girls (Mahony et al. 1998; Delamont 1999; C. Skelton 2001; Francis and Skelton 2005; DCFS 2009a; Elwood 2010). In a reversal of mid-twentieth-century concerns over patriarchal values in schools, girls' success has also been attributed in the popular imagination to feminised school cultures (C. Skelton 2001; Francis and Skelton 2005; Jackson 2006). When academic success is associated with qualities of diligence, perseverance and compliance, traditionally feminine behaviours can be reconciled with schoolroom success. The achieving girl is thus characterised as more successful because she is more motivated, cooperative and compliant than her male counterpart (Francis and Skelton 2005; Jackson and Nyström 2015), rather than simply more clever. And as we have seen, this model of the hard-working achiever historically sits low in the conceptual hierarchy.

The contemporary academic achievement of girls can thus be seen to provide a context for the re-emergence of older discourses of anxiety surrounding feminised achievement, and the achievement of twenty-first-century girls cast within traditional restrictive hierarchies of gendered achievement.

The proliferation of achieving girl discourses in the realms of government policy and popular media has led to a re-examination of the usefulness of gender alone as an educational category. Feminist scholars have been concerned to challenge new gendered discourses which cast winners and losers on the sole basis of gender, demonstrating that data used to trumpet girls' success can conceal significant and ongoing inequalities rooted in socio-economic factors and cultural exclusion (Francis and Skelton 2005; Featherstone, Scourfield, and Hooper 2010; Ringrose 2012). That apparent success stories both conceal complexities and mask inequities in performance which are far greater than those apparent on grounds of gender alone is acknowledged by the Department for Education and Skills, in its commissioned report *Gender and Education* (DfES 2007). As feminist scholars work to recast debates about agency and identity in school within postmodern and post-structuralist frameworks, focus has shifted to an interest in the ways in which multiple forms of gender identity are reproduced in educational contexts (Francis and Skelton 2005; Bradford and Hey 2007; Skelton, Francis, and Read 2010; Francis and Paechter 2015). Scholars seek to counter the rationalist master narratives that identify the causes of inequality based on core premises of gender that bear little relation to the complexity of gender identities in schools (Dillabough and Arnot 2002).

The assumption that achievement is unproblematic for those girls who do well is again a vast oversimplification, and feminist scholars are engaged in uncovering the complexities and inequalities it masks. McRobbie (2004, 257) argues that an apparent culture of choice and flexibility for the 'A1 girls' of the affluent West is in fact bound about with constraint, and the choices are loaded with risk. Ringrose (2007) identifies deep contradictions in discourses of girls' success in that they are both 'wildly celebratory and deeply-anxiety ridden', as girls must learn to unite the binaries. She states the need for research which explores

> girls' experiences in such schooling climates, and the difficulty of nav-
> igating spaces of contradiction and 'impossibility' in these new subject
> positions where girls are to be both bright and beautiful, heterofem-
> inine/desirable and successful learner, aggressor and nurturer among
> other contradictions. (485)

Some of the more recent scholarship on achieving girls in schools examines the performative aspects of achievement, using feminist post-structuralist perspective. Such work focuses on the work girls do in schools to balance social relations and academic achievement in contexts of new and hybri-dised identities that disrupt dominant gender discourses (Renold and Allen 2006; Bradford and Hey 2007; Roeser et al. 2008; Skelton et al. 2010; Allan 2010; Pomerantz and Raby 2011, 2015). It finds that gender work is still a powerful force in 'engaging with, understanding and managing academic success', and highlights the complexities and restrictions of gender. Skelton et al. (2010, 186) observe that it is the most academically highly success-ful girls who find managing achievement alongside 'doing girl' particularly challenging. This study seeks to extend this range of work through exam-ining the ways in which popular as well as school cultures create discursive contexts for high-achieving girls' identity work, and through examining the ways in which they engage with, reproduce and reformulate complex and often contradictory discourses.

The Achieving Girl in 'Gifted' Research

One of the strengths of the archaeological approach lies in its ability to bring together manifestations of a discourse from diverse sites of appear-ance. The field of 'gifted' research sits in something of an ideological bunker in the academy, even while 'gifted and talented' policies have been a feature of many Western government education policies in the late twentieth and early twenty-first centuries (Sternberg and Davidson 2005). However, the essentialism with regard to both abilities and gender which underpins much work in the 'gifted' field, together with a more generalised privileged norma-tivity, works to elide the structural advantage inherent in accounts of mer-itocracy and intellectual destiny (Goldthorpe 1996; Gillborn and Youdell 2000). This failure to address the structural and discursive foundations of 'abilities' forms an epistemological gulf between 'gifted' education research, on the one hand, and feminist enquiry's questioning of both gender and ability as stable categories and overt philosophical commitment to equity, on the other.

In the latter part of the twentieth century, as some girls began to surpass boys in public examinations, some 'gifted' education researchers began to question the validity of focusing research on girls at all. In 2004, an article in the European *High Ability Studies* journal appeared, entitled 'Is Research on Gender-Specific Underachievement in Gifted Girls an Obsolete Topic?' (Schober, Reimann, and Wagner 2004). In her 1998 review of research on provision for the 'very able' in England, and her later (2004) account of cultural influences on gender and achievement for the 'gifted', Freeman describes British girls as becoming increasingly confident, their achievements fostered in classrooms where gendered expectations are higher and curriculum design is girl-friendly. Such acceptance of the performance of girls as unproblematic assumes that all girls are doing well and gender is taken as the most significant category in producing that success.

With girls' apparent success, the focus and concerns of some 'gifted' literature shift from external gendered disadvantage to internal psychological crisis. The proliferation of 'vulnerable girl' text emerging out of middle-class concerns and contexts is exemplified by Kerr's (1997) *Smart Girls* and Pipher's (1994) *Reviving Ophelia* (Baumgardner and Richards 2000). These texts make manifest neoliberal identity discourses in which the responsibility for success – and therefore failure too – lies with the individual. It is within this context that Rose (1999) accounts for the rise of therapeutic cultures, life manuals and self-help guides which enjoin the individual to take on the burden of her own inadequacies and reshape herself into a more fitting subjectivity.

A sense of anxious entitlement pervades much of such literature, in which the 'gifted' girl is described as encountering a range of risks relating to successful social identity, role confusion and psychological security (Reis 1998, 2003). Where the subject may be reasonably regarded as not yet old enough to take on such responsibility, parents and teachers take on the therapeutic mantle in working to reshape the child's subjectivity (Rose 1999; Ecclestone 2004).

There are, notwithstanding such differences, areas of resonance between 'gifted' research and feminist studies. Like much early work on the gendering of genius in the humanities, in 'gifted' research there is a focus on issues of the exclusion of women from eminence, including high-status careers and academic fields. The emphasis is the conflicts and compromises that so-designated gifted women face in satisfying societal demands for feminised lives and behaviours (see e.g. Piirto 1991; Ajzenberg-Selove 1994; Leroux 1998; Bizzari 1998; Kerr and Kurpius 1999). Such research tends to offer a broadly essentialist view of intelligence, creating tension with a cautious interrogation of gender as culturally produced. However, these biographical studies share some of the wider twentieth-century concerns described above, that girls were failing to meet their potential, were meeting discrimination in classrooms and lecture halls, and were struggling with internal conflict in trying to reconcile their gendered with their 'gifted' destinies.

Some key distinctions of gifted girl literature then include the addressing of concerns of 'girl as victim', their intellectual essentialism, their privileged normativity, their focus on individual problems rather than structural disadvantage, and the therapeutic solutions they advocate. These accounts stress the binary of ability as the naturalised and authentic self, against femininity in its populist forms as learned (Spelman 1990; Aapola et al. 2005). The failure of such scholarship to examine 'giftedness' and gender as discursively produced is also a failure to recognise the role of the academy itself in its production. This discursive divide with regard to the achieving girl has some epistemological resonance with that noted above between liberal and post-structural feminist work in the humanities with regard to the female genius.

Feminism's Legacy and Future Directions

As some elements of the second-wave agenda are put into place in visible ways, new opportunities are open to girls in professional and educational fields, in legal and economic terms, and in sexual freedoms. These are balanced by new regulatory modes of being and new pressures. Both feminist activism and scholarship are presented with new dilemmas and new directions.

McRobbie (2009) marks some directions in the routes feminist scholarship has taken and exposes some new dilemmas. She argues that feminism has to some degree effectively dismantled itself, as, under largely post-colonial, post-structural and Foucauldian influences, attention shifted from 'centralised power blocks' to more dispersed sites. The flow of power in discourse and the calling into being of the subject through interpellation led, she asserts, to a 'problematic she' rather than an 'unproblematic we', as assumptions of common feminist concerns and universal female experiences are challenged (13). An element of McRobbie's agenda then is to be cautious regarding claims to agency present in accounts of individualised responses to media meanings, and to question the messages of individuation that such media may carry. This has implications for the ways in which both textual analysis and empirical research with girls are undertaken, in the need to interrogate the nature of discourses on offer, and the need to explore issues of response and agency with caution. Reviewing feminist media scholars' preoccupation with reception and active audience models, she questions the degree to which girls and women studied in the past demonstrated agency in taking pleasure and making social use of mass media texts which appeared to have overtly oppressive messages.

While remaining alert to the exclusive post-feminist address to the ideal (white, middle-class) achieving subject, and the need to 'keep the material and cultural aspects of difference' articulated (Hey 2010, 215), Ringrose (2007, 485) has summarised a need to

> continue working out the complex effects of the post-feminist, neoliberal discourse of achieving girls and to conduct empirical research into

girls' experiences in 'achieving girl' school climates, and the impossibilities and contradictions in new subject positions.

There has been interest in recent years in exploring the subjectivities and experiences specifically of achieving girls in schools (e.g. Renold and Allen 2006; Roeser et al. 2008; Allan 2010; Skelton et al. 2010; Pomerantz and Raby 2011, 2015). There is scope for further exploration of what such identity categories mean both within and beyond school locations. As Grunewald (2003, 10) observes, school discourses and practices can be seen as isolated from the outside world; he advocates a critical reconnection of students within the school with their surrounding environment and concerns.

The linearity of available discourses also opens up possibilities for enquiry, in terms of analysis of the structure as well as the content of the institutional narratives on offer, and those (re)produced by their young subjects. Harris (2004) observes that the old linear models of success trajectories and education policies' fixation with pathways have decreasing relevance for youth in late modernity. She argues for more flexible, less constraining models of transition from youth to adulthood which take into account the complexities of post-industrial society, asserting that 'research and policy need to develop more nuanced interpretations', and this means 'exploring young people's own meanings around adulthood, successful pathways and desired futures' (188).

The spaces of girlhood discourses, especially schools, have been central to theorising identity production (Gonick 2003; Ringrose 2007; Currie et al. 2009). Epstein and Johnson (1998) describe how in school young people draw on the discourses that they live elsewhere, and Schultz (1999) finds that these are given new and specific meanings in school contexts. Currie et al. (2009, 58) describe peer cultures within school as 'semi-autonomous', meaning that youth are active in the construction of meaning in their social worlds. However, such meaning making is mediated by the belief systems, values, and knowledge of 'extra-local' cultures and wisdom.

Issues in Audience Studies

The relationship between textual analysis (the critical reading of texts' inscribed hegemonic meanings) and reception analysis (the study of how audiences make their own meanings, and how they use media texts in everyday life and social relations) remains a focus of tension in the study of girls' relationships with popular culture (Duits and Van Zoonen 2006; Gill 2007b). Debate centres on how far audiences actively construct their own (resistant) readings/meanings in the face of global hegemonic discourses inscribed into texts (Livingstone 1998; Michelle 2007; Philo 2008). There is dispute surrounding the value of small-scale ethnographies exploring the uses audiences make of such texts within contexts of local, often domestic consumption; the claims to agency and resistance that such studies can produce are seen as inadequate in accounting for power relationships inherent in mass production and interpellation (Livingstone 1998; Morley 2006; Gill 2008; McRobbie 2009). In exploring the relationship between popular culture and educational identities, Mendick, Epstein, and Moreau (2008, 5) describes the need to 'cut across the binaries within debates about the relationship between *images* and *identities* ... between active makers of meaning and passive recipients of media messages'. In exploring the circulation of achieving girl discourses within and between (con)texts and subjects, I seek a theoretical framework which neither reifies media texts and assumes monolithic meanings, nor overcelebrates the possibilities for local resistance and agency among audiences/subjects. While warning that no one model can 'bear the weight of audience research' and unite all the theoretical variables, Livingstone (1998, 14) describes the task of the audience researcher as that of exploring the role of media texts in communicative processes and relations; she recommends an expanded view of context, one which is vertical rather than merely locally embedded, and which takes into account conditions of production and recirculation, as well as of reception.

Livingstone's concerns resonate with my aims in undertaking this study; in exploring the different ways and contexts in which girls take up, interact with and circulate discourses of achieving girlhood, I seek to illuminate the nature of the discourses themselves and their relationship to institutional contexts of production. Such an endeavour draws on traditions of both textual analysis and empirical audience studies.

The Achieving Girl on Screen

In media scholarship as well as in education, there has been growing interest in achieving girl discourses, and a range of textual studies have appeared exploring the images, tropes and narratives of female achievement in media texts, including music, film and television (Whelahan 2000; Helford 2000; Inness 2008; Negra 2009; Pomerantz and Raby 2015). In both empirical and textual studies of achieving girl discourses, there is an acknowledgement of the other. Empirical studies in education and audience studies discuss the proliferation of popular texts as a key element of the discursive context in which girls' identity work takes place; media textual studies are underpinned by an assumption of the power of the text to interpellate girls via the images and narratives under discussion.

There is increasing interest in examining the relationship between popular discourses and specifically educational identities among girls. For example, Mendick et al. (2008) explore the ways in which popular culture resources are deployed in the formation of young women's mathematical identities; Gonick (2003) explores girls' mobilisation and appropriation of popular narratives and images as tools for exploring their own identity dilemmas in schools; Mendick and Moreau (2010) examine the online representation of women in science, engineering and technology (SET) occupations and the responses of web users to such representations. Via a range of episte-mological and methodological frameworks, these studies explore ways in which girls' media experiences are woven into their identities in social and educational settings.

This study seeks to extend elements of the kinds of work described above, drawing on traditions of audience studies and educational enquiry, of tex-tual analysis and reception analysis within a wider framework of discourse analysis. This implies an approach which conceives of texts, contexts and audiences as enmeshed in processes of meaning production in which sim-ple relationships and processes of agency or reproduction are not assumed. Aapola et al.'s (2005) work provides a model for considering the voices of girls as texts within an analysis of popular prevailing discourses. While the authors acknowledge the limitations and inevitable selection involved in including these 'intertextualities', they draw attention to the potential of such material to add complexity of thinking. The terming of these excerpts and voices as intertextualities is informative; intertextuality implies not only something interleaved within the text, but a referential relationship between texts. Thus, the 'girlhood voices' are conceived as texts in themselves, placed in an informed and informing juxtaposition with other texts within the wider discourse.

In the field of audience studies, Hills (2005a) offers the possibility of regarding audience accounts of their interest in texts as elements of discur-sive patterns of circulation, as 'claims to agency' rather than as 'truth telling claims as to … experienced realities' (xi). In doing so, he challenges the conventional organising hierarchies of authority between scholars, popular texts and fans by treating each as a site of meaning production of equal interest, and drawing attention to their structural and substantive similari-ties. Like Aapola et al. (2005), Hills (2005a) is able to examine the various accounts as instances of relatable discourse. He shows how these are cir-cumscribed by local and contextual regularities and conventions, but are locatable within wider discourses of aesthetics, gender and cultural hierar-chy. As Gonick (2003, 59) notes of her interweaving of popular texts, eth-nographic field notes and teen-produced video, such discursive treatment of fan, academic and popular texts presents a challenge to the epistemological claims of empirical studies.

The category of 'achieving girl', already acknowledged to be complex, ambiguous and contradictory within schools, opens up possibilities for examining how school identities and discourses are drawn upon in contexts beyond its walls. This study entails such an investigation, through exploring discourses of successful girlhood in an online context where girls discuss school-produced identities and their relationship to popular representations. It also explores discourses of achieving girlhood within television dramas produced for or popular with teen audiences. Such dramas, as Jagodzinski (2008, 97) points out, are representations of high school life crystallised and animated by writers and actors. They are and are not 'lies'; they are narrative processes in which desire is embedded, and they are texts which can be examined within the same discursive field as texts produced by human participants. An archaeological sensibility (Foucault 1969) allows a consideration of such representations in terms of their discursive function rather than as 'truths'; together with young peoples' local meaning making, all are statements within a discourse producing a particular object of knowledge (the achieving girl) across diverse 'surfaces of appearance'.

3   *The Archaeology*
Sites and Stories

In using his *Archaeology*, I am aware that I am adopting a relatively neglected perspective from the range that Foucault's work offers (Gutting 1989). *The Archaeology* not only has failed to attract the degree of interest from feminists that his work on genealogy, power and ethics has done (McNay 1992), but also, as noted earlier, presents particular challenges to the possibility of agency through its relentless insistence on the ways in which discourse creates us (Scott 1998; McLaren 2002). In this chapter, I argue that such an approach enables me to address some emergent concerns in the field of audience studies, and is particularly well adapted to such an interdisciplinary endeavour in contemporary media contexts. I show how *The Archaeology of Knowledge* informs the analytic strategy and the detail of the method.

Foucault argues that a text 'is caught up in a system of references to other books, other texts, other sentences: it is a node within a network' (1969, 23). This concept of a network of meaning, its sites of authority and reproduction, and the possibility of examining a range of statements and narratives as the 'texts' which are its 'nodes' provides a viable theoretical framework for this study in its consideration of 'achieving girl' discourses across a range of sites. However, Foucault presents particular issues for feminist analysis, and these should be acknowledged before a more detailed account of the archaeological framework is given.

Post-Structuralist Feminism and Foucault

Disagreement among feminists as to the usefulness of Foucault's work for both theory and practice is located within wider debate between postmodern approaches and emancipatory agendas. In essence, the tendency of progressive agendas to construct unified categories is viewed by postmodernists as likely to imply exclusion through its normative implications, while postmodernism is seen by progressives as potentially dangerous relativism, denying both the identification of the forces of oppression and the possibility of collective response (McLaren 2002). Yet, even Foucault's critics acknowledge the powerful impact his ideas have had on feminist theory and methods of enquiry (Alcoff 1988; McNay 1992; McLaren 2002). As Taylor and Vintges (2004, 119) observe, 'it was not until the

discursive, constructed nature of the subject had been widely accepted'
that feminists could begin to conceptualise their work as taking into
consideration 'both the subjective point of view and personal agency',
through re-evaluating the self 'as both a strategic, discursive topos that
provides speaking positions on the basis of social experiences of gender
and as a "lived" reality'.

Foucault's 'notorious' exclusion of gender as a category for analysis is
a further point for contention because, it is argued, it ignores the particular conditions of institutionalised, gendered oppression (Alcoff 1998),
it reproduces the inherent sexism of apparently gender-neutral social theory (McNay 1992), and it does not allow for a differentiated internalised
response to the workings of power (Deveaux 1994). However, if there is,
Foucault maintains, no stepping outside discursively constituted domains
of power, the endeavour becomes instead that of 'challenging "truth games"
from a variety of angles within power' (Allen 1996, 287). Alcoff (1988)
suggests a focus on the analysis of gender as a construct that is 'formalisable
in a non-arbitrary way through a matrix of habit, practices and discourses',
which is at once subject to change and located within a particular historical
'discursive constellation'. She argues that

> we can conceive of the subject as non-essentialised and emergent from
> a historical experience, and yet retain our political ability to take gen-
> der as an important point of departure. (433)

The Archaeology of Knowledge as Method

Foucault is notoriously non-specific in terms of methodology, and the
Archaeology of Knowledge (1969) is the closest he comes to outlining a
method. It is nonetheless possible to draw from its principles the strategies, upon which enquiry may be designed (Kendall and Wickham 1999;
Andersen 2003). *The Archaeology* describes Foucault's approach to investigating the history of knowledge as produced by discourses, the analysis of
which can reveal underpinning structures of thought or ways in which the
world can be conceived. This analysis is undertaken via the examination
of discourses as they are manifested in texts, statements and practices at
specific locations in describable ways at particular moments. It is termed an
'archaeological' approach because it seeks to excavate a substratum and to
treat the objects unearthed as artefacts to be described rather than as texts
to be interpreted for their inner meaning or authorial intent.

The Archaeology describes an approach to conducting a history of the
formation of knowledge. It seeks to analyse 'discursive formations' or
groups of statements as ways of organising knowledge which secure dominant relations of power. A discursive formation is built around the following
elements: the *objects of knowledge* which the statements produce – here the
achieving girl, the *enunciative modalities* or manner in which statements are

produced and their status, the *concepts* of which they are formed, and the *strategies* or theoretical viewpoints they develop (Foucault 1969). Examining a discursive formation or group of statements accordingly invites particular attention to aspects of production and appearance, to their relationship with other discourses, as well as to their common or divergent elements (Foucault's 'regularities' and 'disruptions'). While this conveys an idea of the ways in which *The Archaeology* informs this enquiry, it is not used as a sequential set of instructions. It is not within the scope of this study to mobilise each point of analysis that Foucault specifies equally, but to use these as indicators of ways in which an archaeological analytic strategy may be useful. Foucault (1980) himself observes that

> all my books are, if you like, little toolboxes. If people want to open them, to use a particular sentence, a particular idea, a particular analysis like a screwdriver or a spanner to short-circuit, to discredit, to break systems of power, including perhaps even those that my books issue from ... well, so much the better! (in Brocklesby and Cummings 1996, 749)

This provocative offer allows for a considered selectivity from among the tools provided by *The Archaeology*, contextualised within an understanding of the principles of his design.

Discourses, Statements, Texts and Regularities

Discourse, for Foucault, defines and produces knowledge and is comprised of groups of statements. For Foucault, a statement has to be related to or perform a function with regard to other statements within a discourse – it is this that gives it its meaning, not any inherent 'truth'. Graham (2005, 7) describes the Foucauldian statement as a 'discursive junction-box in which words and things intersect and become invested in particular relations of power, resulting in an interpellative event', and which provides the human sciences with objects of scrutiny. My exploration of statements about the achieving girl concerns ways that they function in creating a particular category of girlhood, and the wider power structures inscribed and maintained within them – an undertaking which, as Le Doeuff (2003, 11) exhorts, challenges the understanding of achieving girl as a stable and knowable object and focuses instead on the variable values and categories ascribed to her.

Statements are recorded in documents or texts, which provide the evidence that the archaeologist examines; for Foucault, 'objects of scientific enquiry, and human subjectivity itself, are textually constructed (Soyland and Kendall 1997, 11). These texts go beyond the written word and can include any way in which a statement is recorded, for example, 'accounts, registers, acts, buildings, institutions, laws, techniques, objects, customs' (Foucault 1969, 7) – in short, all those materials with which historians work. I find his expanded notion of texts particularly useful in terms of its ability to embrace visual statements, including the sign systems of television and film, as well as the statements produced by audiences. Further, his inclusive notion of texts takes on particular relevance in the digital age when user and producer divides are increasingly blurred.

Foucault (1969) sees texts not as individual loci of truths, but as part of interrelated groupings in a network of meaning. As a part of his challenge to the obvious, Foucault is particularly concerned with troubling the unities of fields and disciplines and the ways that texts are grouped and ordered within them – and the possibility of creating new ones. The archaeologist's task then is to 'disconnect the unquestioned continuities by which we organise, in advance, the discourses that we are to analyse'. This is achieved through a process of reduction of discourses to their constitutive regularities, and then construction of possible re-formations, of new connections and contingencies (1969, 27).

Archaeological Research Strategy

This study explores texts produced at institutional and individual levels, and considers both mass and localised discourses of feminised achievement. It focuses on three organising principles that Foucault (1969) describes as 'formation of objects', 'enunciative modalities' and 'discursive regularities'. These may be understood as the statements about achieving girlhood, the conditions of production, and the identifiable shared tropes they contain – whether in schools, online or on a TV screen. This allows for a recognition of how power relationships inscribed in institutional discourses are reproduced or reshaped in participant accounts. For example, when group interview participant Amina describes how

> you always, like, hear about how there's so many people competing for the same jobs, like all the time in assembly. And it just pushes you to try harder cause you know that there's gonna be more people out there in the workforce that want the same job,

one can see at work tropes from discourses of self-responsibility and individualised competition within flexible labour forces; within this discourse, education itself and conceptions of ability in children are positioned in terms of their relationship to the economy, as human capital and driven by market values (Ong 2004). In these contexts, a focus on the 'gifted and talented' emerges as an attempt to foster the creation of an international intellectual elite who will ensure the nation's global competitiveness (Tomlinson 2008). Thus, one can locate Amina's statement in the wider discursive field of neoliberal economic policies of free market capitalism (Mohamed 2008) and also identify the school's role in reproducing such discourses via morning assembly. Amina's statement also calls into being that unspoken other against whom she defines herself – the lazy, unproductive pupil who will grow into an adult ill-equipped to meet the demands of the neoliberal labour market, and potentially become a drain on the market and its more productive workers – the benefit scrounger.

The discursive approach I employ then considers the function of Amina's statement in producing the achieving girl as an object of knowledge, and its relationship to other statements in the discursive field; I also consider contexts of production and reception, and how these work to position the statement in the wider discourse. The conditions of a statement's pronunciation effect its identity – it must be spoken in a particular time, place and manner, and if these change, then so does the nature of the statement itself. This allows for a consideration of variation in the nature of statements produced – about, say, 'working hard' – in different contexts of online forums, schools and media texts.

The statements/responses of participants of the study are considered as texts in their own right, and are analysed and grouped with those from popular texts into narratives according to the regularities identified. The organisation of findings by the narratives emerging rather than by discipline, institution, genre or data source is intended to enable the identification of regularities or tropes of the achieving girl discourse across a range of fields, and to use them to create new unities. The juxtaposition of popular, educational and participant texts and statements in newly organised 'achieving girl' narrative categories aims to challenge notions of knowledge of achieving girlhood as being produced in specific disciplines, and to trace the reach of some pervasive contemporary discourses.

The blending of data sources and sites is implicit within the parameters of the archaeological approach, but must also be rationalised within more specific contexts and methodological considerations. Within the three locations, it is possible to define three kinds of achieving girl subject position. In schools, girls are identified by the institution; this creates the achieving girl as a specific institutional subject position through a formal pronunciation that she is 'gifted' (Austin 1976). On the website, participants self-identify as 'smart girls' and establish their identities in a virtual setting through image and written text. In both the group interviews and the online forum, they are invited to describe ways in which they identify with school-sanctioned and popular culture versions of successful femininity. In the television texts, representations 'circumscribe the subject positions' which the girls occupy (Skeggs 1997, 18); here (tele)visual conventions, narratives and technologies work to create identities by which girls may be interpellated in various ways; the achieving girl subject position is inscribed in the text.

Where the Girls Are: Some Notes on Sites and Processes of Enquiry

School Sites

Schools are everyday sites for the local performances of broader cultural femininities, and are thus sites in which exploring young women's interactions with global cultures, particularly media cultures, can enable the 'troubling' of more parochial understandings of gender (Kehily and Nayak 2008, 326). Schools are also sites in which specific local identities associated with achievement are produced and performed. While ability identities inevitably intersect with broader identities of class, gender, ethnicity and individual or family factors, in comprehensive schools it is via such ability identities that pupils are classified and often grouped, and where associated discursive frameworks of expectations and life trajectories are affirmed (Reay 2001b, 34).

The advent of national 'gifted and talented' policies in the UK, and their near-universal adoption by schools since 2000, has led to the creation of a specific category of 'gifted' or highly achieving pupil. This is not to suggest that the 'recognition' of which pupils are likely to achieve most highly is newly produced via such policy; rather, it has led to a new visibility for long-standing practices of categorising students in ways which perpetuate structures of power (Foucault 1979) and to newly heightened subject positions in schools (Francis, Skelton, and Read 2010, 322). The act of nomination of a pupil to a 'gifted and talented' register is in some ways a performative speech act, in that it produces as it pronounces the 'gifted' pupil (Austin 1976, 44). Here I distinguish between Austin's conception of the speech act as an authorised pronunciation which brings a particular object into formalised existence (such as in a marriage ceremony) and Butler's (1990) expanded notion in which more everyday communications (not confined to the verbal) constitute performances which work to define identity, in contexts of cultural consensus as to their meaning. This distinction serves to differentiate contexts and processes in which the achieving girl subject position is formally defined through authoritative statements, and those where it is claimed or negotiated in social and informal communications. The creation of 'gifted and talented' registers, letters home informing parents of 'gifted' status, and records of attainment data for such cohorts all constitute 'surfaces of appearance' for statements at the institutional level in terms of archaeological enquiry. But such 'naming' is not just of significance for the social and pedagogical technologies of schooling; the inhabiting of identity labels in schools is central to youth culture and power (Currie, Kelly, and Pomerantz 2009, 422). The ways in which girls take up such subject positions in their reproduction of local (school) and wider discourses of feminised success forms a core part of this study.

Three schools were chosen to provide, within the confines of the study, a range in which students are specifically identified as 'gifted and talented'.

Although this terminology is not used in all three, they have all partici-
pated in local or national teacher development programmes with a focus
on the area, and maintain annually updated registers of the top 5–10%
of pupils based on a range of qualitative and quantitative data, such as
Cognitive Abilities Tests (CATs), national test scores, teacher nomination
and classwork. The girls participating in this study were drawn from these
registers. It is important to point out that their achieving girl status is therefore relative to their school contexts, and not based on a standard model
of testing. Further, the girls' own experiences suggest that their status on
the registers and in top sets is also dependent on being 'deserving' through
compliance and diligence (see e.g. Kelly, who complains of being removed
from her mathematics class for disruptive behaviour, or Sally, who says she
is unsure if she is 'gifted' because she doesn't actually work that hard to get
her grades, so she pretends to put in more effort than she really does).

The three participating schools are all state-maintained comprehensives:

School A: Sir Walter Raleigh is a large (1900 students) rural 11–18 mixed
comprehensive in one of the shire counties, serving the market town
where it is situated and a catchment area of surrounding villages.
A result of the merging of smaller schools, it has no local competition in the state sector, although the 'gifted and talented' coordina-
tor reports that the more affluent families in a largely conservative
region often choose to educate their children privately. The school is
predominantly white, and a smaller-than-average number of pupils
are from economically deprived backgrounds. Results historically
have been broadly in line with national averages and have improved
beyond these in recent inspections (Ofsted reports 2007, 2011, 2014).

School B: St Ursula's is a Catholic comprehensive school for girls aged
11–16 situated in a Greater London borough. There are approximately 750 pupils on roll. It accepts pupils from a wide geographical
area and is socially mixed. The proportion of students from minority
ethnic backgrounds is higher than average, and is spread across a
number of ethnic groups. However, the percentage who have English
as an additional language is lower than average. The school is over-
subscribed, and results at all key stages are higher than national averages (Ofsted reports 2008, 2011, 2014).

School C: Maple Grove is an inner-city comprehensive of approximately
1400 students where the proportion of those eligible for free school
meals is well above average. Students are drawn from a wide range
of ethnic backgrounds. Nearly 50% are from non-English-speaking
homes, and approximately 10% of students have refugee status. Almost
50% of the students speak a home language other than English, with
a small minority at early stages of fluency. A higher-than-average proportion of pupils joins or leaves the school at times other than usual
transition points (Ofsted reports 2007, 2011, 2014).

Group Interviews

Thirty-six girls were interviewed in the three school sites, in groups of four to six. Interviews lasted approximately an hour, and were both audio and video recorded and then transcribed by me; the decision to interview in groups was made on both strategic and pragmatic grounds. Foremost, it allowed me to access groups of girls in the school contexts that produced them as achieving girls. While groups may not prove ideal for eliciting detailed personal biographical narratives (Barbour 2007, 18), the context-dependent nature of the interview group as a 'site of performance' aligns this method with a post-structuralist epistemology in its treatment of identity production as situated and contextual (Brannen and Pattman 2005, 52). While some group effects of peer and contextual influence are often observed as qualifying concerns (Litosseliti 2003), the interactive and dynamic ways in which meaning is produced in group interviews can be viewed as exemplifying social processes in which identities are elaborated and discourses are circulated (Wilkinson 1999, 225; Barbour 2007, 31). The group discussion context also reflects the social nature and use of much teen television engagement (Murray 1999; Fisherkeller 2002).

Selection of Participants

Girls were drawn from the school years 9 and 10 (aged 13–15) and were all identified as 'gifted and talented' by the schools, that is, placed on the register of the top 5–10% of pupils in their year group. This does not imply a homogeneity of ability or achievement – as discussed earlier, the definitions of 'giftedness' are multiple and methods of diagnosis diverse; the requirement that schools select a percentage means that those in any so-designated cohort will vary according to the broader achievement profile of their peers.

   Determining the social composition of groups was initially problematic, as one school was reluctant to provide such details about the participants as they did not want to 'risk stereotyping'. The school's discomfort with the idea of social categories as significant is worth noting itself as an illustration of the disappearance of discourses of structural disadvantage from national policy down to school practices (Francis and Hey 2009). At another of the schools, the liaising teacher offered me a broad categorisation of their own in terms of social/cultural profile. Because of such variation, and the complexities of subjectivities which resist simple categorisations of class, I decided not to attempt to define categories for participants at the outset, but to pay close attention to ways in which they positioned themselves with regard to the dominant discourses of achieving girlhood under discussion. Such positioning has been found important in understanding the complexities of the relationship between class and educational opportunity, beyond the simplifications of aspirational poverty or financial deterrents (Archer and Hutchings 2000; Reay, David, and Ball 2005). In this context, it was also interesting to note the degree of code switching (Trudgill 2001) in terms of regional accent or received pronunciation in the groups – some participants commenced the interviews speaking in the accents and vocabularies associated with the middle classes but 'switched' into more pronounced regional accents, non-standard forms and informal expressions as discussion warmed up. While this may be attributed to the perceived formality of the proceedings and to their perception of my status, it could indicate a degree of aspiration and possible shame with regard to class, or alternatively that the imperative to share peer language became greater than the imperative to create a particular impression for the researcher. Therefore, the statements and narratives of participants are treated as evidence of the identities and aspirations produced within the contexts of the groups themselves. This approach avoids the imposition of oversimplified categories and aligns with the epistemological stance of the archaeology. It also creates greater resonance with the treatment of statements from online forum participants, whose offline identities similarly cannot be readily categorised and whose subjectivities are treated as contextually produced.

Of the 36 pupils, at St Ursula's one girl was of African-Caribbean heritage, one of Asian-Indian heritage and one of Pakistani heritage, and one self-identified as being of white Irish heritage. At Maple Grove, one girl was of North African heritage, one of Arabic heritage, one of Turkish heritage and one of Chinese heritage. There were no minority ethnic students in the groups interviewed at Sir Walter Raleigh, the rural comprehensive in which there were very few non-white pupils. The remaining participants were white, and two of them positioned themselves as working class through a range of their responses. The other girls appeared to occupy middle-class or aspirational subject positions to varying degrees. None of the girls interviewed stood out as particularly privileged or as occupying the higher strata of the middle classes, which is perhaps unsurprising given that they were all state comprehensive schools.

Media Sites

Before describing the sites and modes of data collection and analysis, I wish to spend a little time outlining the broader media contexts in which achieving girlhood discourses are produced. I want to consider television and online contexts together, before I consider them as separate sites; it is the convergence of these platforms that first prompted this enquiry, when I observed teen fans discussing their ideas about smart girls on a teen TV fan site. In contemporary contexts of media convergence and use, television still forms a significant part of teen media engagement, but its narratives and audience practices are dispersed across diverse media platforms. On these digital platforms, young users enact identities of which the elements are drawn from available cultural resources. Grunewald (2003) advocates a critical reconnection of school discourses with wider culture. I seek to establish such a connection through exploring the ways in which not only media discourses are drawn on in schools, but also educational discourses are drawn on in a virtual setting.

Contexts of Media Convergence and Youth Audiences

'Media convergence' is a complex concept which describes a range of aspects of contemporary digital media production and consumption. These have import for the fashioning of youth subjectivities in relation to technologies, markets and wider culture. It describes the ways in which media technologies converge in multifunctional products; for example, the smartphone is also a camera, a music player, a video screen and an Internet browser. It also describes ways in which media industries attempt to integrate provision across a range of products. A further meaning is provided by Jenkins (2006), who argues that one of the most important aspects of media convergence is not industrial or commercial, but the behaviours of audiences; for Jenkins, 'convergence represents a cultural shift as consumers are encouraged to seek out new information and make connections among dispersed media content' (3).

Despite attempts of established media conglomerates to gain control of new platforms, online youth audiences have proven notoriously fickle and difficult to secure in terms of habits and platforms. The media industries have made successful attempts to establish extended television content as a core element of Internet engagement, in order to increase audience share, fidelity and commercial opportunities through, for example, official show fan sites and associated games (Ha 2002; Siapera 2004; Perryman 2008; Ofcom 2010). This has led to what Jenkins (2006, 21) has termed a new aesthetic of 'transmedia storytelling', a process whereby audiences pursue elements relating to the original text across various platforms. These elements could be, for example, actors, songs featured on soundtracks, merchandise associated with shows, other works by members of the production team, especially writers, as well as platforms for activities such as fantasy role playing and fan fiction. This is most visibly demonstrated in one of the most popular texts among participants in this study – Disney's made-for-TV movie *High School Musical* (see Chapter 5). In a neat variation on McLuhan's (1964, 23) famous claim that 'the content of any medium is always another medium' (23), Bociurkiw (2008, 542) observes that 'the content of the internet is television'. This is affirmed by Buckingham (2008, 14), who describes 'the fundamental continuities between new media and old (especially television)' which 'exist at the level of form and content, as well as in terms of economics'. Teen television dramas and their associated websites – both official and fan-created sites – are among the most numerous and prominent in the genre (Center for Social Media 2001, 2009). Online and televisual worlds are mutually entwined in terms of production, consumption and appropriation.

Conditions of convergence and patterns of consumption raise critical questions regarding identity and the possibilities for agency. The commercialisation of virtual youth spaces and the limitations this places on agency have become a focus of interest as scholars explore the relationship between consumer items and identity (Atkinson and Nixon 2005; boyd 2007; Willett 2008a; van Dijk 2009; Pearson 2010). Although young people may be selective and inventive in their creations of images and identities, borrowing and reshaping resources in works of creativity described as 'bricolage', such symbolic resources are themselves drawn from internationally dispersed (especially from the US) and highly commercialised discourses, making the agency on offer to young people one which is shaped by broader discourses of economic participation and neoliberal notions of the ideal citizen as reflexive consumer (Willet 2008a; Savage 2008; Saltmarsh 2009; Sinanan, Graham, and Zhong Jie 2014).

Such contexts of convergence and the transmedia migration of stories, images and resources invite a specifically archaeological investigation in tracing the regularities that make up contemporary cultural discourses of achieving girlhood.

Contexts of Teen Television: Patterns of Engagement

Television narratives and girls' engagement with them form a central element of this enquiry. This I rationalise in terms of the continuing importance of television in teen leisure time; the dispersal of television narratives across other electronic media; and the conditions created by industry deregulation, commercialised niche broadcasting and new patterns of teen consumption.

In the UK and the US, teenagers are estimated to spend an average of between 6.5 (Ofcom 2015) and 9 (Common Sense 2015) hours a day engaging with various media, and this figure has remained relatively stable this century. Somewhat surprisingly in the face of Internet competition, television watching retains a significant proportion of it year on year (Roberts, Foehr, and Rideout 2005; Ofcom 2013). There is evidence to suggest that time spent on new media involves a re-organisation rather than a replacement of other leisure activities (Wartella and Robb 2008), with a growth in simultaneous media use, for example, of both television and computer or tablet or phone, as household ownership of multiple technologies grows (Ofcom 2013, 2015). In conditions of media convergence, as we have seen above, television content is also a highly visible element of online engagement, as digital platforms are used to extend engagement with television shows, in both commercial and fan-created forms.

It is not only the multiplicity of media engagements that is of interest: conditions of engagement are also changing. A pattern that has been described as 'the privatisation of media use' indicates increased intensity of experience through increased immersion, repetition and isolation in viewing habits (Roberts 2000, 9). This happens as households adopt multiple devices on which to watch, record, replay and engage with visual media. The later twentieth-century teenage girl had to watch television with the family and negotiate her programme choices; she was limited to three channels until 1982 and unlikely to have the technology to record a broadcast until the mid-nineties. However, by 2009 77% of teenagers were estimated to have televisions in their bedrooms (Thomas, Mulligan, and Wiramihardja 2000; Ofcom 2010). Patterns of watching are shifting again as increasing numbers of teenagers report watching TV on personal digital devices such as phones and tablets (Ofcom 2011, 2013). While much television watching still nonetheless occurs in the living room, teens increasingly consume their chosen media both differently and separately from family and adult worlds (Livingstone 2009; Ofcom 2010, 2013). Before this era of private consumption, adolescent television viewing decreased as youth sought separation from their family groups (Roberts et al. 2005; Eggermont 2006). New viewing habits and broadcasting trends, however, offer the adolescent separation via increased screen engagement in conditions of increased intensity and repetition (Livingstone 2009).

The advent of new television technologies, media deregulation, multiple channels and online content has led to changes in the nature of broadcasts to narrowcasts, from family to niche-orientated shows as mass audiences are fragmented and a plethora of channels fight for smaller shares. This shift from what Eco (1983) has termed 'paleotelevision' to 'neotelevision' also marks a philosophical shift in the provision of public service–orientated broadcasting and public ownership to market-orientated broadcasting and commercial ownership (Scolari 2009). The UK in particular demonstrates a strong take-up of new television technologies and, unlike access to high-speed broadband, this take-up has been distributed fairly evenly across higher and lower socio-economic groups, although lower socio-economic groups spend more hours watching (Adda and Ottaviani 2005; Livingstone 2007; Stamatkis et al. 2009; Keaney 2009; Ofcom 2010, 2013).

Segregated viewing patterns and the shift to market-orientated broadcasting are central to the growth of teen TV genres. Bolt (2008, 94) describes how teen TV came to occupy its own particular niche through its address to a demographic which defines itself as alienated from the mainstream – adolescents. However, such address to a defined demographic is framed within commercial imperatives: teen shows are often characterised as quality or intelligent television (Wee 2008, 50); they assume sophisticated levels of media literacy (Osgerby 2004, 77) and a high level of formal education in their attempts to secure audiences with the greatest disposable incomes (Davis and Dickinson 2004, 8). The identificatory possibilities offered by such texts are therefore likely to be dominated by hegemonic groups: the affluent, white and educated (Meehan 2002). This is of significance in the light of suggestions that wishful identification with aspirational figures is as important a factor as peer identification in teen viewing – in other words, teen television choices and identification figures are dictated by the offer of models not just like them, but those whom they wish they were like (Brown and Pardun 2004, 268). The ways in which formulaic, commercial TV culture works within the experiences and imagined futures of young people is important to our understanding of the ways in which they negotiate identities (Fisherkeller 1999, 2002); as Fisherkeller observes, it is not only the presence of televisual technologies in the home, but the ways in which young people grow up within television *culture* that demonstrates the integration of television into their lives (2002, 3). Given contemporary concerns regarding the restricted address of achieving girl discourses and the gendering of achievement, the nature of identities and narratives on offer in teen television as a central site of cultural engagement must be of interest.

Online Contexts

I describe above how the line between televisual and online content has become increasingly blurred as narratives are dispersed and industry ownership converges, and also that the consumption of popular culture products has become a means of identity display in online settings. The creation of online identities, particularly in relation to television consumption, thus presents itself as an area for focus. Early studies of online identities are often celebratory in their accounts of the Internet's potential for identity reconstruction in contexts liberated from the cultural restrictions of experienced reality. Such identities are seen as the technological manifestation of post-structuralist notions of fragmented, discursively constituted selfhood (Braidotti 1994; Turkle 1994; Lister et al. 2009). Later work focuses on the connections and continuities between real-world and virtual identities, finding that raced, classed and gendered subjectivities are reproduced online (boyd 2011), and on exploring the continuities and need to keep a story going in the performance of online identities (Merchant 2006). Merchant distinguishes between anchored and transient identities, as those which are

> profoundly influenced by a long history of socio-cultural practices (such as gender or religion) and those which are more easily made, remade and unmade, such as fandom. (239)

This distinction is not a simple binary division, but rather represents either end of a continuum; transient and anchored identities may overlap, change and develop through maturation, experience, peer influence and circumstance. Such a distinction is of interest with regard to gendered ability identities in contexts where the new identity of 'achieving' may be grafted onto the relatively anchored category of 'girl'; for example, one participant, Kirsty, describes how she

> didn't really know it til I got my SAT results and I got like the highest in my class. And then in Year 7 when I got the letter [announcing

her placement on the school's 'gifted and talented' register] then I kind of knew.

It is also of interest where a girl finds an identity as a visible achiever more difficult to manage as she enters adolescent cultures in which emphasised femininities are valued, like Anna, who describes how 'it's kind of like, I don't want to act smart in case a certain group of girls don't like this and will go back to the boys and tell them this'. The degree of transience or stability of the 'successful' element may vary as it intersects with other subjectivities, such as those produced by class and 'race'. The formal identification of 'giftedness' is a relatively new practice in schools; for girls, this may represent a stable subject position they have comfortably inhabited for some time – as online participant *Pandora* claims: 'It means everything to be smart. Because that's who I am' – or one which may be novel, partial, fleeting and context dependent.

Online contexts present new opportunities to examine girls' discursive practices as they take place in visual and textual modes. There is a body of work from the early days of youth online engagement to the present exploring the gendered nature of engagement and identity construction online. Common findings include girls' use of online spaces to experiment with wishful or idealised identities, to seek authenticating affirmation from peers for aspects of selfhood, and to appropriate popular culture images and narratives as resources in identity construction (Savicki 1996; Arnold and Miller 1999; Calvert 2002; Stern 2004a; Subrah-manyam, Greenfield, and Tynes 2004; Mazzarella 2005; Guzzetti 2006; Manago et al. 2008; Willett 2008a; Monaghan 2010; Paechter 2013; Sinanan et al. 2014). The study of online fan activities in particular has provided insights into the ways in which girls use television to explore their subjectivities and construct self-narratives (Murray 1999, 222).

The investigation of online identities lends itself particularly well to a Foucauldian archaeological approach in its focus on the textual manifestations of discourses, rather than on the lived experiences of subjects as individuals (Foucault 1969). The researcher's concern then becomes not 'How can I be sure that online participants' identities are representative of an authentic, embodied offline identity?' but rather, 'How are participants positioning themselves with regard to wider discourses? What cues and resources are they making use of in the construction of identities?' As such, this highlights the element of *all* claims to lived experience and authenticity as reported, rather than empirically verifiable truths.

Virtual Sites: The Online Forum

I briefly outlined my rationale for building my own teen TV forum in the introduction; the decision to do so raises epistemological, ethical and practical issues. The process of creating and moderating the site also presented challenges and possibilities in terms of the researcher–subject relationship and the nature of knowledge produced.

The epistemological stance of archaeological analysis is, as discussed above, one which foregrounds the discourse rather than the subject, and which gives primacy to the text as the manifestation of knowledge. It would thus seem that Internet enquiry, in which subjects can only be known by the texts they produce, is well aligned to such an approach (Mann and Stewart 2000). As Hine (2000) observes, a 'textually inflected' approach may be particularly appropriate because

> a textual focus places emphasis on the ways in which contributions are justified and rendered authoritative, and on the identities which authors construct and perform through their postings.... The reality which texts construct can be evaluated on its own terms, without recourse to an external, pretextual reality. (53)

However, treating subjects as texts in this way may elide ethical issues surrounding informed consent and the status of Internet interactions as private or public (Lotz and Ross 2004; Eynon, Fry, and Schroeder 2008). These issues become particularly acute when researching youth online (Stern 2004b).

I therefore treat participants epistemologically as authors, but ethically as human subjects. This distinction between authors and subjects is made by the Association of Internet Researchers in their ethical guidelines for online researchers (AIoR and Ess 2002). It is made in terms of material which is meant for public consumption (e.g. blogs, essays, news sites) and material which appears to be person-to-person interaction, such as social network site and chatroom postings. This distinction is not without difficulties; the status of some online material is ambivalent. It also raises difficulties for non-participant observation of online social worlds where declaration of presence and intent may influence outcomes (Mann and Stewart 2000, 52). The potential vulnerability of participants is also a key factor. The diversities and complexities of online worlds make attention to specific contexts central to approaches to research ethics (AoIR 2012).

Fan sites where participants post are ostensibly public spaces, but the ethics of using such postings in research remains debated (Lotz and Ross 2004; Whiteman 2012; AoIR 2012). In earlier days of researching youth online, some researchers treated treat teen messages, blogs, homepages and forum postings as publically available data – for example, Murray explores an online fan site for a teen TV show (1999) and Merskin studies teen Wiccan Internet communities (2007); both discuss, quote and screen-grab the words and images of site users, while neither appears to have sought consent or engaged directly with participants. While the easy availability of data and the naturalness of the setting are strong inducements to the practice of 'lurking' as a researcher (Whiteman 2012), it is increasingly accepted that the diversities and complexities of online worlds make attention to specific contexts central to approaches to research ethics (AoIR 2012).

An alternative practice is that of joining an online forum or community openly as a researcher and directly seeking consent from site owners and participants. I had indeed originally intended to garner my data from existing teen TV fan sites. However, using existing websites as data sources presents particular problems. First, there are problems of scope and defining the field (Hine 2009). Creating my own web forum provided a practical means of defining boundaries in that it provided a single defined location for research, and the site was designed for and overtly devoted to the purposes of the research. However, the other visible functions it came to perform and the relationships developed thereon were subject to the organic, social processes of engagement, and while less easy to define in terms of boundaries, they provided interesting material for reflection.

Gaining Consent

A further issue in researching existing communities is that consent is more easily sought than gained (Fischer, Lyon, and Zeitler 2008, 541). In the early stages of this study, I identified a range of possible UK-based teen TV fan sites and emailed the sites' owners describing my research and requesting permission to ask questions on their forum boards as a declared participant-researcher. Only one readily gave consent; while others did not express hostility to the study itself, they did not wish their communities to be used for research. Concerns were expressed regarding participants' privacy and what was seen as adult intrusion into teenage space – a consideration also noted by Stern (2004b), boyd (2007) and Livingstone (2008). Another explained that allowing a researcher access may result in losing members in the fickle world of TV fan sites. Creating my own site thus enabled me to overcome a range of practical and ethical problems raised by attempting to garner data from existing sites.

As noted above, the Internet is often seen by teens as a private space. They not only may be reluctant to share their own online practices, but also can be unwilling to involve their parents in the process of getting consent forms signed, seeing this as a challenge in itself to their online autonomy (Stern 2004b). Rather than attempt what other scholars have found to be a largely fruitless endeavour, I decided to focus instead on gaining the consent of participants themselves, and on security, anonymity and transparency, so that for participants and for those parents who monitor their offspring's Internet use (Livingstone 2007), the purpose, nature and outcomes of the study would be clear, as would the care taken to ensure no harm comes to participants. As the AIoR (2002) guidelines observe, because there is debate about the capacity of minors to give informed consent, it is incumbent on the researcher to ensure the safety of participants.

Recruiting Participants

Getting the design right was key to recruiting and retaining participants. The site was created with the collaboration of a small group of girls known to me personally who fit the target subjectivities of the site in that they were identified as 'gifted and talented' by their schools and were enthusiastic television watchers and Internet users. This group was consulted at various stages about the website name, appearance, accessibility and content in terms of appeal and relevance. Their forthright and helpful suggestions proved invaluable in constructing a site which attracted users in an age of stiff Internet competition, particularly in terms of TV fan sites; one cannot assume with a youth-orientated website that if one builds it, 'they will come' (Montgomery 2008, 28). It was this group who suggested the name 'smart girls'; while this usage of 'smart' is American, as opposed to the traditional UK meaning of 'smartly dressed', it illustrates the pervasive nature of US television culture as observed above. It is also sufficiently removed from school terminology for the site not to appear, as one of my young consultants put it, 'dorky'.

Some 137 members in total registered and remained on the website forum. My recruitment strategy adhered to the EU Kids Online Best Practice Research Guidelines for recruiting older children in using both existing online networks and communities, and putting to use other offline contacts (Lobe et al. 2008). I posted notices (with site owner permissions) in a range of similar or related Internet sites as also recommended by Gaiser (2008, 294). I also approached those TV fan sites which had not been hostile in turning down my initial request to use their sites, and asked if they would be willing to add a link. A number of participants were recruited in this way, and as the study progressed, some participants asked permission to post links to other forums they themselves had created, particularly those for TV fantasy role play linked to the shows under discussion. I also asked both government and commercial teacher websites to add links to my site and was successful with a range of these; for example, the National Strategies, Teachit.co.uk, National Association of Teachers of English, National Academy for Gifted and Talented Youth, and a range of Local Authority websites all agreed. Furthermore, an unanticipated degree of 'snowballing' occurred; I was approached by other sites asking permission to feature my site on theirs, with a reciprocal link on mine. These included sites in New Zealand, Australia and the US, including NASA.

Because of the online/real world nature of the study, I also recruited via schools. I sent details of the site and the project to every school with which I had any sort of contact. The actual site design included incentives to visit in addition to the research participation – for example, a page of quotations suggested by participants, and a page with links to other sites of possible interest to which participants could add. In designing the website, I used a range of images of TV and film smart girls and women. I had made sure that these included non-white representations; in the 'links' section I had also included blogs and websites run by and for minority ethnic groups.

Access and Digital Participation

I also had to take into consideration issues of access and inclusivity. These issues have both technological and cultural dimensions. In terms of technology, while fast Internet access in secondary schools is now almost universal in the UK (Becta 2010), the quality of information and communications technology provision and levels of access in school vary widely (Lee 2008), and there remain unresolved issues in terms of class, access and use beyond school (Lee 2008). The digital divide within the context of the global West is increasingly becoming one of use and integration rather than just practical access (Peter and Valkenburg 2006; Livingstone 2007; Ofcom 2010, 2015); boyd (2011) observes ways in which social networks are becoming increasingly defined by class and race in the US. Other scholars observe that online engagement is influenced by a complex mixture of social, psychological, economic and practical factors (Chen and Wellman 2004; van Dijk 2005; Selwyn and Facer 2007; Moyo 2008; Walker and Logan 2009).

It is therefore important to be aware that participation in any web forum is likely to be shaped by both technical and cultural issues, and not to assume a universality of youth or gendered practices from its participants. In such a forum as this, which explores popular representations of achieving girlhood, the restrictions in such representations are likely to be played out among its participants too.

The Researcher's Role Online

The creation of a purpose-built forum for online research raises some of the same issues as presented by real-world group interviews, in that such a forum is an artificial construct, and therefore discussion and statements produced are inevitably shaped by this (Wilson 1997, 217). However, the nature of forum technology, the asynchronous character of the process, and the cultures of practice within online forums highlight the co-construction of knowledge. This implies a need to reflect on the researcher–subject relationship in new ways that align both ethically and epistemologically with feminist post-structuralist approaches (Lotz and Ross 2004). Such reflection reveals ways in which creating such a forum approaches more nearly to Pollock's (1976) ideal of research, which comes as close as possible to the conditions in which opinions are formed, and offers new possibilities to the television audience researcher concerned with engaging with audiences in the contexts in which they produce readings (Morley 1992).

The nature of forum technology itself challenges the primacy of the researcher in directing the focus and managing the contributions of participants. The asynchronous nature of online discussions means that they will continue when the researcher is not actually present to shape them. While this can be regarded as a problem in terms of loss of control (Gaiser 2008), it can also enrich the process. While I initiated a range of the discussion threads myself, participants were encouraged by the forum facilities not only to respond but also to start their own; of the 64 discussion threads, I initiated 22 and the remaining 42 were started by forum members. This is part of the usual culture of TV fan sites, and the forum technology also rewards member activity through heightened status (from 'newbie' through to 'hero member'). Forum participants' awareness and valuing of such status was demonstrated to me early on by their requests for clarification of the tariff, and advising me to adjust it more generously to encourage more posting. They also had the facility to start mini-surveys through the standard forum technology, which they made use of early in the life of the site, setting up surveys on favourite characters, chocolate and how participants knew they were smart. Such technologies and practices, while they may imply a loss of control on the researcher's part, contributed to the co-constructed nature of the meaning-making process.

My own presence on the site presented some initial issues in terms of transparency. A requirement of the site was the use of a pseudonym, and personal avatar photos were not allowed. However, it was important for disclosure that my status as researcher, not fellow participant, was apparent when I asked questions or responded on threads. I resolved this through choosing 'Michele the Researcher' as my screen name, and using an avatar of a character pictured undertaking some kind of experiment, thus underscoring my research agenda. The character is from a TV show mentioned by participants, *CSI* (2002–2012). This also helped to address the issue of implied consent as renewed each time a member logs on and comments, through reminding them of the research purpose of the forum. Participants wanting to know more could follow a link through to my university web page; this provided reassurance as to the status of the project. Such practices are among those recommended by Eynon et al. (2008) in their discussion of ethics, transparency and disclosure in researching online.

The management of the forum, as well as the design of the website, raised new issues. The nature of the discussion led me to reflect on some of my practices as moderator. In real-life group interviews, discussion was often moved on by a prompt from me and all questions were responded to; online, if a question had not hit the mark, it was simply ignored, and participants often took on the lead questioning role. In contrast with school group interview subjects, online participants also displayed curiosity about me and my motives for undertaking the research. They also debated the forum ground rules; for example, one ground rule related to use of language that might offend. This was challenged by two participants, and after discussion we agreed that perceived offence was to be the guideline; participants had the facility to send a direct message to me to raise issues or complain about any aspect of the forum.

The forum thus became a much more overtly shared space between me and its users than I had anticipated; this was also evident in the creation of the third board. Having created separate boards for their discussion of TV engagement and their real-world experiences of smart girl subjectivities ('Smart Girls on TV' and 'Smart Girls off TV'), I found that participants were increasingly using the forum as a general social space. To cater for this while keeping the focus of the 'researcherly' threads, I created a third board simply entitled 'Anything/Everything Else', which was used by members for general chat.

While some researchers find the tendency of online research spaces to be used for socialising problematic (Gaiser 2008), I found it contributed to the aims of the study. Not only did such interaction affirm the success of the forum as a space which participants wanted to use, but it also allowed for the emergence of unlooked-for but relevant material – Gaiser (2008, 297) discusses such 'bonus insights' as evidence of the need to retain flexibility in terms of the design and conduct of such online enquiry and the researcher's role. This is not to overvalorise all such contributions – sometimes users went online just to chat, and contributing to my agenda was not always a part of theirs. The brevity of some contributions and difficulty in asynchronous modes of expanding responses through the 'flow' of follow-up questions, as observed by Gaiser (298), could also be frustrating. A further issue in online research encounters noted by scholars includes social cue impoverishment (Gaiser 2008; O'Connor et al. 2008); this, however, is mitigated by the use of emoticons and other textual cues (Dresner and Herring 2010; Taesler and Janneck 2010). These were tools with which my participants were obviously familiar, supplementing the array available from the forum package with their own.

Online Identities

Online forum identities are textual constructs which carry with them the real bodies and structures from which they emanate (Bury 2005). For the purposes of this study, I explore the ways in which online participants occupy the subject position of smart girl which they have taken up in this particular context. Issues of identity which are relevant are not then those of verifying online with offline embodied selves, but the ways in which participants enact and discuss identities on the forum. Issues of authenticity among participants themselves did not arise explicitly during the study. As noted by Cheseboro and Bertelsen (1999) and Gurak (1997), group bonding and credibility online are often built up through shared values and identities rather than demonstrable authenticity. While the idea of the entirely disembodied identity has been largely dismissed – an old Cartesian manoeuvre, reclothed for digital times according to Stone (1996, 13) – the concept of virtual groups as meaningful communities of practice has fared better, particularly with regard to female fan communities (Bury 2005). A range of studies find that girls' online selves involve a new and expanded sense of audience, and complex impression management which is influenced by a desire both for authenticity leading to disclosure and to take opportunities for display of an ideal form of selfhood (boyd 2007; Manago et al. 2008; Maguire 2016). In analysing the interactions produced online for this study, it will be important to keep this tension between the ideal and the authentic in mind, and to treat forum statements as contextual discursive strategies and performances within wider discourses of gender and ability.

Textual Sites: Defining Teen TV

In terms of defining the field, choosing which TV texts to include in the analysis would at first seem a simple task, in that it would be logical simply to select from the teen TV genre most discussed by participants; certainly this was a key criterion in selection. However, if one of the aims of the archaeological study is to challenge existing unities, then the uncritical selection of texts according to existing genres would seem at odds with this. Furthermore, the defining of the genre of teen TV itself is not a simple process – Davis and Dickinson label the task a 'blatant dilemma' (2004, 5).

The concept of genre operates at both popular/audience and academic/theoretical levels (Larsen 2002, 132). In popular terms, it broadly defines groups of texts which are recognised as likely to contain familiar narratives, characterisations and values (Lacey 2000, 133). Predictability is central to the concept of genre; at the same time as providing narrative security in the unfolding of anticipated events in a predictable order, popular genres also reaffirm prevailing cultural ideologies (Dunn 2005, 126). However, television genres as cultural categories are formed in different ways and for different purposes by broadcasters, scholars, critics and fans (Mittell 2004, vii).

Teen TV could be defined by its content, themes and target audience, but also by other factors, such as its actual viewership, its intertextual relationships and its channel location. Feasey (2006, 4) complicates any easy definition by arguing that shows characterised as teen TV may also have strong adult viewership, and conversely, shows considered adult may share a range of features defining the teen TV genre, such as music and intertextual references designed to be intelligible to younger audiences. Feasey argues that the blurring of generic boundaries between teen and adult shows can be seen as an outcome not just of the development of teen shows as 'quality TV', but also of the material conditions of young people's lives in late modernity: prolonged education, job insecurity and housing crises mean that 'adolescent' states of identity and material insecurity are prolonged well into adulthood.

In this study, the blurring of age-related genres is evident in both group interviews and online discussion, where the frequently watched and discussed shows include young adult shows such as *Friends* (a US sitcom broadcast from 1994 to 2004, but continuously repeated on digital channels and owned as DVDs by several participants) and children's shows such as

Dora the Explorer, (an American cartoon for younger children which features Spanish instruction, broadcast on cable in the UK). A further generic complication is the inclusion of film and made-for-TV film. Many of the participants discussed films seen on TV as well as actual TV programmes, and among the most popular texts was *High School Musical* (2006), a Disney production originally made for television, but the success of which led to the cinema release of sequels, and the sequential DVD release of the suite of films.

Fans themselves may classify a text in different ways according to their own unities or discursive formations. Young viewers create their own TV taxonomies not only through textual features, but also through insider knowledge and production team fandom (Pearson 2005, 11). Thus, genre becomes an intertextualised audience strategy, rather than a marketing/broadcasting taxonomy (Mittell 2004; Hills 2005b), but as such, it is then absorbed back into industry constructs of genre. As the streaming of TV shows becomes more common with increased high-speed broadband access (Ofcom 2015; Pew Research Center 2015), genre becomes a process of personalised curation through personal data analysis (Amatriain 2013). Acknowledging such variations and instabilities in genre construction resonates with the archaeologist's aim of questioning discursive unities.

Issues in Viewership and Selecting Texts

Issues in terms of audience figures, syndication, private ownership and repeat viewing further complicate the process of defining the field of enquiry. In her review of *Geek Chic: Smart Women in Popular Culture* (Inness 2008), Brabazon (2008) observes that most of the shows discussed in the essays are US productions, and critiques this narrow focus. However, one cannot assume that such TV shows are not integrated into local television cultures and identities in the UK and elsewhere (McCabe 2005). New technologies and audience behaviours offer new possibilities for this; digital formats, the technologies of multiple viewing and cross-border reproduction have changed television reception. This means that shows which are barely mentioned in mainstream TV guides can nonetheless have a strong following, and other shows can retain viewership long past their original broadcast date (Hartley 2009).

This was evident in this study as participants nominated and discussed shows not well known in the UK but broadcast on niche digital channels, and also shows which were no longer in production but which were readily available through streaming, download, DVD or syndication. Participants' consumption of US television not actually broadcast in the UK but available on the Internet or via DVD was evident too in their citing of shows that had never been broadcast in the UK. These are in addition to more expected sources broadcast on major British channels and with a specific youth address mentioned by participants, most notably *Doctor Who* (2005–).

Where US shows are broadcast on mainstream UK channels, this is often later than the American air dates; participants describe watching them online in order to keep up and, importantly, to be in the know. As one group interview participant comments on the preference for Internet streaming, torrent downloads or boxed DVD sets as ways of consuming TV shows: 'If you have to wait like, a week, that's annoying'. One of the shows (*The Vampire Diaries*, 2009–) was mentioned specifically as 'Friday night conversation' because it is broadcast in the US on a Thursday night but not available to UK audiences until Friday morning.

Thus, viewer cultures and industry practices, both online and off, make the identification of possible texts for inclusion of such a study as this an exercise in tracking through links and discussion threads online, as well as following up such references from group interviews. The old technologies of mass broadcast and their assumed audiences can no longer be relied upon, and traditional sources of viewing figures, such as the Broadcasters Audience Research Board (BARB), can no longer be viewed as accurate indicators of watching (Curtin 2009); most of the girls I interviewed reported consuming at least some of their television via computers, personal digital devices, or DVD, rather than as broadcast on an actual television set, and what they did consume through these alternative means was most likely to be teen-orientated.

A noticeable feature of viewing habits among the group interviewees was the adoption and repeat viewing of certain shows by local friendship groups; these included shows that had aired some time ago but which remained favourites, such as *The OC*, a teen drama which aired from 2002 to 2007, but certain seasons of which were owned by one of the groups. The 2003 film based on the teen TV series *Lizzie McGuire* (2001–2004) was viewed in the same way by some members of another group. In this way, local audience behaviours resembled those of online fan groups, in that girls wanted to discuss shows with which they had a shared familiarity and shared familiar responses, such as jokes and character likes and dislikes. The selection of shows for such group viewings seemed dependent on what was owned locally rather than by contemporary national broadcast trends. More contemporary shows, such as *Doctor Who* (2005–), the British family sci-fi, and *Grey's Anatomy* (2005–), a US adult medical drama, were likely to be watched apart from friends or with family, but discussed among social groups nonetheless.

It is important to note that this study is not a traditional reception analysis of audience responses to a particular text or texts; the archaeological purpose is broader in seeking to identify regularities within wider discourses. Therefore, while many of the shows in this study are those raised by participants in schools or online, others are included for their discursive relevance to the narratives identified by the girls. A further criterion for inclusion is the texts previously singled out for academic analysis of their representation of achieving girlhood/young womanhood. The relationship between perceived

quality, longevity and durable formatting of teen TV shows has been noted a
by Davis and Dickinson (2004, 5) as contributing to a sense of 'worth'; this
works to filter some teen TV rapidly into the academic canon.

The field in terms of TV texts then includes those discussed by participants, those noted in online fan sites as featuring achieving girls, and those
attracting academic interest for their representations of achieving girls. This
gave me a long list of 40 texts (see filmography). I obtained copies of these
and watched, the first time taking notes of broad narratives and key details.
I then selected particular episodes, scenes, narrative threads or characters as
which were representative of specific participant interest or that resonated
with themes emerging in discussions. I watched these again, transcribing
dialogue along with descriptions of features of costume, performance and
plot, as outlined below. This was a lengthy but valuable process; the broad
narrative notes enabled me to identify patterns across and between seasons
of long-running shows, while finer details and transcribed dialogue could
then be coded in the same way as the interview and forum transcriptions.

Analysis of Discursive Regularities in Texts: Narratives and Tropes

When approaching any kind of textual analysis, there is an obvious tension
between recognising the potential for a range of readings and seeking to
identify the structures of texts that lead to certain inscribed meanings. It
is therefore important to recognise that the text as read by the researcher
or other reader is not fixed and unitary, but contextual, intertextual and
variable (Fiske 1987; Steier 1995). By narratives, I mean events told in an
imposed sequence in 'concrete circumstances in particular sites … with an
audience in view' (Silverman 2013).

The relationship between identity and narrative is complex, and provokes ongoing debate broadly divided along essentialist and constructionist
lines. In examining the identities and narratives in achieving girl discourses,
I adopt a perspective from post-structuralist narrative enquiry in which
identity is seen as an outcome of stories of selfhood, rather than an essential
selfhood as the source of stories (Currie 1998; McNay 2003; Kraus 2006).
This accords broadly with the archaeological conception of the subject as
produced by discourse; it is in the materials for such production that the
archaeologist's interest lies. However, narratives are not just drawn from
personal accounts; their wider distribution means they can 'bridge' the institutional and the everyday, creating constituencies in their address and reproduction (Reissman 2001). Popular texts lead us to ask questions about the
kinds of stories that girls 'turn into lives', and the kinds of stories that girls
'turn life into' (Gonick 2003, 48). Although personal narratives may lack
the coherence or consistency of media narratives, they are also nonetheless
shaped by the conventions of genre (Krause 1996). Tracing generic conventions of achieving girl narratives in both media and participants' accounts

can reveal inscribed educational and life trajectories, enabling consideration of their relevance, possibilities and limitations – a concern noted by Harris (2004) – as well as the emergence of new and competing accounts.

I also address issues of absence; Potter and Wetherell (1994) emphasise the need to be alert to both what is naturalised within and what is absent from regularities; in this study, this includes, for example, the predominance of white middle-class representations. For as many achieving girls who have a sanctioned speaking voice in pronouncing on conditions of subjectivity, the very rationing of 'gifted and talented' identities in schools and the privileged address of much teen TV means that there are more who are silenced and excluded by the discourse – and their absence is central to its shaping (Canaan 2001).

The Researcher as Meaning Maker

It is important to acknowledge that in the analysis of texts I am constructing a reading in a particular context and for a particular purpose. Within the post-structural endeavour, the researcher's role in the construction of narratives is foregrounded; as Nespor and Barylske (1991, 806) are careful to stress, 'representation is not just a matter of epistemology or method, but a matter of power'. Even in the rejection of hermeneutics implied in the *Archaeology* (Foucualt 1969), it is important to recognise the researcher's role in the choice of focus, in selecting and discarding data and in constructing new narratives through its organisation (Blumenreich 2004, 78).

Atkinson and Delamont (2006) remind us of the importance of the researcher's authority and positionality in representing others' narrative accounts. In eliciting, selecting, coding and re-creating the narratives for this study, my own experience and understanding as an academic, a woman, a television watcher, an Internet forum user, an ex-teacher and a former achieving girl from a background of social exclusion, as well as specific experiences of conducting research and writing, are built into the context of meaning making (Stacey 1988, 24).

Steier (1995, 140) stresses the ethical responsibility of social scientists and media theorists to 'grant the human constituents that populate their reality constructions at least the same cognitive abilities they claim for themselves in constructing them'. This resonates with Buckingham and Bragg's (2004) concerns that young audiences' critical capacities should be recognised. This implies an acknowledgement of participants' abilities to construct their own realities, to be creative and critical when engaging with media and other texts, and to be reflexive about the process. This is even while recognising subjects' capacity to do so as inevitably bound by the limits of the discursive field they inhabit. In organising the reporting structure of this study into a typology of achieving girl narratives emerging from participants and institutions, narrative is recognised as a representative technology for the research subject, as well as for the researcher (Nespor and Barylske 1991,

806). However, as McNay (2003, 2) cautions, the construction of narratives is not in itself evidence of agency; we should not overlook the role they 'may play in sustaining relations of domination'.

For what Foucault (1969) describes as 'regularities', I prefer the more familiar term 'tropes'. Although it has more specific definitions with the various fields that employ it, the term 'tropes' broadly describes recognisable elements of spoken or visual texts that function as a kind of shorthand in what they convey, or that carry readily recognisable meaning. Derived from linguistics, the term is now commonly used in literary, media, narrative and discourse studies. In the same way that the archaeologist is concerned with making taken-for-granted knowledge strange through identifying the regularities of its production, scholars have found tropes useful in identifying shared behaviours, meaning and definitions across settings, and also in exploring ways that these can be disrupted (Spiggle 1998, 164).

Drawing broadly on studies of media and cultural rhetoric, and of narrative enquiry (Potter and Hepburn 2008), this study involves identification of the following tropes:

- Narrative events, structures and genres
- Identities, characters and relationships which suggest achieving girl subject positions
- Verbal and visual language
- Mise-en-scène and media technologies (in TV texts)

These elements are traced within and across media and participant narratives, identifying ways in which they draw on common discursive repertoires. This attempts to overcome the 'now artificial distinction between textual and extra-textual interpretative approaches' which characterises traditions of examining media texts and the accounts of their audiences differently (Mailloux 2000, 21). Data sources were coded in the same way. An initial coding system was developed which revealed a multiplicity of regularly occurring themes and images, such as 'competition', 'life trajectories', 'authenticity', 'caring', 'media critics' and 'self-responsibility'. These groupings were then organised into the wider discursive groups that form the chapter headings of this work, and informed the genealogical investigation of the opening chapter.

Presenting Findings

Organising the accounts drawn from group interviews, the web forum and the media stories into categories presents issues concerning interpretation and the imposition of meaning. Such an organisation inevitably involves selection and omission, creating synergies and fissures and thus significance which may not have been consciously intended by the producers of these statements and texts. For the feminist researcher, this becomes particularly problematic in that it can create a distance from the voices of girls themselves, and imposes a kind of meaning upon them. One of the strategies I have adopted in an attempt to achieve a recognition of participants' voices is using the words of the girls themselves as an integral part of the text, directly quoting as far as possible, rather than presenting verbatim data separately (Corden and Sainsbury 2006). I have used the words as transcribed, and in the case of the online contributions have preserved original spelling and grammar.

While the focus of this study is discourses and narratives rather than individual subjectivities, the archaeological design in some ways attempts to mitigate the colonising nature of the researcher's meaning making, in that it is conceived as a method of recording, describing, contextualising and ordering statements, identifying patterns and disruptions. Foucault sees hermeneutic interpretation as the imposition of secondary meaning upon an original text, one which seeks to render a superior level of meaning intended but not fully realised by the text's creator (1969, 7). However, even the descriptive categorisation itself inevitably involves processes of selection and omission in which interpretation is implied, from the delineation of sites of enquiry through to the identification and coding of regularities. In the presentation of these results, therefore, while I attempt to avoid the interpretation of girls' statements in terms of suggesting a secondary level of meaning somehow hidden to the girl as producer but revealed by me as researcher, I do discuss the cultural significance within the patterns of discourse of which such statements form a part, while I acknowledge that it is the researcher's will to order that has recognised the statements as a part of a wider discursive pattern.

4 Girls Reading Girl Texts
Genres, Tropes and Trajectories

This chapter is principally concerned with those aspects of discursive formation that Foucault (1969) terms 'surfaces of appearance' and 'enunciative modalities'; that is, it focuses on the relationship between what is said about the achieving or 'smart' girl and who says it, and the relationships between these and the wider discursive contexts. I am particularly interested in the ways smart identities are produced and endorsed in local contexts, and how girls use their authority to position themselves within wider discursive hierarchies. I am also interested in the ways in which participants online and off engage with media techniques, as well as the discourses they carry, as evidence of the nature and limits of criticality and agency. It is important to recognise that many of the participant statements are not just about achieving girls; they are statements about texts about achieving girls. Post-structuralist audience studies recognise that being called upon to interpret a text is not a simple matter of 'truthfully' representing a received impression; commentaries and interpretations are performances of readings which strive to appear 'right' (Allington 2007, 46) and are a means for defining identities and positions within reading communities (Merrick 1997, 55). In this chapter, I attempt to explore girls' statements and negotiations as those authorised to pronounce both on media texts and on achieving girlhood itself. I move between their statements and claims about television and about what they commonly term 'smart' girlhood, to television texts themselves to show how some narratives and performances are endorsed, how girls mobilise both school and popular discourses in establishing their authority. As Nyström observes (2014, 88) observes, interactions between peers as well as with teachers work to validate pupils' identities with regard to their abilities.

Smart Girl Tropes on Screen and in Schools

Through their discussion of television characters and their own school contexts, participants showed themselves to be minutely aware of ways in which gendered ability identities are coded, and of how such codings function within both on-screen genres and school identities.

Participants use popular culture categorisations in the framing of their own and others' identities, and also invoke their own experiences when discussing mass-produced texts. Group interview participants move easily between discussion of screen and school contexts, to the point where at times it is unclear whether they are discussing their own experiences or their television viewing; when I ask them to clarify which, I am more than once met with the answer 'both'. This illustrates the ways in which popular representations carry a 'forceful significance' within schools as manifestations of cultural language and assumptions, because they provide ready categorisations in the very contexts in which subjectivities connected with ability and achievement are elicited and regulated (Gonick 2003, 137).

It is important to note that many of the examples discussed by participants relate to American television shows and so draw on a context where powerful and pervasive discourses of nerds/geeks, 'popular' students and jocks exist, constructed along existing lines of social division (Gonick 2003, 144; Mendick and Francis 2011, 19). However, the terminologies, tropes and positionings connected with more abject 'geek' identities appeared regularly in the school contexts, as well as in the television shows discussed.

The terms 'geek' and 'nerd' were common across school, online and television settings, and 'swot' and 'boffin' were used in all three school sites. There were some creative local variations too – for example, at Sir Walter Raleigh, 'apple polishers' describes pupils who regularly engage in teacher-pleasing behaviours, and at Maple Grove, the term 'neek', a combination of 'nerd' and 'geek', was in popular usage. On screen, the terms 'nerd', 'geek', 'egg head' and 'ghost world' were all attached to smart girl characters. The term 'geek' was the most common across all sites, used to describe an identity that was both social and intellectual, and earned through dress and behaviour rather than just through achievement itself.

Terms such as 'nerd' and 'geek' are not solely assigned as abuse, but are also voluntarily adopted. As one TV smart girl character instructs her friends, 'It's the computer age. Nerds are in' (*Buffy the Vampire Slayer* 1.1). 'Geek' is now frequently paired with 'chic' as a style choice (Florin et al. 2007; McArthur 2009), albeit a choice more likely to be available to privileged students (Mendick and Francis 2011). At Sir Walter Raleigh, participants describe how 'geek' at their school can be applied to girls who are both clever and rebellious, but that 'boffin' is reserved for the merely studious.

Even for girls who appear to adopt the label as an act of defiance, such appropriation of the term does not strip it of its original pejorative meaning; their power to reclaim the term is limited to their own local power to outface it, and the responses of others in the group suggest, as Budgeon (2011) notes, that intended subversion is not always read as such by the intended audience. Moreover, the politics of embracing the originally pejorative term are not necessarily those of critical appropriation (Shugart, Waggoner, and O'Brien Hallstein 2001).

The adoption and assignation of geek and smart identities is subject to powerful regulative positionings of the subject within discourses of gender and class (Mendick and Francis 2011). For example, more confident middle-class girls were more likely to report not worrying about being called a geek or finding it amusing, than girls who appeared less confident within the group or who were less securely aligned with middle-class discourses. For those girls whose identities are already more marginal, aligning themselves with transgressive or abject positions is altogether more risky (Walkerdine, Lucey, and Melody 2001; Currie, Kelly, and Pomerantz 2009). Less confident or less securely positioned girls may also appear to accept being called geeks because it is harder for them to object. As did Skelton, Francis, and Read (2010, 189), I found most girls adopted identity positions within conventional femininities, with only a small minority appearing to adopt the nerd/geek terminology, and then with a degree of distancing humour.

The distributing and inhabiting of such identity labels in schools is central to youth culture and power (Currie, Kelly, and Pomerantz 2006, 422). This is evident in girls' discussion of the workings of such power within the film *Mean Girls* (2004). Stella (Sir Walter Raleigh) describes how the film's popular coterie of girls has 'so many different labels for people. There's like Burn-outs, Cool Asians'. Kelly, Suzanne and Georgina join in, offering further categories from the film, such as 'Asian Nerds', 'Plastics', 'Girls That Don't Eat' and 'Girls That Eat Their Feelings'. Suzanne explains the popular coterie's naming as a process of normalisation and othering:

> Like for them, they're the only people that are perfect. Everyone else has something wrong with them. Cause they're the ones that make all the labels.

She recognises the power of naming, both on screen and off, as lying with those with the highest standing within peer hierarchies in school. Girls discussed the labels in their own schools, as well as the geek variants, 'goths', 'emos' and 'chavs', featured across different sites. 'Chav' is a pejorative word currently popularly used in the UK to describe the working class poor and also to signify conspicuous and tasteless consumption (Hayward and Yar 2006). The term appeared particularly at Sir Walter Raleigh, where one participant, Kelly, used it to identify herself while naming another participant as a 'goth'. Kelly aligned herself with some working-class discourses and identities during the interview, and appeared to take up the 'chav' label as part of a performance of authenticity, as a means of defining herself against the dominant middle-class profile of the group (see below for further discussion of discourses of authenticity and class), and also as a means of establishing her authority to make statements about achieving girlhood from a critical distance.

Geek Girl Tropes

The visual vocabulary for abject achievers in school is well established (see Gonick 2003, 72; Skelton, Francis, and Read 2010, 189); certain visual tropes were identifiable across all sites. Participants frequently describe, and television texts show, geek girls as wearing spectacles, their dress and hair as immature or childish (especially pigtails) and likely to be ginger – as Stella explains, we can tell which sister is clever in the TV show *8 Simple Rules* (2002–2005) because 'hair colour is a big issue. Kerry's got really red hair and she's really geeky, and her sister's really blonde but really stupid'. Braces are mentioned by participants at Sir Walter Raleigh and online by *Pandora*, who calls them 'the stable accessory of geeks' (see Figure 4.2). At Sir Walter Raleigh, participants also describe geeks as being 'dressed by parents' and their clothes as being too small or too short – the term 'ankle swingers' is used to describe pupils whose clothes were perceived as 'geeky' in this way.

The geek girl is thus coded through costume as trapped in or embracing a childhood state and failing to achieve endorsed femininity. This suggests a postponing of the business of feminised maturation in ways that are particularly associated with traditional white middle-class schoolgirl identities in their innocence, modesty and 'niceness' (Reay 2001a; Archer 2005). Investment in hyperfeminised heterosexual identities has historically been associated with working-class girls' resistance to the cultures and technologies of schooling which would produce them as failures (McRobbie 1978; Hey 1997; Archer, Halsall and Hollingworth 2012). The coding of the stereotypical geek girl can thus be understood as a classed coding in its rejection of heterosexualised maturity. Her behaviour and appearance indicate an attitude of deferred gratification to the supposed pleasures of adolescence. Such codings of the 'nice', pre-sexual, geek girl can, as Allan (2010, 40) observes, be mobilised by schools themselves in the version of girlhood they depict in their promotional materials. Sally (St Ursula's) identifies this coding in some of her own school publicity photographs; she describes the photographer hailing her as 'You with the glasses!' and wanting her to look 'clever' in the foreground.

Participants also recognise how the geek girl is identified by tropes of performance. There was noticeable congruence between behavioural tropes cited as identifying girls as geeks in schools, and the performances used to enable role recognition on screen. On-screen girl characters identified as geeks include Hermione Granger from *Harry Potter* (2001) (Figure 4.1), Willow Rosenberg from *Buffy the Vampire Slayer* (1997–2003) and Betty Suarez from *Ugly Betty* (2006–2010) (Figure 4.2). The tropes include compliant and teacher-pleasing behaviours such as putting her hand up (Figure 4.1), reading and carrying books (Figure 4.3), doing homework and using a computer. As well as the conspicuous place in the classroom, common screen settings include the library and her bedroom, which for the smart girl is primarily a space for doing homework.

That such signs have an identity-creating function which does not necessarily represent an underlying 'truth' is recognised by participants at Sir Walter Raleigh:

Figure 4.1 Hermione Granger with hand up.

Figure 4.2 Betty Suarez.

KELLY: There is a difference between being clever and being, like, geeky, cause like, being clever you could just be determined but geeky, you gotta fit the stereotype.

SUZANNE: Geeks are not always clever. You can look like a geek without being a geek.

STELLA: If they fit that stereotype and they look the part, it doesn't matter if they are clever or not.

KELLY: They could be really thick and still be a geek.

Suzanne, Stella and Kelly demonstrate understanding of the geek identity as a performance, and one which can be undertaken regardless of the aptitudes that are assumed to underpin it as long as other intelligible signs are present. As noted above, an individual may take up 'a position which is already determined by the rules of the discourse' (Gutting 1989, 241). As those who, by virtue of a range of school technologies, are secure in their speaking positions as clever girls, Stella and Kelly can pronounce on those who are not.

As well as costume and performance, tropes in terms of narrative outcomes are identifiable across all settings. These narrative regularities can be seen to serve a pedagogic purpose in illustrating the risks involved in investing in non-endorsed identities, whether played out in fictional settings or in participants' claims to experience – they illuminate the 'zones of inhabitability', as described by Butler (1993, 3), that define the limits of the subject, and against which she establishes her own claim to identity. Typical events include social isolation, being subjected to bullying and mockery, being exploited by teachers and peers, and romantic rejection. At St Ursula's, girls describe the potential social costs of smart identities:

RINA: They're usually like, on their own.

ALISON: They might get bullied.

MONICA: They sit right at the front of the classroom.

RACHEL: If you are really pretty then you are gonna be more popular and you can be more who you are and people won't like bully you or whatever but, I don't know, if you're a geek then like, they won't go out with you.

TINA: You'll never be accepted.

Investment in feminised aspects of identity is a key compensatory strategy for achieving girls (Jackson 2006; Renold and Allan 2006; Allan 2010; Skelton et al. 2010). Rachel's observation that attractive girls 'can be more who you are' resonates with Francis, Skelton, and Read's (2010) finding that looks are an important factor in managing to sustain an identity which is both achieving and popular.

Participants as Critical Readers

Participants demonstrate not only a detailed familiarity with the ways in which the achieving girl is coded as a geek in popular dramas, but an understanding of the narrative function of such stereotyping. Indeed, the performance of a knowing and critical awareness of the strategies of television characterises both on- and offline discussion and, through the workings of postmodern stylings and self-referentiality, of some TV shows themselves. The groups and the forum operate as the audience 'reading communities' that can provide a means of defining identity (Merrick 1997, 55). Girls establish their claims to their own smart identities through both their critique of the shows and their stated identification with smart characters. This is not to imply that such critique is necessarily resistant; as Willett (2008b, 422) warns:

> By celebrating girls' active resistance to or transformation of popular culture, we can simplify the powerful structures in girls' lives and overlook the complex ways girls are negotiating those structures. More importantly, we can overlook particular narrative codes which the girls are buying into.

However, such awareness as there is indicates that girls' relationship with media texts is not simply one of passive take-up of their pedagogies and subjectivities, nor one of an active, subversive localised resistance. It points rather to the complexities of the audience–text relationship, which includes consideration of the pleasures that can be taken from media texts alongside awareness of their technologies and ideologies. One must also take into account the conventions and pleasures of undertaking critique itself; in the group interviews and online, girls were invited to offer their readings of the texts and appeared to take pleasure in displaying critical awareness.

Girls in this study expressed both critical awareness of and identification with some stereotypes. They were less likely to recognise some textual pedagogies than others, and their alignment with some discourses was not expressed as knowingly as it was with others. It was also noticeable that forum participants discussed stereotyping and other aspects of their TV watching in more detail and more frequently than group interview participants. On a website badged as a forum for discussing TV, this is unsurprising and may reflect the recruitment strategy, in which I had established links with other TV fan sites run by girls. Participants joining from such sites were more likely to be experienced in the kinds of detailed conversations discussing and deconstructing shows which typify online fan activity, and which work to establish hierarchies of insider knowledge and connoisseurship (Mittell 2004; Hills 2005a).

The ubiquity of achieving girl stereotypes is commented on by both forum and school participants. At Sir Walter Raleigh, Rachel describes how 'they're a specific group … lots of stereotypes'; Anna agrees, describing how 'in anything you watch there'll be like, a little "nerdy" [makes an air quotes gesture] character'.

In the online forum, stereotyping was a popular topic of discussion and spread over five separate threads. *Jadoremusique* comments that

> most TV shows that i watch do stereotype smart Women though occasional there are smart women who aren't stereotyped.

As practiced media consumers, participants demonstrate awareness of the ways in which the complexities of character are reduced to schema for ease of audience recognition. At St Ursula's, Monica explains:

> It's because when you're like watching a TV programme you don't get a chance like to actually get to know a character so you obviously have to make them, the audience, know.

Online, in the thread 'Stereotyping the smart girl', *HatStand*'s comment distinguishes between media worlds and reality:

> Characters in television programmes [particularly those aimed at teens and younger audiences] need to be exaggerated to get a certain image/idea across. Though I do agree that it seems that the majority of smart girls in real life have the capability to be smart as well as socially successful; unlike a lot of those seen on television.

Pandora agrees and offers a lengthy description of the roots of girl stereotypes in fairy tales. She concludes that

> fairytales characters are often simplified so young children can follow the plotline. Something similar happens in 'TV-land' not necessarily to make the plot 'easy to follow' but possibly to make the character dynamic more interesting.

Discussing *Ugly Betty* (2006–2010), *jen.nzgirl* shows understanding of the entertainment function of such stereotyping, commenting thus:

> I reckon that all the characters on Ugly Betty are stereotyped, but to a deliberate, over-the-top, -larger than life extent, like they are acknowledging these stereotypes and mocking them at the same time. It makes the show so much more hilarious.

She goes on to warn the forum that they 'are not to be taken seriously'.

Participants also identify some narrative functions of the geek girl as providing a gendered foil to the feminised appeal of more central characters and also as a means of advancing the plot through using her enhanced reasoning abilities. This latter is identified as a feature of genre by scatter-brain online and by Isabel at St Ursula's, who both observe that the popularity of procedural crime dramas such as *CSI* (2000–) and *Bones* (2005–) means there are more roles for women playing scientists and characters with good problem-solving skills. This observation is interesting in the light of recent research seeking to establish whether girls' identification with TV scientists is more likely if the scientists are women who are attractive and demonstrate caring qualities as well as intelligence (Steinke et al. 2012). At Sir Walter Raleigh, Lucy comments that she likes *CSI* because

> the women seem to be really … perfect and glamorous … even like when they're mucking around with dead bodies their make-up's impeccable!

The shows, the focus of the research and participants' comments are indicators of the pervasiveness of discourses of a specifically feminised intelligence and achievement, and of the ways in which television genres provide contexts for their circulation.

The Regulative Function of Smart Girl Tropes

Participants also show awareness of the regulative function of smart characters as a form of heteronormative conduct guide. In a thread called 'Ugly Betty's Inner Beauty', *Oipoodle* describes her experience of watching *Ugly Betty* thus:

> When I saw the adverts for this show I was worried it would be another stereotypical view of smart girls and that the show would be making fun of Betty. However I was pleasantly surprised as although they've made her look like a "nerd" they have made her character well rounded and loveable. Often smart girls are relagated as the best friend of the pretty one and are usually rather dull but Betty is witty, kind and fiesty. I think she's a really good role model.

Andrea agrees, stating that

> we relate more to Betty because so many girls out there watching TV never believe they are beautiful enough. There is always something about our physical selves we dislike. To compensate, we use our social skills such as wit, charm and intelligence to get by. That's exactly what Betty does in every episode and we love her for it. She proves that you

don't always need the looks to make a positive impression on those around us. You need the smarts!

The 'make the most of yourself' message, with its exhortation to use 'smarts' to be witty, charming and lovable as a kind of compensatory feminine performance, is embraced by some participants. However, others are more dismissive: *Pandora* finds Betty 'overly exaggerated and stereotyped' complaining that 'she struggles to be popular and wears braces'; *Gabriellamontez* agrees, stating, 'I think they are over stereotyped by a mile! Ugly Betty is smart so ugly. Models are pretty and thick'. Such disagreement suggests that the relationship of smart identities with more mainstream and commoditised forms of femininity is subject to negotiation among audiences as well as within the TV texts themselves.

If the regulative function of the geek girl is to demonstrate the social costs of pursuing alternative identities or forms of gratification and to establish the limits of legitimate femininities, such regulation must include instruction as to how such failure can be recovered from. The most well-established means is via the narrative staple of the transformational makeover. Gonick (2003, 107) positions such makeovers within the narrative genre of the Cinderella romance, and links this to the post-feminist pedagogies of self-improvement genres in their mobilisation of shame and desire. As Gabriella Montez, the lead character in *High School Musical* (2006), states, 'I don't want to be the school's freaky genius girl again'. Her statement positions her ability as excessive, a spectacle of which she is ashamed and an identity by which she is uncomfortable being defined in its non-normative gender coding. The film is the story of her attempt to find a new and more acceptable form of visibility through her singing talent. Girls recognise that in these narratives the geek girl perceives her shortcomings, feels appropriate shame and seeks to remedy them. The successful transformational makeover leads to a reclassification of an individual's identity. At Sir Walter Raleigh, Hermione Granger's geek identity is the subject of debate and negotiation:

SUZANNE: Like Hermione, she is really good at magic. She's really clever.
TINA: She kind of does rub it in people's faces.
STELLA: She doesn't understand why people are annoyed with her
KELLY: She looks quite like … not geeky but she looks quite like …
LUCY: It kind of shows that whatever you are like you can have a chance to shine.
TINA: They portray her as being quite a geek.
ISABEL: She is quite geeky.
TINA: But she's really clever.
ISABEL: She doesn't always dress like a geek.
JOANNE: She gets her teeth fixed [*taps her teeth*].
RACHEL: Yeah, she's really clever but she like, breaks the rules and stuff as well.
TINA: She's like Rachel! [*laughs*].

This exchange shows some different identificatory and narrative tropes which the girls mobilise in negotiating identity labels. While Suzanne, Stella, Tina and Isabel argue that these combine to define Hermione as geek, Rachel and Joanne dispute the categorisation. When Joanne reminds them that Hermione has in effect a magical form of corrective surgery makeover, this evidence of investment in feminised self-improvement works to rescue the character from the 'abject' category.

They are referring to *Harry Potter and the Goblet of Fire* (Rowling 2000; Warner Bros. 2005), the fourth book/film in the series; participants moved between the two formats without discrimination. In this text, Hermione, having heretofore exhibited tropes that mark her as geek, undergoes a trans-formational makeover to attend a ball where her femininity is endorsed by attention from a visiting sports star and elicits jealousy. This marks a signif-icant shift in her narrative role and identity in the series from geek to poten-tial love interest. After the ball, she decides to retain elements of her magical makeover – this is made more explicit in the book than in the film. Partici-pants' negotiation of the meaning and weighting of different aspects of the performance demonstrates ways in which geek/girl identities are assigned in processes of situated and negotiated label making.

Geek Identities, Heteronormativity and Transgression

The geek identity as both abject and threatening in terms of hegemonic heteronormativity finds its apotheosis in the character of Willow Rosenberg in *Buffy the Vampire Slayer* (1997–2003). Responses to this character illus-trate anxieties with regard to the affirmation of heterofeminine identities, but also ways in which tropes from a traditional narrative medium (televi-sion) can be appropriated and used to destabilise hegemonic discourses via newer media (online fan sites). Although not mentioned as frequently as some other shows, Willow Rosenberg is the only lesbian character identified as such by participants.

Willow appears as a stereotypically geeky sidekick in the first two sea-sons of the show (Wilcox 1999, 2). Almost all the previously identified tropes are employed: An exceptionally hard-working and highly achieving student, Willow has a particular facility with computers; she gets on well with teachers; her clothes are chosen by her mother, including shapeless dresses, childish knitwear and dungarees in primary colours; she wears her (ginger) hair long and often in plaits; her performance is defined by childlike vulnerability and social awkwardness; in the pilot, she is introduced as a social outcast and a victim of the popular coterie's bullying (1.1 'Welcome to the Hellmouth').

The geek girl as unmatured woman trope is played out through Willow's development arc across the show's first three years. From schematic geek, by high school graduation she evolves into a subculturally cool figure; her appearance shifts to suggest subcultural cool and she acquires a sim-ilarly subculturally cool boyfriend. This new, cooler geek chic identity is threatened when her boyfriend leaves her in Season 4: The importance of this as an identity-defining event is established when soon after, she over-hears herself referred to as 'some egghead who tutored me a little in high school. I mean, she's nice, but, come on, captain of the nerd squad' (4.11 'Doomed'). When Willow recounts the insult, she reminds listeners of her recent, more successful heteronormative identity through its endorsement by her high-status boyfriend, pointing out: 'I haven't been a nerd for a very long time. Hello! Dating a guitarist, or I was' (4.11 'Doomed'). The need for successful compensatory performance of femininity in the avoidance of more abject forms of geek girl identity is dramatised, and the need for vigilance reinforced.

However, in a development arc which would appear to challenge the show's mobilisation of the geek girl heteronormative conduct guide, Willow's next relationship is with a female student, a relationship she ultimately chooses above being reunited with Oz. The smart girl narrative here turns away from the Cinderella/makeover genre, and has been identified as displaying the tropes of 'a not uncommon coming out narrative' (McAven 2007).

Some responses to Willow's sexuality suggest a challenge to heterofeminine identities, which as a result require affirmation. On the smartgirls.tv forum, when Charlotte nominates Willow as favourite smart character, at the same time she distances herself from Willow's lesbian identity and states her own liking for Oz (the character's boyfriend).

In contrast, fellow forum participant *Dark Angel* sends a link to a widely circulated Internet meme that suggests fan awareness of the ways in which intellectual identities intersect with those of gender and sexuality. This meme commonly shows Willow in the library or carrying books and bears the legend 'Reading leads to witchcraft and lesbianism' (see Figure 4.3). Reading, which stands within the narrative for all intellectual endeavour, is thus positioned in opposition – and celebrated by fans as a form of resistance – to hegemonic femininities. As Renold and Allan (2006, 466) and Francis (2009, 663) observe, girls' investment in academic success without simultaneous investment in feminised behaviours is seen as transgressive. One can read fans' responses to Willow as both a celebration of transgression and, at the same time, mocking the rules and anxieties which render those identities as transgressive. This critical appropriation of the smart girl narrative redefines the subject position for fans, suggesting the discursive agency through playing with cultural narratives posited by Weedon (1987). The reading/lesbian meme is particularly interesting in the light of Francis's (2009, 664) finding that lesbianism is the 'discursive unsaid' of the geek girl stereotype, hinted at by students in her study but too shocking to be articulated. It is similarly unspoken in the group interviews in this study and referenced somewhat obliquely through the meme on the website, which was sent without comment.

   The Internet offers opportunities for the mass circulation of counter-hegemonic discourses which may begin to offset the historical weight of patriarchal discourses. As Warf and Grimes observe as early as 1997, there is 'nothing inherently oppressive or automatically emancipatory about the internet' (259); however, it has developed a history of 'jamming' practices, of which the circulation of such memes forms a part, as a means of 'subverting meanings … using humour, mocking, satire and parody' of the hegemonic (Cammaerts 2007, 72). The discourses and anxieties surrounding feminine and intellectual identities expressed in the group interviews and mocked by *Buffy* fans can be seen as a continuation of historical anxieties. In exposing and ridiculing the premises of a gendered order of intellect, fans are aligning themselves with Le Doeuff (2003, x) in their undermining of apparent truths as they appear in the popular domain – or those things 'not worth learning in what generally passes for knowledge'.

Figure 4.3 Willow with books meme.

Geek Girls and the Affective Transformation Arc

The narrative of the geek girl's feminised maturation can appear as emotional as well as physical. This variant reflects the gendered maturity model proposed by Gilligan (1982), who posits a 'morality of care' as characterising girls' development, as opposed to the 'morality of justice' proposed by Kohlberg (1973). Gilligan famously claims that Kohlberg's theory models and universalises masculine moral development and subjugates the connected, relational and empathic as feminine and inferior to more abstract and absolute ethical reasoning. While Gilligan has been criticised for proposing an essentialist gender model that assumes a universalised girlhood (Woods 1996), and it should be noted that she writes from the perspective of developmental psychology rather than social constructionism (McKinley 1997), her work reflects, and indeed has been important in the development of, wider discourses of gender and maturation in which girls grow into a more connected and empathic relation with the world, while boys grow away from it. Her findings further illustrate the process of 'casting off' (Le Doeuff 2003) of less valued attributes, such as emotionality onto women, described in Chapter 1. Such casting off is reproduced both in popular narratives of achieving girls and in participants' discussions.

A trope which I shall term the 'caring achiever' is ubiquitous in teen TV, and is recognised and endorsed in the web forum as an affective development arc for girls. *AlwaysTakeBackup* and *Oipoodle* debate whether the development of the eponymous heroine of *Veronica Mars* (2004–2007) is credible as she moves from being 'cold' and 'guarded' to confiding and accessible; *sisteract* describes how Neela, a young doctor in the hospital drama *ER* (1994–2009),

> was early on being portrayed stereotypically as book wormy and out of touch with patients feelings and has been allowed to grow to being warm, moral and sexy.

Sisteract's positioning of learning as rational and masculinised, 'out of touch' and in opposition to the emotional, sensual and ethical as more evolved and feminised aligns with Gilligan's feminised ethics of care, and reproduces the complementary female intelligence model (Alaya 1977), particularly as it takes place within the highly technological and rational setting of the hospital. Participants identify other female doctors performing similar roles; for example, *Oipoodle* states that

> Cameron was always my favourite character in House, whereas all the others are pretty cold she was always the heart of the show, getting too emotionally attached to patients.

Not all participants absorb the pedagogies of complementarity uncritically; on the forum, *Oipoodle* starts a thread entitled 'Changing smart girls' characters' in which she protests that some smart girl characters, such as Veronica Mars, change beyond recognition as their 'flaws' are ironed out and they become friendlier and softer. *Charlotte* agrees, declaring, 'It's fantastic to see a character try to hold it all together and keep her image'. This indicates that for girls, emotional transformation narratives can create tension with narratives of authenticity, a topic which I discuss in more detail later.

It should be noted that while *Oipoodle* and *Charlotte* express dissatisfaction with the transformation/makeover aspects of some shows, their dissatisfaction is expressed within terms of neoliberal, post-feminist discourses of confidence and autonomy. In this respect, participants' responses accord with Willett's (2008b, 432) findings that while girls may reject particular narrative codes, they are inevitably buying into others which frame their very resistance. As Driscoll (2002, 12) argues, the concept of resistance is not necessarily a useful one in seeking to understand girl cultures because there are sites where 'resistance is often just another form of conformity and conformity may be compatible with other resistances'. However, there is a need for caution regarding the degree to which girls' statements represent a definitive 'buying in' to one discourse or another; rather, it is evidence of participants using available discursive tools and positions to produce a response or a reading which is appropriate for the context in which it is expressed.

The Rise of the Alpha Girl

The geek girl is not the only available subject position for the achieving girl. Within contemporary contexts of neoliberal post-feminism, there is now the necessity of maintaining a feminine identity while achieving success as the 'can do' girl (Harris 2004), also known as the 'A1 girls' and 'glamorous high-achievers' (McRobbie 2004), the 'top girls' (McRobbie 2011) and the 'alpha girls' (Kindlon 2006). Osgerby (2004) describes teen TV as having been, from its origins in the 1950s and 1960s, characterised by 'consumerist hedonism' and by the speed with which it has taken up 'new social identities' associated with consumer pleasures. The alpha girl can be located within an industry tradition that has produced young femininity in terms of pleasure, certain kinds of social freedom and consumption within both the UK and the US. The alpha girl's appearance and rise can be contextualised not only within the contemporary post-feminist imaginary, but also within the conditions of media industry deregulation, niche broadcasting and address to affluent audiences, described in Chapter 3. She is the popular representation of a mode of being in which success and femininity are not only possible but required.

McRobbie (2009) argues that the feminised achieving girl occupies new positions of visibility and agency through her participation in consumer femininities, as well as in education, and that her performance of hyperfemininity is necessary to secure the patriarchal order under the threat of women's increased presence in the labour market and growing economic power (70). In its popular representations, we can see the alpha girl figure as modeling participation in consumer regimes and in education, but also as defining the means and setting the limits of achieving girlhood itself. Recent research into the ways achieving girls construct identities in schools suggests that the performance of hyperfemininity has become a normative pressure and a peer approval strategy for middle-class girls (Allan 2006, 2010; Renold and Allan 2006; Raby and Pomerantz 2015). For the alpha girl, academic success is not incompatible with femininity; rather, 'her intellectual capital is an important part of her production of a desirable and desiring self' (Featherstone, Scourfield, and Hooper 2010, 190) and indeed has become a key means of marking her distinct from white working-class and lower middle-class women (Hey 2010, 215). This can be seen in Pomerantz and Raby's (2011) multiply capable girls, who work to maintain both social and academic profiles, and in Francis et al.'s (2010) HAP (highly achieving and popular) girls. Ringrose describes the difficulties for girls attempting to occupy such subject positions 'where girls are to be both bright and beautiful ... heterofeminine/desirable and successful learner' (485).

Such difficulties arise regularly in group interview discussion with regard to both popular dramas and girls' own experiences. For example, at Maple Grove this exchange takes place:

SONIA: I think these days people ... not even just those on film ... care a lot about their appearance and things. Cause I think, like, in school you're often judged by the way you dress or how pretty you are. Stuff like that.
DORA: I think that people that are at like a young age are influenced by that.
POPPY: You try to have a mixture of all three. It's really hard though, to try and be, sort of, everything.
DORA: It's very difficult. Because you don't wanna be judged ... but then, if you judge other people like that, well there's no getting away from it.

This illustrates participants' awareness of the circulation of alpha girl discourses between media and audiences, and suggests this has been a constant feature of their girlhood from a young age. It highlights their experience of impossibilities of the position, but also suggests girls' awareness of their own role in circulating such discourses – Dora's last comment illustrates her consciousness of having internalised and reproduced them.

As well as the abject geek girl, participants identified a range of TV characters as socially and academically successful alpha girls. These are the on-screen embodiments of girls who are self-managing and smart, groomed and appealing. They represent the most contemporary form of feminised achievement. Group interview participants readily recognise their defining qualities:

AMINA: Like in Gossip Girl, they're all in University. And like Blair's really, really hardworking.
MAY: It's like Neighbours, this girl called Natasha. She's like, obsessed with her looks and stuff but then she's got an amazing talent for maths.
JESS: In Being Human, Nina, she's a doctor and you need to like, obviously be clever about that, and also a werewolf, and now she's pregnant. ... Multi-tasking!

The effort that goes into the maintenance of success is described alongside their feminised appeal. The hard work, highly visible femininities and 'multi-tasking' necessary for sustaining the alpha performance are identified across genres and (Western) national contexts of production: Mentioned in this exchange are an American teen TV drama, an Australian daytime soap and a British urban gothic drama series.

Two of the more recent alpha girl incarnations popular with participants and causing something of a moral panic among some feminists are the shows *Gossip Girl* and *90210* (see Figure 4.4). Naomi Wolf, for example, does not allow her own teen daughter to watch them (New York magazine 2007). These shows focus on the lives of friendship groups of highly privileged teenagers in New York and Beverly Hills, respectively. Both shows start in high school and move on to college as their ensemble casts grow up. The casts themselves are exceptionally attractive young people among whom extreme consumption, hyperfeminised appearance, intense heterosexual competition and frequent and varied sexual activity are all foregrounded as normative behaviour (Van Damme and Van Bauwel 2012). In their glossy high-end perfection, they are the small-screen embodiment of the discourses of consumption and hypersexuality described by McRobbie (2009). Wolf (2007, n.p.) comments that the world of the shows is one in which sexual activity is another commoditised pleasure. The actor Leighton Meester describes the *Gossip Girls* creators' instructions with regard to playing the character Blair Waldorf:

> They were like, "Be bitchy and nice, ugly and pretty, young and old, stupid and smart, innocent and slutty, blond and brunette. Can you be all those things?" (Gay 2009, n.p.)

This confusing list encapsulates the multiple and oppositional identities that the socially successful achieving girl has to inhabit, the 'balancing act' in relation to gender and cleverness (Reay 2001a, 157) and the 'massive contradictions' (Ringrose 2007, 474) in the discourses that constitute her. A Season 3 promotional poster featuring Blair has the copy 'Trying to live up to expectations without cracking from the pressure', indicating how the very impossibility of the alpha subject position has permeated popular discourse, and is sufficiently recognisable to be mobilised to interpellate mass teen girl audiences.

The Alpha Girl and Gendered Learning

Although a relative newcomer on the popular culture scene, the alpha girl mobilises some deeply entrenched discourses of gender and learning, as outlined in Chapter 1. Despite her identity as hyperfeminised consumer whose every desire is quickly gratified, the alpha figure works to reinforce the model of female talent as produced by effort rather than inspiration, and to define the limits of feminised performance as a success strategy. There are cautionary plot lines in both *Gossip Girl* and *90210* in which the alpha girl characters are shown to attempt to win academic prizes through exploitation of the very heterofeminised desirability which defines them. In *Gossip Girl*, Blair attempts sexual blackmail in order to pressure a teacher to withdraw a negative reference on her Yale application (2.1. 'Carnal Knowledge'), while in *90210* Naomi Clark (see Figure 4.4) uses sex in an attempt to gain a college place (2.5 'Environmental Hazards'). On each occasion, the characters are found out and punished.

Although extraordinarily privileged, for alpha girls, like geek girls, academic success is achieved via application rather than innate ability. This is underscored when Naomi experiments with an approach coded as masculine; having failed to work on an important assignment, she undertakes a last-minute, intensive all-night study session. At first it seems successful and she gains an A for the paper. However, her teacher is suspicious and investigates further; it transpires that Naomi's boyfriend edited and improved the work when she dozed off (*90210*, 3.21 'The Prom Before the Storm'). The work is indeed a last-minute A out of the hat, but it isn't her A. Naomi is expelled for cheating; although it is made clear that she did not deliberately cheat, the audience is invited to recognise her attempt to adopt a masculinised model of success as foolish and risk laden. When she applies herself in the proper hard-working girl manner, she is successful.

Thus, alpha girl narratives, as well as offering positions for wishful identification and pedagogic function with regard to hyperfemininity and consumption (Brown and Pardun 2004; Meehan 2002), also reinforce models of feminised success as produced by application rather than inspiration. This they share with geek girl narratives. The variation between geek and alpha then lies in the degree to which compensatory performances of femininity are invested in. What they have in common is the model of their academic achievement itself, the gendered, subordinate 'hard-working' model traditionally and persistently gendered as female.

Producing the Achieving Girl: The Functions of Ability Recognition

The identification and measuring of ability are processes central to the production of the achieving girl as an object of knowledge, and in endowing her with the authority to speak from the 'achieving girl' subject positon. Such assessments have the discursive function of the examination as described by Foucault (1977, 192), in their 'fixing … of individual differences'. 'Examination' here is an expanded definition which includes processes such as the medical and psychiatric examination, in which the individual is 'described, judged, measured, compared with others, in his very individuality', and is turned into a documented case. Foucault identifies the examination as the key technology in creating the individual, and it is indicative of 'a modality of power in which each individual receives as his status his own individuality' (193). In schools, the examination includes formal testing, but also other elements that make up the school report, such as behaviour, sociability and broader aptitudes. The procedures and practices by which schools are advised to identify their 'gifted' pupils[1] include a range of indicators which together can be said to constitute a Foucauldian examination in nature and purpose: They constitute the student as a particular kind of individual and bestow a particular kind of status.

Figure 4.4 90210 alpha girls. Naomi Clarke (second from left).

The examination is thus a cultural as well as a 'scientific' process; the features and 'marks' which individuals display are social and performative, and are read in cultural contexts. It is the process by which students are hierarchised and distributed 'according to their aptitude' in ways that create as much as predict their prospects in later life (Foucault 1977, 183). The examination therefore is central to the processes by which the individual achieving girl is produced as an object of knowledge within particular domains of power.

A variety of processes that produce girls as achieving are evident in popular and participant texts; they range from formal, high-stakes testing to informal processes of 'recognition' by others who have the authority to pronounce. For example, Summer Roberts (*The OC*, 2003–2012) is identified late in her school career by a high test score; Buffy Summers (*Buffy the Vampire Slayer*, 1997–2003) also achieves a surprise high test score and is regularly pronounced clever by teachers; Rose Tyler (*Doctor Who*, 2005–) has her thinking skills tested and affirmed by the Doctor before he invites her on the Tardis; Joan Girardi (*Joan of Arcadia*, 2004–2005) is pronounced smart by no less an authority than God. Among participants, tests, placement on 'gifted and talented' registers, teacher affirmation and ability grouping are all named by girls as means by which they acquire their achieving identities in schools. These various technologies and practices serve the discursive function of placing the girl within narrative trajectories which offer expanded opportunities for success. However, such trajectories are not equally accessible to all girls even when so identified, and are in themselves shaped by relational orders of gender and class. This is a disturbing trope both on and off screen.

The Narrative Functions of Ability Recognition on Screen

The role of school mechanisms and teachers as both recognising and producing ability identities as a kind of a speech act is a recurring trope in teen TV. This trope performs two key narrative functions: It serves to position characters as successful and aspiring, proper objects of identification for commodity niche audiences. Further, characters' responses to identification offer a regulative guide as to how such recognition may be appropriately managed without compromising feminised (consumer) identities.

Kelly and Suzanne at Sir Walter Raleigh draw my attention to the operations of ability recognition in the teen TV series *The OC* (2003–2007). The example they cite is that of Summer Roberts, a privileged and popular high school girl who fulfils all the stereotypes of a socially successful and feminised identity. Suzanne describes her as a character who is

> really clever but she doesn't like realise for ages it because she was like the one to go shopping and had a really superficial life. She was really clever but she got wrapped up in everything else and didn't really care that much.

A core source of drama is the surprise identification of Summer as smart and her response to this identification. This starts when she receives an unexpectedly high SAT score (the Scholastic Aptitude Test, which is the US college entrance exam). Her score places her in the top 0.3% nationally (Sat scores, no date) and above her high-achieving geek boyfriend, Seth. The test score works to place the character on a new trajectory of success, and functions as a kind of perlocutionary act, calling into being as it pronounces (Austin 1976). As the episode and the season progress, Summer's appearance, her ambitions and the terms in which she describes herself change, suggesting ways in which the technologies of ability coding can act upon subjectivity and self-narrative.

Pronouncing (a girl as smart) is shown to be potent; the identity which it produces can be overpowering. Moreau, Mendick, and Epstein (2010) describe the colonising effect of mathematical ability on characters in popular representations, in that it overrides all other aspects of personality and life narrative. A similar effect is played out with regard to a more generalised ability in Summer. The next time we see her, she is costumed as a 'band geek', carrying a French horn in an attempt to create an identity profile attractive to a college recruiter. In a following scene, she appears to have undergone a reverse makeover, costumed in dowdy brown clothes and horn-rimmed glasses (*The OC*, 3.8, 'The Perfect Storm'), This colonisation by ability is a recognisable and long-standing trope of teen TV. A well as those already discussed, *My So-Called Life* (1994–1995), *Freaks and Geeks* (1999–2000), *Malcolm in the Middle* (2000–2006), *Joan of Arcadia* (2004–2005), *High School Musical* (2006) and *90210* (2008–2012) all feature students whose ability identities override all other aspects of character. Such colonisation in effect reverses the 'makeover' process and creates a narrative crisis. As with the geek narratives discussed earlier, the 'colonisation' effect has the pedagogic function of stressing the need for both compensatory femininity and constant vigilance to survive identification as 'achieving' with feminine identity intact.

The transformations that such characters go through, the crude and abject portrayals of alternatives to hyperfeminised consumer identities (strident, unwashed and unloved), especially those that embody political and feminist dissent, work to offer dramatic conduct correctives to the viewer, and are often played for laughs. For example, to the horror of friends and boyfriend, at one point Summer eschews personal hygiene (toiletries, leg shaving) as a protest against environmentally damaging cosmetics and consumer stylings (*The OC*, 4.4 'The Metamorphosis'); there is a similar narrative incident in in another teen show, *Joan of Arcadia* (2.21, 'Vanity Thy Name Is Human').

This illustrates the active invocation of hostility to assumed feminist positions from the past, identified by McRobbie (2009, 18), 'in order to endorse a new regime of sexual meanings based on female consent, equality, participation and pleasure'. Such hostility has been identified as a particular characteristic of contemporary popular texts aimed at girl audiences (Kelly and Pomerantz 2009). Through the humorous undermining and anxious stigmatisation of behaviours and identities positioned as too marginal, too political, too smart and insufficiently 'girl', the viewer, together with the TV smart girl, is guided back toward more hegemonic, and importantly consumer, modes. Responses such as Kelly's and Suzanne's at Sir Walter Raleigh, and those from participants at Maple Grove, express admiration for characters who manage to successfully manage the tensions inherent in sustaining achieving and feminised identities, even while acknowledging the difficulties – I explore this further below.

The transformation that Summer Roberts undergoes on *The OC* (2003–2007) can be seen to serve a range of purposes. In terms of dramatic function in ensemble cast teen TV, establishing characters as college capable ensures members of the cast are credibly able to pass as a group from high school to university as a series progresses, and is a common teen TV device. The identification of central characters as smart is also an audience-positioning device. Academic success and higher education participation are central to the narratives of more affluent and aspirational classes. Having a recognisably college-bound cast of characters serves as a means of ensuring a show's continuing address to an affluent young target audience (Brown and Pardun 2004; Wee 2008). Participants show some awareness of this, for example, in Suzanne's (Sir Walter Raleigh) comment on *The OC* in terms of wishful identification: 'The OC makes everything seem perfect'. The address to the university-bound, or those who aspire to be, reinforces particular trajectories in ways I shall discuss later.

Complementary Intelligence and the Post-Feminist Contract

As well as establishing characters on success trajectories, the narrative trope of surprise ability recognition on screen provokes a crisis in terms of gendered identity and the patriarchal order. Effortless, innate achievement such as high test scores achieved without work are, as we have seen, a specifically masculinised attribute. The proper resolution of this crisis in terms of address to audience is that of a successful reconciliation of achievement with endorsed, consuming femininities. For example, in *The OC* it is quickly established that Summer's intelligence is a threat to her boyfriend:

RYAN: I think it's really great that Summer's a genius.
SETH: Whoa, whoa, whoa, whoa, whoa! Dr Kim said she had some untapped potential. No one went around using the G-word.
RYAN: Don't do this man.
SETH: Do what?
RYAN: Compete with Summer.
SETH: Why? [*looks scared*]. Because do you think Summer would win?

The anxious invocation of the 'G-word' suggests a masculine preserve under threat; the casting of this as competition, and the threat of her possibly prevailing, is presented as precipitating an identity crisis for Seth, who is characterised from the outset by both his innate abilities and masculine 'geek' performance. The threat is defused by constructing Summer's intelligence on a specifically feminised model, which allows Seth to retain his dominant position as the 'real' masculine intellect. We can see this in, for example, her response to success in her university interview, which is to 'go get a mani-pedi'. As elsewhere in the drama, although Summer experiments with alternative identities, her 'girlness' is consistently foregrounded.

This endorsing of a model of complementary feminised intelligence is an increasingly popular trope in post-feminist depictions of female success – for example, Amina (Maple Grove) describes Elle Woods from the film *Legally Blonde* (2001) as an example of being both girly and achieving (see Figure 4.5). She describes Elle's thinking processes in proving a case as specifically feminised:

> Cause she's like, really girly … the way that she figures it out, it's about the design of her shoe or something like that … it isn't exactly something that everybody would think.

The central comic premise of this film is that a girl who majors in fashion and is described as a 'dumb blonde with a credit card' secures a place at Harvard Law School and once there beats her fellow students and wins cases through a combination of specifically feminised thinking and self-belief. It is the post-feminist contract writ large, with Elle consistently constructed in ways that reduce her threat, and teaching the more conventionally successful, less feminised women law students – who are described as 'boring and ugly and serious' – how to be more successfully girl. The discursive premise of the film is that 'girl knowledge' is just as powerful as, but essentially different from, male rationality and expertise, and therefore non-threatening. For example, her acceptance to Harvard is based, like Summer's college acceptance in *The OC* (2003–2007), on an exceptionally high test score. The potential threat here is balanced by her resume, which lists appearing in a Ricky Martin pop video and designing faux-fur underwear as her extra-curricular achievements. The threat is further removed by the fact that she only applies because 'going to Harvard is the only way I'm going to get the love of my life back'. This in effect places her outside of masculinised competition.

All of Elle's knowledge derives from 'girl cultures' of the boutique and the spa, and this knowledge is mobilised via cognitive processes which are also framed as feminised in those ways described by Victorian commentators (Buckle 1872); she is irrational, lateral and emotionally connected in her thinking. Elle's hybrid feminine–professional identity recirculates older discourses of complementarity which position women's particular talents as 'socialising genius' in their empathy and connectedness (Alaya 1977); this is updated in terms of an economic rather than a domestic identity, one that is fulfilled through successful participation in the rituals of gendered consumption: Elle wins her first case through her knowledge that a woman who has just had a perm would never get into the shower. She had previously almost lost the case by refusing to disclose the client's alibi because it involved liposuction and she promised the client that she would never tell. This she justifies to her law professor on the grounds of 'sisterhood', thus invoking discourses of feminism in ways that take them 'into account' within the pleasures of the exaggerated hyperfemininities of the post-feminist masquerade (McRobbie 2009).

While Shameem (St Ursula's) reads Elle's success within the neoliberal framework of self-actualisation and endorsing hard-working girl discourses, saying, 'I think that the movie more shows that you can achieve what you want to if you really put hard work into it', Carrie (St Ursula's) frames it within an understanding of the post-feminist promise as offering girls pleasures and freedom. She declares, 'I think it's you don't have to be a geek to be smart ... it's kind of saying both, you can be'.

Here in popular forms, it is thus possible to identify a recirculation of much older discourses of anxiety surrounding achieving women, and also of the ways they have been resolved through the casting of specifically feminised modes of intellect as complementary and subordinated. In post feminist teen dramas, the performance of threat-reducing femininities and intellectual complementarity is the condition of women's entry into previously masculine fields. This is presented as both pleasurable and empowering.

Figure 4.5 Elle Woods.

The Narrative Functions of Smart Girl Identity Markers Off Screen

In participant accounts, identification as smart can be seen to serve similar purposes to those on screen; test results, placement on 'gifted and talented' registers and ability setting perform the same discursive function as TV identification tropes in that they operate to call the achieving girl subject into being and to place her within success trajectories that are bound up with wider social identities and structures. Among group interviews, identity produced as an outcome of test results is described by participants in all three schools. For example, at St Ursula's Kirsty describes how she 'knew' she was 'gifted':

> I didn't really know it til I got my SAT results and I got like the highest in my class. And then in Year 7 when I got the letter [announcing her placement on the school's gifted and talented register] then I kind of knew.

Online, the source or confirmation of smart girl identities emerges as a matter of interest to participants themselves. *Hyperpinkdramaqueen* starts a thread with the question, 'Does it mean anything to be smart?' She answers it herself starting with the statement 'I think it means you have a good grade'. *Kitty_Kat* starts a poll entitled 'How do you know your smart?' The three options she offers are:

- Get good grades
- Get told
- Feel smart

No respondents select the 'feel smart' option. *Gabriellamontez* endorses the school-produced nature of her identity in her response: 'I voted for 2 because I couldn't decide between being told and getting good grades', while *Jurda* and *hyperpinkdramaqueen* define their smartness through the levels they achieve in maths and English.

The poll and the responses suggest that for girls, the production of ability identities draws more on external than on internal resources. Both online and in the group interviews, girls refer to their place on registers, their grades and their test scores, not only as measures of their achievements but also as placing them in a hierarchy of authority to speak about achieving girlhood. This resonates with Allan's (2010) findings in her study of high-achieving girls in an elite independent school, where girls 'seemed to signal a belief that their success was only recognisable once it had been measured and tested in a quantifiable manner' (46).

Participants are acutely aware of the pressure to establish themselves within success trajectories, and the relationship between identity and narrative expectations. On the forum, *Pandora*'s claim to a smart identity is established through claims to both pleasure and authenticity, but also indicates a reliance on external markers to support her sense of self. She stresses the importance of grades as identity markers, and the part they will play in her life trajectory:

> To me … it means everything to be smart. Because that's who I am. All of the time I obsess about grades, they are VERY important to me as I need good GCSE's to go to University and to study what I want

to study. I am doing private study because I enjoy it and it doesn't feel like studying.

Similar anxiety is also evident among some group interview participants. At St Ursula's, Sally is 'not really sure' what she wants to study, but getting to university is central to her vision of her future:

> At least I wanna get through university. Cause I have this funny feeling that, where if I don't like, get to a certain place I'll never get anywhere. So I really wanna get things right, like, in order.

Sally's is a clear account of success as a narrative of established sequence, of the way that university operates as an identity marker of success, and of the anxieties that accompany it. It would be tempting to interpret this as a standard, if fairly acute, example of middle-class anxiety with regard to the role of education as the means of maintaining and reproducing status (Walkerdine et al. 2001; Reay 2001b). Sally's self-presentation elsewhere in the interview would accord with such an interpretation – she is the most apparently confident and articulate of the group, the girl whom her primary school teacher predicted would be head girl, and the one to whom the others frequently defer. However, her relationship with the success narrative and her claims to authoritative voice are less secure than first appear, as she explains:

> Cause my mum didn't go to university and my Dad didn't go to university and my dad's like really clever and stuff but he didn't go to university, so I just want all the stuff I can get, to be completely prepared for where next.

I ask Sally if the idea of getting to university makes her feel secure. She replies, 'Exactly. You can't go any further back'. The spectre of social demotion haunts the success narrative; Sally's comment regarding going 'further back' suggests a lurking anxiety regarding her ability to sustain forward momentum, to stay on track. Walkerdine et al. (2001, 136) have identified the 'powerful fear of failure' operating within middle-class families, which is built on assumptions that entry into the professions is a precursor to happiness, and that education is necessary to sustain privilege and to ensure such entry; accompanying this fear is an anxiety that any softening of purpose or effort in themselves or in their children will result in failure and downward mobility.

Sally is not the only one of the group to demonstrate awareness of the success script, nor anxiety regarding her placing within it. Her comments prompt the following discussion:

JUSTINE: You kind of feel like if you don't go to university then you haven't really finished it all.

SHAMEEM: It's like, primary school, high school, college, university.

SALLY: It's expected of you as well.

JUSTINE: If you just stop it … [*grimaces*].

KIRSTY: I think it's like expected that we'd go on to university and not just stop after school.

These exchanges illustrate the pressure girls feel to stay on the 'conveyor belt' of education as described by Walkerdine et al. (2001), and the defined paths which they learn to pursue 'in a rational and determined manner' (Aapola, Gonick, and Harris 2005, 87).

Variations in the Success Narrative

Discursive variants within an apparently straightforward success narrative ('primary school, high school, college, university') are evident. At Maple Grove, the success trajectory, and particularly university, is framed as an institutional expectation by Sonia, as opposed to a family expectation by Lydia:

SONIA: I think I'm pretty sure I want to go to university and like pass A levels and stuff. Because, like, what's the point in working if you're just like … because I think, these days, like government requirements to get a job, they judge you more on like if you've been to university. If you haven't really been to university it's like … I dunno.

LYDIA: I think, definitely. I talked about this with my brothers. I really want a gap year because if I'm gonna work really hard and get good GCSE's and A levels then I want, like, a year off.

Jess expresses the same intention. She describes a similar context to Lydia's for her own narrative, saying, 'I've got older cousins and stuff and I always hear about their gap years'. This is in contrast with Amina and Nicki, who intend to go straight on from school and describe their anxieties regarding entering a competitive job market if they don't.

Sonia's expectations seem formed by institutional discourses, and it is interesting that she locates the source of these as the government level rather than the school, suggesting the permeation of policy discourses in schools down to the level of student interactions and narratives of self. This is in contrast with Lydia, who frames her expectations in terms of her family's encouragement and her own sense of entitlement to a gap year, an established feature of the middle-class educational narrative (Heath 2007). The gap year, however, does not feature as a narrative regularity, but merely as a means of giving the deserving hard-working student a break: As Heath argues, 'the gap year also provides an important means of 'gaining the edge' over other students in the context of increased competition for entry to elite institutions' (89). Jess shows awareness of the potential advantage, recognising that 'you can get like different experiences that might help you with university'.

Within this study, participants' inclusion of the gap year correlates with the degree of anxiety or security that they express with regard to university, with ultimate career ambitions and with motives for applying. This reveals the 'going to university' narrative as having variants in which girls place themselves according to their cultural resources – these include family, school expectations, careers advice and confidence – and such resources are unequally distributed across social groups. As Reay (2008b) notes, 'As more and more groups get caught up in the race for educational credentials, new internal differentiations are emerging'.

At Maple Grove, Elaine says she thinks university will be 'scary!' She draws on a range of popular narratives and expresses doubts about her ability to manage their competing demands:

> You like hear stories about those people who get into loads of debt, and partying hard, then it's like you have to kind of balance out the school work … so it's like, confusing.

Differing levels of knowledge and kinds of expectation are also evident at St Ursula's, for example, in this exchange:

MP: What do you think university will be like?

TANYA: Really long!

MP: How long's really long?

TANYA: I dunno. Some people wanna be doctors like and they'll be in university for seven years.

MONICA: That's what I thought about til I found out what my sister was doing … like, going out every night!

Kirsty too describes her expectation of enjoying university both academically and socially, with specific knowledge about the way university life works. She locates this within family rather than school-derived insights:

> My cousin just went and she said that she loves doing her … like she has lectures. She said, once the lectures are done you can just have fun. Cause she only has like five a week, and then they all, like, have their own little rooms next door to each other so she said once they're, like, over, it's really fun.

Expectations with regard to university are not only created in different contexts, but are created differently within those contexts. Discourses of enjoyment with regard to higher education have been found to circulate almost exclusively among white, middle-class students with expectations of attending higher-status universities (Hutchings and Archer 2001). In this study, participants suggest that while the expectation of going to university is established by their schools, expectations of pleasure are circulated within families and are dependent on a history of participation.

In participants' accounts, we can see processes of governmentality operating in different ways; Sonia shows direct uptake of the language of policy as promulgated by the school, while Kirsty and Lydia reproduce discourses of the normalised middle-class subject. These not only illustrate different points of entry to the higher education narrative, but also show the operation of the two modes of governmentality proposed by Foucault as

> processes by which the individual acts upon himself. And conversely ... the points where the techniques of the self are integrated into structures of coercion and domination. (1993, 203)

Kirsty and Lydia's accounts illustrate how those technologies of the (middle-class) self – narratives of expectation, the reproduction of advantage through education – have become integrated into structures of coercion within national policies, such as 'gifted and talented'. Sonia's account, however, suggests the point where government technologies have direct impact on the ways she acts upon herself; middle-class values are in this way normalised through the institutional structures of schooling. In this way, governmentality promulgates inequalities of power. It is not just a process whereby all individuals self-monitor according to the same disciplinary regulations; rather, the kinds of knowledge which produce such regulation are drawn from the normative values of more powerful groups.

I was interested to see the way that the group interview itself became a forum for such reproduction and for competitive display of cultural resource. Sally, as noted earlier, is accorded a degree of deference by the rest of the group with regard to her intellectual status in the school. She has said earlier in this exchange that she is anxious to go to university, to get things 'in the right order', and that her parents didn't go; after Kirsty's description of her cousin's enjoyment, she qualifies her earlier position remark saying:

> Yeah, it's like another thing, I wanna have the university experience as an experience and as a baseline, but I'm not sure if I'm gonna find it easy or hard to keep motivated. It's like, there's always the pull to like, get into university life [gestures dismissively at Kirsty].

Here she suggests that in describing her earlier anxieties, she had already taken the temptations offered by the student life into account and hints that Kirsty and her cousin have not been able to resist them, thus exerting claim to both existing prior knowledge and superior strength of character. It suggests the role that the going to university narratives as a discursive resource can have in the social positioning of self among girls, and that this positioning is relational and competitive within peer groups. It illustrates the intra-subject circulation of discourses in the social operations of governmentality.

Only one participant expresses any doubt as to the importance of university itself: on the forum *AlwaysTakeBackup* comments:

> I don't think University means much any more ☺ It's not just the elite that go there ... it's mainly people with the funds that go.

This comment is interesting in its context – it appears in a discussion thread concerning contestants on that season's *Big Brother*. The contestants in question are identical twins Sam and Amanda, middle-class young women distinguished by their hyperfeminised performances. Participants discuss the fact that they are also university students and whether their performance is part of a conscious game plan. *AlwaysTakeBackup* calls the twins 'tacky' in the same thread. In terms of attitude to university, she appears to define the 'elite' academically as differentiated from the merely affluent – the fact that her posting is made in the same year as the announced increase in university funding may be significant; it calls to mind the 'Uni for Boffs Not Toffs' ('Boffs' being British slang for the studious and intelligent, 'Toffs' for the rich and aristocratic) protest banners (Figure 4.6) which encapsulate students' attempt to establish a discursive separation between privilege and academic performance, and to reinforce discourses of meritocracy.

Figure 4.6 'Boffs Not Toffs' student banner.

Boffs and Toffs: The Achieving Girl as Raced and Classed Narrative

In this study, both participant accounts and TV texts are characterised by narratives of success built around a classed developmental model, and participants themselves are dominated by white, middle-class girls. As in Pomerantz and Raby's (2011, 554) study, the accounts produced by girls tend to ascribe academic success to factors other than 'structural privileges and oppression'. This is not to say, however, that connections are entirely absent, and it is interesting to look at how class and 'race' appear where they are directly invoked. There is a tendency of those who belong to dominant groups to fail to recognise the power relationships inscribed in their positions or the workings of privilege and disadvantage in terms of class and race (Frankenberg 1993; Gillborn 2005, 2008). This is true of many of the participants in this study, yet class is invoked in the authority they claim to pronounce upon the smart girl. The testing regimes and schedules described above only go so far in identifying the smart girl; these must be allied with classed and gendered performance for the subject position to be fully recognised, and its benefits fully realised. Harris observes that 'while some privileged young women are reaping the benefits of new opportunities, those without cultural capital are slipping through the ever-widening holes in what remains of our social safety nets' (2004, xvii). Yet girls who both do and don't speak from positions of privilege are active reproducers of discourses of self-management and hard work as the key to success. Elision of class and structural disadvantage is characteristic of the neoliberal ideologies central to the development and proliferation of discourses of both 'gifted and talented' and those of the new universal 'future girl'. This has been remarked within accounts of the successful self-managing subject (Furlong and Cartmel 1997) and those of the achieving girl which both produce the achieving young woman as the ideal neoliberal subject and assume a default white middle-class subjectivity (Walkerdine 2003; Francis and Skelton 2005).

The ways that public discourses shape the sense that individual girls make of their lives and opportunities are complex, and operate in local as well as institutional contexts. Work to tease out the complexities not only exposes the structural differences elided in the classless neoliberal vision, but also reveals the psychological labour involved in developing compensatory strategies through which the individual can make sense of their own positioning with reference to dominant discourses: Bradford and Hey (2007) examine the ways in which government discourses are worked into the subject's psychological self-conception, in processes whereby the very desire to improve the self (regardless of actual opportunities, risks and barriers) becomes the most significant form of capital. Such desire elides consideration of – and thus resistance to – oppression via structural limitations such as class and race. Budgeon (2003), Allen (2008) and Zaslow (2009) explore ways in which young women take up discourses of femininity, creativity and success, and the difficulties for the individual in reconciling neoliberal narratives of choice with their own experiences of restricted opportunity. Explorations of girls' lived experience focus on the limitations of discourses of flexibility and self-invention, especially for those marginalised and excluded along the axes of class and race.

On the forum, class is at first addressed via a discussion of favourite TV characters. Only three are named in terms of class and disadvantage:

Oipoodle describes Joey Potter from the serial teen drama *Dawson's Creek* (1998–2003) and Veronica Mars as 'having to get jobs to support their ambitions of higher education and having to cope with the snobiness of the other characters'. She describes them as both socially and economically disadvantaged, although in many respects they are constructed as middle-class characters in straightened circumstances rather than as working-class. *Pandora* nominates Rose Tyler, the ninth Doctor's companion (*Doctor Who*, 2005). *Pandora* describes her as

> not smart in an academic way (this is exaduated greatly in the series) but asks questions and picks things up very quickly.

The fact that *Pandora* sees Rose's identity as exaggeratedly 'not smart' is telling. Rose is clearly coded as working class: She lives with her mother in a council flat on an inner London estate, works in a shop and has a strong regional accent. Furthermore, the character is played by Billie Piper who, via a process of transmedia identity, brings particular resonances of classed femininity through her existing profile as pop star and 'ladette' partner of a celebrity DJ. At Maple Grove School, participants refer to her as 'Billie Piper' instead of Rose, indicating the degree of identification of the celebrity with the character she plays. The actress herself has referred to the character of Rose as 'a bit of a chav', a derogatory term which casts the working class as the abject other (Jones 2011). Yet, Tyler's comment is ambivalent as she also mourns that since *Doctor Who*, she has mainly played 'posh birds', a statement which expresses alignment with Rose in terms of class positioning (interview with Singh 2008).

Each time Rose is nominated, whether online or in group discussions, her nomination is justified in the face of her class status and lack of academic markers. This suggests the persistent association of the markers of privilege with those of ability. For example, at Sir Walter Raleigh Joanne says, 'She's got a lot of common sense, not, um, like academically, book clever. She's, sort of, smart', and Tina offers the perspective that 'she's had to fight to get what she wants. It's not been plain sailing'. This accords with Archer's (2005) 'distance travelled' model of relational success which describes the achievement of girls whose background or profile would more usually indicate failure.

Elaine and Jess (Maple Grove) comment specifically on the character as occupying a non-normative class position in terms of the smart girl narrative:

EMMA: Billie Piper. She didn't seem that clever but when you got to know her more, she became, like, clever.
MP: Why didn't she seem that clever at first?
JESS: She was blonde and off a council estate.

When Amina and Jess nominate Cheryl Cole as smart, some of the others in the group laugh. Amina defends her choice, saying,

> She didn't grow up with the best … like she grew up in a council flat and stuff. And you wouldn't really expect someone … like not in a rude way, but to become as successful as her.

Cole is coded in the same way as Rose Tyler/Billie Piper, via the markers of council housing and strong regional accent that make their success what 'you wouldn't really expect'.

The role of class, accent and education as markers of smart identities is highlighted in the protest of some web forum participants to the nomination of Rose as smart, and the defence of Rose by others. *Pandora* defends her as a quick learner with natural curiosity, saying, 'She doesn't just want to sit around eating chips. She realises there is more to life'. This evokes the same sort of 'sofa slacker' as Sally at St Ursula's evokes, and casts the smart girl as morally active in the construction of her own ability identity in a way that is strongly connected with class. *Jurda*, however, is forceful in her objection, stating:

> Rose is not smart, she is thick. She also pitys aliens that later try to kill her (also the darlek soldier). I hate the way she speaks (nuthin').

This statement excludes working-class girls from the possibility of achieving identities on grounds of both gender and class. *Jurda* rejects connected and empathic forms of knowing, those very qualities cast as feminised (Gilligan 1982) and celebrated in affective geek transformation narratives (see above); she also excludes Rose for her verbal display of her class origins. *Jurda*'s objections are also particularly interesting in the light of her complaint in a thread on class that she herself has been made to take elocution lessons.

On the same day as the Rose debate on the forum, *Dark Angel* starts a thread asking the question, 'Do you have to be posh to be smart?' Her phrasing of the question invokes a popular series of adverts in the UK starring upper middle-class actress Joanna Lumley, for which the slogan is 'You don't have to be posh to be privileged'. These advertisements position the (not posh) viewer as able to enjoy the privileges of the upper classes (here car insurance) while mocking the upper classes themselves as ridiculous. In transmedia terms, Lumley's own identification with the sitcom *Absolutely Fabulous* (1992–2012), which mocks the pretensions of privileged celebrity worlds, makes her an authoritative voice on what is and is not ridiculous. *Dark Angel*'s invoking of the advert thus also invokes the actress, and displays a use of media to suggest her own position – that is, not posh but possessing certain advantages usually pertaining to the privileged.

Dark Angel describes her experience of having her potential overlooked at her school sixth form, where she was the only student from her council estate to stay on for A levels. She says, 'I felt out of it a lot of the time' and locates her sense of alienation in not dressing or speaking in the same way as other students. She says her predicted grades were always lower than her actual results, and ascribes this to teacher stereotyping on grounds of class. *Jurda* responds:

> It's the opposite with me, I live in Hull and most have a strong accent but my parents (so cruel) taught me to speak differently so I get classed as posh ☹.

This revelation gives a context for *Jurda*'s objection to Rose's identification as a smart girl noted above; it appears her parents' resources and her own efforts are devoted to erasing one of the key markers that defines Rose as working class: her accent. This is also clearly at some social cost to *Jurda* if the 'so cruel' aside implies that she is mocked for speaking 'differently'.

The shame that achieving working-class girls associate with their class origins as described by Walkerdine et al. (2001) is suggested in *Jurda*'s dismissal of Rose as 'thick' and her hatred of Rose's speech. It sets classed and gendered terms for inclusion in terms of smart identities that she indicates she herself cannot meet. These also indicate the conditions of shame and desire that underpin the transformational makeover narrative (Gonick 2003; Ringrose and Walkerdine 2008), and which her elocution lessons evoke. However, *Jurda*'s use of the frowning smiley (☹) at the end of her comment indicates she is not happy to be 'classed as posh', suggesting a similar ambivalence to Billie Piper's being cast as more privileged.

This ambivalence toward dis-identification with working-class origins indicates that neoliberal discourses of aspiration and self-invention are not an easy mantle for working-class girls to assume. Even when the twin incentives of desire and shame operate as powerful motivators, the debate over Rose Tyler's smart identity, *Dark Angel*'s feelings of being overlooked and *Jurda*'s elocution lessons all indicate that, far from being a redundant category in the individual's self-construction project, signs of class can operate to inhibit the individual's ability to take up an achieving girl subject position.

Spectres of Class and the Elision of Race

While *Dark Angel* and *Jurda*'s responses to the question 'Do you have to be posh to be smart?' would seem to confirm that indeed you do, other responses from *hyperpinkdramaqueen, Gabriellamontez, lalagirl, jadoremusique* and *jen.nzgirl*, who represent a spectrum of private, state and public school experience from New Zealand and the UK, are all brief but emphatic denials. It would seem then that class is not seen as an issue except by those participants who have consciously experienced its deleterious effects as the impact specifically of class. As Skeggs (1997) observes, class awareness emerges most strongly in those whom it most constrains.

In one of the Maple Grove groups, *Gilmore Girls* (2000–2007) is cited as an example of a show where class is addressed:

JESS: Rory, she grew up and her mum was really young when she gave birth and so they didn't and so … Lorelai wasn't exceptionally, she dropped out when she was sixteen.

MAY: She didn't really go to school much and then Rory goes on to Yale and gets amazing … she graduates.

Their discussion positions the Gilmores' story as a narrative of overcoming underprivilege through judicious effort, one in which the hard-working girl, with the right kind of parental support, overcomes the disadvantages of her birth and goes on to win accolades and a shining future. The fact that in this drama Lorelai's rich, quasi-aristocratic parents pay for a private education for Rory, that Lorelai herself is rich in cultural capital and in well-paid and fulfilling work, and that Rory's wealthy father re-appears and funds her Yale education mean less to them than the narrative significance of Lorelai's early pregnancy and single motherhood. For Jess and May, the warning spectre of teen mother trope overrides all other signifiers to render this above all a narrative of upward mobility, of disaster overcome.

At Sir Walter Raleigh, Lucy also invokes the teen mother, describing how

> even if like you're clever and you make a mistake you can be seen as being really stupid. My cousin got pregnant when she was 16, a big 'No', and she was really clever.

This resonates with Walkerdine et al.'s (2001) discussion of the spectre of the pregnant teenager as haunting the middle-class girl as a figure of excess and failure. Focusing on the enactment of discourses of class on the feminine body, they find early motherhood offers role and status to some working-class girls who do not follow successful educational trajectories, while middle-class girls postpone reproduction in favour of achieving educational and professional goals. While working-class girls achieving success face loss of class identity and community, the figure of pregnant young mother haunts the middle-class girl as a figure of excess and failure. Thus, they argue, through the unequal availability of success narratives, middle-class and working-class girls have become one another's feared 'other' (Walkerdine et al. 2001).

These discussions offer a view of class in its most crude contemporary configurations. The council estate 'chavs' Rose Tyler and Cheryl Cole and the teen single mother are those tropes which have come to signify working class in popular discourse (Jones 2011), and they are the means by which participants frame their claims to achieving identities and accounts of the ways class might make a difference to narrative trajectories. The absence of apprehension of the workings of class beyond such figures of exclusion is notable across all three sites of enquiry. This absence is significant in a discourse which creates success as available to every girl if she will make the required effort. This ties the achieving girl subject yet more closely to neoliberal self-improvement discourses.

In terms of race, there was similar elision. Of all the many TV drama characters nominated by participants as smart girls or women, few were non-white. These were Martha Jones, a Black British medical student who is the 10th Doctor's assistant after Rose Tyler, (*Doctor Who*, 2005–2012); Miranda Bailey, an African-American doctor in the medical drama *Grey's Anatomy* (2005–2012); Carla Espinosa, an Hispanic-American nurse in the medical sitcom *Scrubs* (2001–2010); Christina Yang, a Korean-American doctor also in *Grey's Anatomy* (2005–2012); Gabriella Montez, the Hispanic-American star of *High School Musical* (2006); and Dora, the Hispanic-American cartoon character from *Dora the Explorer* (2000–2006). Of these, only Carla Espinosa and Miranda Bailey are named by participants specifically in terms of their ethnic identities, and Dora in terms of her bilingualism.

When I ask each group about the white profile of most TV smart girls, I am met with slightly embarrassed shrugs. At Maple Grove, Elaine says, 'I don't think about it … you don't think about it with your ethnicity at the forefront of your mind', illustrating the tendency of majority white positions to be normalised and thus neutralised in their consideration of race. May (who is of Chinese heritage) and Jess agree. Farida explains:

> Well if you watch like Arabic TV then there's all like, there's no white people. So you shouldn't really criticise the English TV for having everyone white.

Gonick (2003) describes how in her study minority ethnic girls aligning themselves with discourses of success could be faced with the dilemma of a 'dis-identification with racism' (Mercer 1992, in Gonick 2003); this discursive dilemma may also be at work here within the specific context of an identified smart girl group exploring the nature of claims to this identity both among themselves and with the awareness of a wider audience (me as the researcher in school, with the added awareness of the forum as a public space online). Of course, white students are not faced with the dilemma of dis-identification with discourses of normalised whiteness, although one can see glimpses of such a process at work in terms of negotiation with class identities.

Online participants' forum user names often reference their favourite shows and change with their preferences. One of the most prolific posters, *Gabriellamontez*, originally joined as *Buffysummers* (white, American, middle class), then became *Rose_Tyler* (White, British, working class), switched to *Marthajones* (Black, British, middle class), and then to

Gabriellamontez (Hispanic-American, middle class). When I ask her about Gabriella's Hispanic identity in particular, she replied: 'I don't know she doesn't speak with any particular accent and in it she moves around a lot so not clear where she came from'.

The elision of ethnicity and race as factors in group discussion and in this participant's serial identifications across identity signifiers is interesting. It is indicative of the assumed neutrality of race as a category typical of young women from dominant groups (Frankenberg 1993), and also suggests a take-up of neoliberal discourses of global girlhood in which self-inventing individuals carry no culturally significant markers across borders of nation, class and race in their quest for upward mobility; the characters chosen for forum names are the 'de-raced and de-classed' young women responsible for their own success or failure as described by Ringrose (2007, 481). It is only when an obvious marker of structural difference intrudes (such as Rose Tyler's accent) that the normative, exclusive nature of the discursive regulations is thrown into relief. It was interesting to see the debate in some quarters in December 2015 prompted by the casting of Black actor Noma Dumezweni as *Harry Potter* smart girl Hermione in the theatre adaptation, *Harry Potter and the Cursed Child*. Rowling asserts that she never specified Hermione's ethnicity (BBC News 2015), while some fans have been representing Hermione as Black for some time on fan sites (see e.g. Bennett's [2015] post on Buzzfeed). The response by the liberal press that Hemione's race 'doesn't matter' (*Independent* 2015) serves to underscore the elision of race as a significant factor in structural oppression.

However, it should also be remembered that the technologies of television literacy work to enable identification with central characters; *Doctor Who*'s companion is the audience's point of access to an unknown universe. The narrative unfolds from her viewpoint and the camera works largely through her eyes. In short, in *Doctor Who* it is not the Black or working-class girl who is constructed as alien.

Genre, Class and Gender

Of the television shows discussed, it is only in *Veronica Mars* (2005–2007) that the role of class in producing academic success is specifically addressed; as Hayes (2006 n.p.) put it, this is a show in which

> everything that happens is presented and viewed through a class lens. A war is raging between the haves and the have-nots, Veronica says, and you have to choose sides.

Veronica Mars is highly popular on the online forum, with more participants choosing usernames relating to this show than to any other. It is one of only three shows in which class/disadvantage is directly raised as an issue by participants (see above). This distinction, also noted by media academics

(Bolt 2008, 107), makes it worth examining further, particularly in terms of the circulation of discourses of class and femininity within the restrictive framework of US prime-time teen drama.

This show is set in the California town of Neptune where the affluent have benefitted from the dot.com boom and social divides are deep. In the pilot episode, Veronica provides voiceover context which evokes class as a significant factor in the narrative from the outset, saying:

> This is my school. If you go here, your parents are either millionaires, or your parents work for millionaires. Neptune, California, a town without a middle class. If you're in the second group, you get a job. Fast food, movie theaters, mini marts. (1.1 Pilot)

Racial tensions are constructed along WASP/Hispanic lines, with poor Hispanic students shown as being involved in gangs, violence, drugs and the prison system. Rich white students are also shown to have vicious and deviant propensities, but are protected by their wealth and status. It is part of Veronica's role as schoolgirl and private detective to see that justice is done, earning her the soubriquet 'rich-dude kryptonite' (2.14 'Versatile Toppings').

Veronica's own class position is ambiguous, and this ambiguity is consistently articulated; her father used to be the town sheriff, and she was formerly accepted by the popular rich crowd due to her best friend's and boyfriend's core membership status. Following her father's loss of his job in unpropitious circumstances and his reincarnation as a PI with a shabby office and some seedy clients, she becomes an outsider, eating lunch alone, scorned by the rich and threatened by the poor. The character herself is constructed as acutely aware of class positioning and frequently comments on it, as does her father. She and he (her mother, an alcoholic, left the family) live in a small flat in a depressing building; when he wins a case, he buys them steak to barbecue, saying, 'Tonight we eat like the lower middle classes to which we aspire!' (1.1 Pilot). Veronica is thus established as well qualified to comment on issues of social division.

Braithwaite (2008) argues that such outsider status is central to the noir detective genre upon which the series is styled, and allows the character to provide direct comment from an external perspective; Veronica's outsider stance is frequently invoked to critique the class-based inequalities of the school system via voiceover address to the audience. The show's positioning with regard to class can thus be seen as deriving from traditions of the noir genre, which has its own narrative tropes of exposing the unattractive underbelly of bourgeois suburban life (Spicer 2002).

Veronica's downward mobility and identity transformation are represented in costume and performance through flashbacks in the first episode, a visual series of 'then' against 'now' continuity cuts. These illustrate an abandoning of investment in the alpha girl subject position (which is no longer sustainable because she is no longer recognised/affirmed by her peers nor supported by the financial resources necessary for consumer femininity), and the inhabiting of a newer, more transgressive identity. She has cut her long blonde hair into a spiky chopped style; her dresses have been traded for jeans and biker boots. Her performance in the flashbacks is hyperfeminised – smiling, naive, affectionate, friendly and social. In the present, she is rebarbative, defensive, cynical and isolated. In terms of the noir genre, Veronica can be identified as an example of the 'good–bad girl' trope whose hard-boiled exterior hides a good heart (Wolfenstein and Leites 1950, 28) – Veronica's closest friend in fact calls her a 'marshmallow' when he gets to know her.

The unifying constant between the character's then and now identities is her academic performance and the sustained effort she puts into it. Rather than rejecting her achieving identity when she loses her social status, she switches between possible subject positions from a variant of alpha girl – highly achieving, popular, feminised – to the more transgressive masculinised stylings, autonomy and authenticity which typify some achieving girls who do not invest in feminised performance (Renold and Allan 2006; Francis 2009; Allan 2010). That adopting such stances/identities is risky is suggested in the ways that it makes Veronica a frequent target of bullying, including the sexualised bullying which some achieving girls who do not invest in compensatory femininities have been found to experience (Braithwaite 2008; Francis 2009). Veronica's intellectual credentials are established simultaneously with the ambiguity of her class position. The pilot episode opens with her staying up late to catch an adulterer on camera and seeing off a bullying biker gang with a brand of crude wit and a pit bull dog both more than equal to the task, all the while worrying about finishing her trigonometry homework. The next day in class, we see her quoting from Pope's *Essay on Man* from memory and with weary cynicism; this places her for the audience from the show's outset as a tough girl living a seedy life who is nonetheless serious about academia.

Both within the show's reality and for the audience, Veronica is positioned as a disruptor of discourses which elide the role of structural advantage in producing school success. However, *Veronica Mars* can also be seen as aligned with pedagogic discourses which position perceived masculine behaviours as transgressive and risky for girls. Because the show is positioned as noir/detective as well as high school drama, it has more generic latitude than most teen TV in terms of its discursive possibilities; it can offer a smart heroine who is neither alpha nor geek, and who can construct an identity as a PI that would code her as 'bad' or excessively masculinised in purely high school genres. As Sibielski (2010) observes, Veronica's toughness is implicitly linked to gender transgression through the unconventional (for an adolescent girl on TV) appearance and behavior she embodies, while that gender transgression becomes linked to female empowerment through the agency that her rejection of hegemonic femininity confers upon her (325).

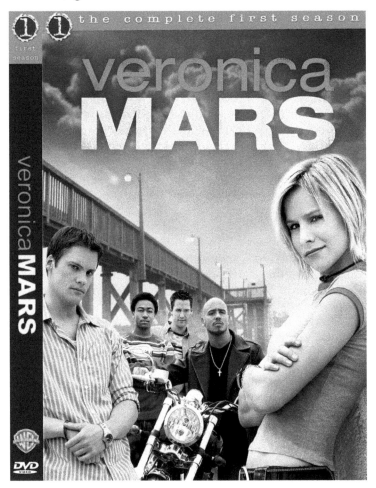

Figure 4.7 Veronica Mars: Season 1 poster.

Of course, the noir genre has its own restrictions and limitations, and the lone private eye figure is one originally constructed on a premise of nostalgic/hegemonic masculinity; this creates problems when recasting the role as female. *Veronica Mars* can be seen to employ typical strategies (as defined by Mizejewski 1993) for the 'chick dick' in resolving them; these include domesticisation (her relationship with her father is core), the imposition of a romantic subplot ('her boyfriend might be her brother' and 'her boyfriend might be a murderer' are two long-running subplots) and heterosexual partnership. However, in the first season at least, the show appears to work against the glamorisation/fetishisation of the female detective also identified as a noir trope[2].

As noted with regard to the TV alpha girls, the adoption of historically masculine positions by girls or women requires a compensatory investment in hetero- and hyperfemininities (McRobbie 2009); this can be seen to operate in terms of genre where women characters are allowed to occupy traditionally male narrative roles in return for not invoking feminism to challenge the patriarchal order; their performance of enhanced femininity is their reassuring pledge.

The relationship between genre and gender/class constructs is, as Gonick points out, one of convention (2003, 115); the tropes and structures of genres mobilise discourses and create subject positions which reflect and therefore can reveal common cultural assumptions. While the genres discussed by participants are produced within broadly the same cultural settings (Western teen TV), within them there are variations which may be accounted for in terms of genre history, target audience and cultural status. It is beyond the scope of this study to offer a full account of the various generic conventions, but it is worth observing that the purely high school drama genre appears to be more restrictive in its classed and gendered representations than the sci-fi, noir and medical genres discussed by participants.

Veronica Mars as a hybrid high school–noir text also allows for a starker take on the optimism of 'girls can be anything they want' discourses in its generic obligation to turn over the stone and examine the dank underside. Thus, we see Veronica's ambitions and those of her poorer classmates are repeatedly unfulfilled or, worse, thwarted by the more privileged in unfair competition. A key feature is the way that school is shown to perpetuate disadvantage; at Neptune High, privileges are accrued in ways which exclude poorer students. The role of schools in creating elites through extra-curricular activities that confer institutionalised power on popular students is identified by Thompson (1995, 50, in Gonick 2005, 47) and further explored by Gonick (2003, 2005). While *Veronica Mars* is by no means the first teen TV show to depict school socials, committees and sports teams as formalised mechanisms for bullying and elitism, it makes a connection, rare in more popular discourses of schooling, between extra-curricular opportunity, academic advantage and class. At Veronica's school, it is not only social privileges that are accrued through out-of-school activities; pupils at Neptune can increase their grades by participating in expensive courses like sailing, which carry honours-level academic credit, but which for many students are financially impossible. This advantages the richer students in competitive scholarships to fund college education. Rich students are shown as beating poor students (including Veronica herself) for whom scholarships represent survival, not just status, through unfair practices and inherited advantage.

Extra-Curricular Advantage and the Limits of Meritocracy

The specific function of extra-curricular activities in creating middle-class subjectivities is noted by Gonick (2003), and their role in reproducing cultural advantage among youth is explored by Scardigno (2009) and Covay and Carbonaro (2010). Such activities are regarded as not only providing skills and knowledge (such as learning a musical instrument) which count as cultural capital, but also as providing contexts where the values, behaviours and discourses associated with class cultures are shared. It is interesting, therefore, that a teen show should focus on issues of extra-curricular opportunity as a means of exploring wider disadvantage; this focus provides a readily intelligible framework for its young viewers to access ideas about social justice.

As noted earlier, direct discussion of class is largely absent from participant accounts, as it is from most generic high school dramas. However, discourses of fairness are also invoked by participants specifically with regard to the extra-curricular opportunities which are available to them because of their identification as 'gifted and talented'. These lead to some comment on enhanced expectations/success trajectories. Given that explicit discussion of advantage/disadvantage was otherwise absent, this suggests that it is via access to tangible benefits seen as specifically provided by the school that students can find a starting point for understanding education's role in maintaining social structures.

Both groups of participants at Maple Grove raised these issues. In the first group, Becky observes that 'you get more choices at GCSE if you're smarter', and Dora adds, 'In school terms I've noticed you get more opportunities to compete or take part outside of the curriculum activities', and Poppy specifies going on trips. Here choice, competitive advantage and cultural enrichment are all raised as privileges they enjoy. The second group identifies similar advantages, but with more ambivalence:

AMINA: You kind of know that you're gonna be more, like, successful when you're older, and that you're gonna get the best grades.
ELAINE: We kind of get chosen, like, for example, going on trips, we'll probably be um, the ones to go on it, which is not, um, which is good, basically, yeah … . Sometimes I think it's unfair, like, to other classes, but … it's fun … to go on trips.
OTHERS: Yeah!
KARA: I think we get more choice.

The group participants are aware that they are advantaged in terms of short- and long-term rewards (grades and future opportunities) and that this brings them even further advantages in terms of preferential treatment with regard to trips, but Kara's comment is not celebratory in tone. Elaine's honesty in admitting that the trips are 'fun' is balanced by her discomfort at the idea that others cannot share the benefit. Bradford and Hey (2007, 596) describe the ways in which initiatives such as 'gifted and talented', as well as aiming to

> raise standards … have been designed to demonstrate the capacity of the state system to both maintain and reproduce middle-class

advantage *as well as* advance the promise that other young people (the 'socially excluded', for example) can achieve some educational and social mobility.

The awareness and enjoyment by girls of the advantages that their smart status brings them suggest understanding of intended benefits; however, their qualified responses and invocation of discourses of fairness suggest that their participation in discourses of meritocracy does not extend far enough to see all the benefits as their just deserts. Negotiating perceptions of fairness and social justice within school contexts that offer disconfirming evidence for the very meritocracy they appear to espouse adds yet another layer of tension and complexity for girls struggling to make sense of the achieving girl subject position. In Chapter 5, I explore further the idea of the hard-working girl as a contemporary meritocratic ideal.

Notes

1. See, for example, the DfES (2006) publication *Identifying Gifted and Talented Pupils: Getting Started*.
2. See Sibielski (2010) for discussion of the show's problematic 'backlash' third season.

5   The 'Girls Work Hard' Narrative

I began Chapter 4 with a focus on the ways in which girls claimed authority in speaking as achieving girls, and the ways in which they used this to pronounce upon aspects of the discourse itself, on its tropes and exclusions, with varying degrees of awareness. In this chapter, I explore the most pervasive and widely endorsed narrative to emerge from all sites of investigation – one that I have called 'girls work hard'. This narrative can be seen as a contemporary rendering of the historical discourses of diligence as feminised and subordinate in a gendered hierarchised binary explored in Chapter 1. Its continued circulation has been noted with concern; for example, Walkerdine (1989, 4) finds that in teachers' views of achieving children, 'girls were felt to lack something, even if they were successful', while 'boys were felt to possess the very thing that girls were taken to lack', while Jackson and Nyström (2015) note that girls are unlikely to be celebrated for effortless achievement in the ways that some boys can be. In its insistence on success being produced via the efforts of the individual, it is readily accommodated by neoliberal discourses of self-regulation and educational discourses of meritocracy, without presenting a challenge to patriarchal structures, and is taken up within 'equal but different' post-feminist discourses of gendered complementarity.

In this chapter, I explore ways in which the hard-working girl narrative reinforces concepts of ability as developmental and supports classed models of 'good' parenting, as well as mobilising popular self-improvement tropes and claims to morality via discourses of meritocracy. For some girls adopting the 'achieving' subject position, there may be tensions with some peer-approved identities, but these tensions are lessened according to class and contextual factors. There are also rewards: These include endorsed claims to authenticity and autonomy. I draw attention to some ways in which girls knowingly engage with its tropes, which include claims to hard work which they acknowledge are not representative of the actual effort they put in. I argue that the hard-working girl discourse works to produce compliance and reinforces gendered and classed school behaviours, but also carries associated risks of loss of femininity and social prestige. This suggests powerful motivations underlying the hard work necessary to sustain the subject position, the labour of both 'doing girl' and 'doing success' (Skelton, Francis, and Read 2010, 186).

The association of ability with hard work in schools also re-activates some historical connotations of moral decadence inherent in innate genius (Stadler 1999; Hemingway 2002); for example, in discussing the uptake of the term 'gifted' in UK schools, Smithers and Robinson (2012, 16) describe teachers' concerns that its implied innateness smacks of elitism because pupils so described 'need make no effort'. The girls in this study make some of those claims to morality in their discussions, claiming both authenticity and superiority in their willingness to assume the hard-working identity. However, their statements also suggest that the effort required to sustain this visible profile renders the identity of 'achieving girl' itself precarious; not appearing as 'hard working' can result in demotion from top sets and exclusion from classrooms. This precariousness works both to produce compliance and to reinforce gendered and classed school behaviours. The rewards described by participants include endorsed claims to authenticity and morality, as well as anticipated future benefits.

It is interesting to note that, despite what Jackson and Nyström (2015, 2) describe as 'the love affair' of the West with ideas of innate intelligence, these have been challenged in the popular realm, and alternative practice-based models posited through both discourses of meritocracy and, more recently, the popularisation of neuroscience. For example, Coyle (2009) uses neuroscience to argue that brilliance in performance is learned through practice and fostered through context; Colvin (2008) makes the same broad argument based on observation and biography of highly successful individuals. However, the strength of popular investment in the idea of innate ability is demonstrated in responses to such contemporary reappraisals of what constitutes genius. In the *New York Times*, Brooks (2009) reviewed both Coyle and Colvin, and provocatively asserted that they demonstrate innate genius to be 'hocus pocus', and that genius is simply 'the ability to focus for long periods of time' combined with the right context for support. Brooks (2009) contends that

> the key factor separating geniuses from the merely accomplished is not a divine spark … it's deliberate practice. Top performers spend more hours (many more hours) rigorously practicing their craft. (n.p.)

Brooks's column received 370 online comments on the day of publication, many oppositional and some heated. These illustrate the playing out of competing discourses of genius in the public domain through essentialist, sociological and religious argument. One respondent declares that 'to deny genius as an honest-to-god phenomenon is like denying the law of gravity', while another exhorts us to 'let everyone have a chance to maximize their latent genius by ensuring that health care, education and a level economic playing field support and enable each citizens growth' (Brooks 2009). In the field of psychology, 'expert performance theory' developed in the latter twentieth century in an attempt to explain exceptional attainment via effort and commitment, but found it difficult to shed the association with an inexplicable innateness, and harder still to assess within viably testable conditions (Ericsson and Charness 1994), although it is taken up with some enthusiasm in 'gifted' education.

Even before one takes gender into account, discourses of ability as innate, developmental or produced by individual effort are in themselves paradoxical and held in a state of tension and uncertainty in educational settings. As noted in the introduction, there is some investment in ability as an essential, inborn quality, evenly distributed even if potentially masked by social disadvantage, and realisable through the intervention of good teaching. Such a broadly essentialist conception is evidenced by Tony Blair's statement in his address to the Labour Party conference in 1996:

> We believe that people should be able to rise by their talents, not by their birth or advantages of privilege. We understand that people are not all born into equal circumstances, so one role of state education is to open up opportunities for all, regardless of their background. This means we need to provide high standards of basics for all, but also recognise the different abilities of different children, and tailor education to meet their needs and develop their potential.

Here we have an uneasy mix of essentialism and sociology as Blair seems to imply that talents are both an accident of birth and an outcome of education. Youdell (2004, 421) describes notions of ability in schools as 'generalized, encoded in genetics, constrained by home environment, and open to a restricted degree of enhancement through school intervention'. One can see a similar intermingling of science, subjectivity and sociology in the plethora of general and subject-specific checklists for identifying 'giftedness' circulating on educational websites and in policy documentation at national and very local levels, in their mixture of standards and behaviour-based criteria. While this represents an opening up of notions of ability to more qualitative models beyond that produced by testing regimes, as well as a stated focus on potential rather than raw performance, there is a failure to acknowledge that both tests and classroom-based checklists are themselves measures of learned behaviours, not innate abilities (Gillborn 2006). Smithers and Robinson's (2012) attempt to clarify and refocus using the term 'high ability' as measured in national testing does little to resolve the issues regarding the role of structural advantage in producing test success, and indeed represents a retrograde step in their recommendation of a return to more selective schooling and more selective practices within comprehensive schools based on the outcome of national tests taken at age 11. They find that currently some schools, mainly those serving low income homes, have very few high ability pupils, even on the current broad definition adopted by the DfE. We urge the government to consider the plight of these pupils and make provision for them. (iii)

This either assumes an innate ability which is not distributed evenly ('very few high ability pupils' in schools 'serving low income homes') or acknowledges that ability is produced by privilege, in which case the rest of their recommendations serve to secure that privilege.

Despite such competing accounts, the hard-working achiever continues to be seen not only as a debased form, but one which characterises female achievement rather than male. It is interesting to see girls in both the school interviews and the online forum consider ideas about their abilities as innate, produced by their families or by their own efforts.

'Girls Work Hard' as Developmental Narrative

Within the girls work hard narrative, the smart girl is made, not born. It constructs ability as developmental rather than innate, engendered through particular kinds of home support and maintained through application. The absence of a narrative of a naturally 'smart' girl was conspicuous. While this can create a tension with conservative views of ability, the hard-working achieving girl is readily accommodated within essentialist views of femininity as compliant and conscientious, and within neoliberal and post-feminist discourses of self-produced success.

When asked where their 'smartness' comes from, group interview participants offered an overwhelmingly developmental view, one in which family, teachers and their own efforts all play a part: At St Ursula's, Adele's reflection is typical:

> I think it kind of starts with like, support from your family ... and then if you're recognised at school as good at being able to do something then you get pushed by your teachers, and it just goes on from there.

The hard-working narrative starts early in Monica's account of where ability comes from: 'I think it's like when you're little, d'you know like when you get reading, um, you actually get ... you work at it'. This becomes entwined with a narrative of early encouragement:

ANNA: If it's something you enjoy when you're little, you kind of build up on it when you get older ... you think like I'm obviously good at that so I'll use it.

MONICA: I think it's like when you're younger you do something right, and you get so much praise for it, so you think, oh I did that right so I might wanna do it again ... it comes naturally.

These comments describe a model of ability which is formed through early pleasure, encouragement and effort. It is both externally recognised and exploited as such, and internalised through repetition and affirmation in such a way that it feels innate.

While also citing accident of birth, *Marzipanna* offers a largely similar view in the online forum under the thread 'Where do smarts come from?'

> I think it's a bit of everything. I think some people are born with the ability to be smart but it depends on how they are brought up and encouraged by school to how they end up. My parents weren't smart but I think there might have been something in my genes. I think I was helped a lot by how I was brought up, my grandparents often took me to interesting places, museums, stately houses. I know that sounds geeky but that's just how it was.

The idea of the supportive, involved and informed family offering varied cultural experiences suggests some awareness of the role of class, although most online and group interview participants were quick to deny any link between class and ability when asked directly (see Chapter 4). Some do attempt to articulate a difference between achievement as a result of innate ability and that earned through hard work. However, the narrative of the nurtured child given a head start through parental support, structured home learning activities and the inculcation of school-compliant habits was common, for example, in this exchange:

SALLY: I was taught to read and write before I went to school, so it all kept me motivated … . There was a certain routine when I got home … like I've never been used to going home, sitting in front of the TV in my school uniform and not doing my homework. It was always, 'Come on then! Take off your uniform and do your homework, and then do whatever you want for most of the evening' so ….

SHAMEEM: I think it's more about, like, how your family brings you up to learn, and how they help you when you're learning, like in school, and like, I have like, I'm the youngest in my family out of both sides and all the cousins, so I always had like their help when they were growing up.

SALLY: It can be difficult. But like, when I was little my mum and dad were really insistent that I did everything that it's possible for me to do. Like they put me into PE and like, and like, intellectual stuff because they didn't want me to just be a total boffin.

Sally emphasises the labour involved in bringing up the child to be educationally successful, from early reading and regulation of leisure time to ensuring the child is developed into a fully rounded subject. Her invocation of the badly parented other, who might be permitted to sit around in her uniform watching TV and ignoring homework, provides a contrast to her own and to Shameem's family, which 'brings you up to learn' and in which you get 'so much praise' that it makes achievement feel as if 'it comes naturally'.

It is this developmental view on which discourses of the 'ideal' middle-class parents as the producers of educational success are constructed and which pathologises working-class parenting practices as producing academic failure. Reay (2008a) describes how (ideal, middle-class) parents now play a central role in children's academic development and are viewed as 'co-educators'. This shifts the locus of responsibility away from the structures that produce inequalities and into the homes of working-class families (Lucey, Melody, and Walkerdine 2003, 289). Such a view can be seen as central to discourses of aspiration and intervention in New Labour Education policy, including 'gifted and talented' initiatives (Reay 2008a, 642). The advantage this gives middle-class children on entry to the classroom is such that it makes a distinction between innate ability and learned behaviours difficult, even if one were inclined to try and make one.

The above exchanges also indicate how girls position themselves with regard to such classed discourses of parenting, where the middle-class model of 'parent knows best' is privileged and normalised and the working-class approach of leaving educational decisions to the 'child as expert' is pathologised (Reay and Ball 1998). Whereas Archer, Halsall, and Hollingworth (2007) find that one of their working-class subjects takes up this discourse and sees her parents' approach as inadequate, at Maple Grove, schoolgirls who have elsewhere demonstrated investment in middle-class subjectivities now defend their parents' more hands-off approach:

DORA: There's all these parents' that work their kids really intensively and my parents don't really care if I get an F or an A, and that's helped because I don't feel pressured.
SONIA: My parents don't really care if I do homework or not, but I still do it.
LYDIA: I think that if … the more pressure, the more somebody hammers on to you about doing something, the more you just don't wanna do it.

These responses seem to indicate that alternative, non-authoritarian models of parenting persist in the midst of the increasing anxiety, surveillance and determination over children of a middle class under threat. However, the girls' stance also allows them simultaneously to approve their parents' approach while aligning themselves with neoliberal discourses of individual responsibility and self-management.

The blurring of developmental and the innate models of intelligence, and also the role of classed parenting styles in producing ability are recognisable tropes in the television shows discussed by participants. For example, Nicki (Maple Grove) raises the importance of the mother's role in *Gilmore Girls* (2000–2007). She describes the closeness in age as important in the relationship, and Jess also ascribes it to the support of the mother who 'dropped out and had a baby at sixteen' and 'didn't really go to school much', but nonetheless sends her daughter to Yale. In this exchange, Nicki and Jess readily identify the two defining features of the show: the mother–daughter relationship is central, and central to this relationship is the passing on of cultural capital. This is achieved not just through the sharing of knowledge, but also through the competitive conversational style between the characters, which is sharp and rich in cultural and subcultural references. Thus, in this show we see the middle-class mother's role as providing the basis for rational argument as well as emotional safety (Walkerdine, Melody, and Lucey 2001, 178).

The character of Rory Gilmore is defined by her achieving status and studious habits. The excerpt below is from a scene where her mother, Lorelai, is trying to persuade Rory not to take a heavy book bag to school. What on the surface appears to represent parental concern about backache in fact serves as a mutual display of cultural capital, in which reading becomes a marker of both moral worth and class as they put each other through their paces with regard to canonical authors and genres:

LORELAI: You don't need all of these.
RORY: I think I do.
LORELAI: Edna St Vincent Millay?
RORY: That's my bus book.
LORELAI: Uh huh. What's the Faulkner?
RORY: My other bus book.
LORELAI: So just take one bus book.
RORY: No, the Millay is a biography, and sometimes if I'm on the bus and I pull out a biography and I think to myself, 'Well, I don't really feel like reading about a person's life right now', then I'll switch to the novel, and then sometimes if I'm not into the novel, I'll switch back.
LORELAI: Hold on. What is the Gore Vidal?
RORY: Oh, that's my lunch book.
LORELAI: Uh huh. So lose the Vidal or the Faulkner. You don't need two novels.
RORY: Vidal's essays.
LORELAI: Uh huh. But the Eudora Welty's not essays or a biography.
RORY: Right.
LORELAI: So it's another novel, lose it!
RORY: Unh-uh. It's short stories.

(2.07 'Like Mother, Like Daughter')

The only child of a single mother who had her at 16, the relationship between Rory and her mother Lorelai is characterised by a sibling-like closeness (Gamber 2009, 119). The character of Lorelai is constructed within a discourse of 'adultescence' (Feasey 2009). This is recognisable as both a condition of late modernity in which parents hold on to the pleasures and identities of youth (Ruo and Toro 2011), and an audience-garnering tactic of teen television in its bid to sustain address to an ever-broadening definition of youth demographic (Feasey 2009). In *Gilmore Girls*, generational blur-ring and bonding is further signified, for example, by a mutual preference for junk food and a frequent sharing of pop culture references. However, in terms of class these allusions could be misleading; examination of the music references locates them in punk/new wave/alternative genres of the seventies and eighties, their taste for TV and film is retro-chic, and they are never seen anywhere near a fast food chain but consume their burgers and coffee at the funky café of a close friend. These references are part of the bid to appeal to an expanded 'youth' but also to a nonetheless privileged audience, and rather than associating them with blue-collar lifestyles, they serve to mark Lorelai and Rory as 'cool' within their highly conservative social context. In fact, the Gilmores belong to a high-status and wealthy family. Both rep-resent the kind of 'cool' achiever described by Raby and Pomerantz (2015).

Despite its pop culture appeal, the show works to reinforce conservative class values and the claims to privilege of an intellectual elite; poetry and philosophy are as readily referenced as punk rock and pizza. Rory's desire to go to Harvard and her mother's determination to help her display an anxiety to reclaim a class identity which Lorelai herself has compromised through her teenage pregnancy and lone motherhood. The resources Lorelai deploys to ensure her daughter's future are not just financial (she accepts money from her parents to pay for private schooling); the parental role here is seen as the passing on of cultural capital, and models the 'parent as expert' who can also simultaneously sustain her own heterofeminine youth-ful appeal. A *New York Times* reviewer commented when the show came to the end of its seven-year run, 'No mother in the history of television was ever cooler than Lorelai Gilmore' (Bellafante 2007, n.p.). The discursive function of such cool combined with the show's 'unabashedly elitist values' which foster Rory's success is identified as

> a rebuke to the striving parents of the overweight and merely average. This wasn't the show's intent, but it was certainly its effect, a televised delivery of inadequacy syndrom.
>
> (Bellafante 2007, n.p.)

What Bellafante describes as 'televised … inadequacy syndrome' can be expressed in academic terms as popular culture's circulation of classed par-enting models, their location of the causes of success in the home and the pathologisation of parenting styles which fail to deliver according to such a model.

Participants' awareness and reproduction of such discourses is evident. For example, Sally describes how her parents support her learning and enjoy discussion at home; she also relies on her parents rather than her teachers for academic advice (see below). **Marzipanna** (see above) gives an account of her own success as produced by family encouragement. At Maple Grove, when Farida says that her mother did not go to university, Dora is quick to interject, 'But she's done really well!' This reassurance works to emphasise the girls' own awareness of the importance of having the 'right' kind of parental support from the 'right' kind of parents.

Girls Work Hard: Recognition and Risk

Teachers play a central part in the 'girls work hard' narrative's construct of ability in both participants' and popular accounts. Through recognition of the markers of 'ability' (Nyström 2014) and a continuation of the processes begun at home, the girl identified as able is shaped into the 'hard-working girl' through a combination of teacher affirmation and expectation. However, such recognition is dependent on classed and gendered performances which render it unequally available, and with it come social risks that illustrate some core contradictions in feminised achievement discourses.

Participants show understanding of the home-school developmental continuum, and of the ways in which it differentiates them from fellow students. At Maple Grove, when I ask what made girls realise people thought they were clever, Elaine and Amina answer almost simultaneously – 'The expectations' (Elaine) and 'The set they put you in' (Amina) – while at St Ursula's, girls describe a range of ways in which teachers play a role in shaping distinct identities and expectations:

ADELE: If you're recognised at school as good at being able to do something then you get pushed by your teachers, and it just goes on from there.

JUSTINE: I think it's just in school … they kind of like expect more from you in classes. …

ADELE: Teachers expect you to push yourself more and may push you more than … they expect a lot of you, more than they do of the rest of the class.

SHAMEEM: *They expect you to achieve more than a normal person in the class would, but, then again, like, they push you. … School's always like there to push you … and it's not a school that will just like, ignore any ability you have. They always like, find something in you.*

These responses suggest how identification as a smart girl works to position girls simultaneously in terms of their learning contexts, narrative trajectories and teacher relationships. The encouraging/pushing teacher is a recurring role in girls work hard narratives and is a key figure in positioning subjects within particular academic and life discourses.

Online, **Ikkin** describes the 'extra pressure' that is put on her by being 'constantly told you're going to have to get a certain grade or result', while **Smiliestar** describes the particular pressure of being entered for her GCSEs a year early, and the pressure from teachers to do well. As Gonick (2003, 134) observes, the achieving girl identity is 'an active and conscious production' in which teachers collude. They play a role in confirming or denying a 'positive visibility' that is not equally attainable for all girls; it is structured around a circumscribed repertoire of behaviour of which classroom interactions form a key part.

Girls identify a range of ways in which their own behaviour and teacher actions work to identify them as smart. Teacher actions included nomination for prizes, inclusion in extra-curricular opportunities and letters home; their own behaviours included compliance, visible hard work and crucially, answering questions in class: At St Ursula's, Sally describes her teachers' treatment of her as consciously different, saying, 'If, like, adults know that you're [makes air quotes] "able" they, uh, talk to you differently' and relates how, at her primary school leaving disco, her teacher approached her and said, 'Five years' time. Head girl. No pressure'. Sonia describes how 'they always expect you to say something in lessons ... they always expect you to put your hand up and say what your views are', while Shameem mimics in a bass voice a teacher approaching her and saying, 'You're going to be a lawyer, aren't you?' This illustrates how teacher identification can operate to place the girls within very specific trajectories, and work to construct a view of the self through affirming particular kinds of visibility.

Classroom Discourse, Participation and Class

Some participants themselves are aware that such recognition is not equally available to all students, but frame their awareness in ways that allow them to be reconciled to the privilege of their position. On the forum, *maths_ genius2192* describes how when she talks in class, 'my words are only understood by my teacher and maybe two other students', while *jordi-horses* describes a fellow student as 'really jealous' saying, 'Whenever I answer a question, she acts very pissed off'. Francis (2009, 660) discusses how such narratives of jealousy work to mobilise the moral discourses of meritocracy, allowing the hard-working 'geek' to claim the moral high ground associated with deferred gratification while positioning the jealous classmate as feckless and undeserving. This claiming of moral ground is also evident in participants' framing of others' lack of success, as discussed later.

Middle-class, white students are more likely to participate in the same cultures and forms of discourse as their teachers. Their shared language and culture can intimidate and exclude working-class and minority students (George 2007). At St Ursula's, after I ask whether being identified as smart in school makes a difference, Sally describes how

> I can go off at a tangent and have a bit of, um, a debate on stuff, and my teacher and me, we've always like got ideas that we wanna put forward and stuff. So it does make a difference in the fact that people ask for your opinion and they value your opinion more because apparently you're smarter than everyone else.

Her description of her classroom interactions with her teacher as a debate and her use of 'we', implying a degree of equality in this relationship, are interesting. Kirsty responds by observing,

> *Yeah, yeah, in RE Sally is like, always the one who puts forwards ideas and they get, like started on stuff and everyone else contributes after Sally.*

While Sally has described her ability to interact with her teachers on levels of equality as a source of pleasure, she goes on to describe the more negative social outcomes:

> *I think it does make a difference on how other people in your group view you, even outside of school.*

Of course the degree to which this is experienced is highly dependent on context, the demographic of the classroom cohort and the degree and nature of teacher encouragement or otherwise. On the forum, *Pandora* describes how her classroom language creates problems with her teachers and her fellow students:

> In many of my lessons at school it is unacceptable for me to act 'smart'. Even the teachers seem to dislike me speaking the way I do at home, one actually pulled me back after class to tell to stop. Apparently I was 'making the other girls feel stupid'.

This demonstrates ways that teachers can distance themselves from unpopular students regarded as geeks or 'boffins' as a way of preserving their own relationship with other more popular students (Mendick and Francis 2011, 18). The need to navigate carefully between acceptable and unacceptable performances of achieving girlhood with teachers as well as peers adds another layer of constraint to an already complex subject position. This is reflected in TV representations too; for example, in *Lizzie McGuire* (2003), a film popular with participants at Sir Walter Raleigh and Maple Grove, the head teacher refers to compliant and highly achieving students as 'sneaky brown-nosers with a hidden agenda'.

Within the St Ursula's group, other girls' responses to Sally's language displays can have a similar effect to that which *Pandora* describes above:

ADELE: People, like call me clever because of the marks I get, but then if I'm having a conversation and I don't understand anything they call me stupid because I don't actually understand it. But like, Sally's really clever in everything [*smiles at Sally*] I'm not being rude. I'm sorry but like, cause even now she's having … a really good conversation.

SHAMEEM: In depth. Intellectual.

ADELE: Yeah yeah [*gestures at Sally*]. But I don't know that many big words in a sentence.

The anxieties displayed and Adele's deference to Sally suggest an insecurity of tenure in terms of Adele's own smart identity. Such insecurity is created with regard to language as the visible marker of in- and out-group class membership. Gonick (2003, 134) describes these sanctioned forms of classroom discourse as 'necessary speech displays which are at once terrifying and the source of recognition of smart self'. Girls must undertake such displays to ensure identification and secure their smart subject position, but as public performances they are sources of anxiety, especially as failure to perform correctly is so highly visible.

Moreover, even if successful in terms of securing the smart identity, the visibility of the performance means girls risk social censure. This operates in the same way in popular narratives; at Maple Grove, Nicki and Jess discuss an unabashedly intellectual character from *Gilmore Girls* (2000–2007). This character, Paris, has the narrative function of foil to Rory's more successful blending of erudition and popular femininity. Nicki and Jess describe her as 'snotty' and 'self-involved'. At Sir Walter Raleigh, Stella refers to Hermione's classroom displays as 'rubbing people's faces in it'.

Participants describe other negative aspects of teacher recognition. It bestows what can be unwelcome visibility and increased expectations. At Sir Walter Raleigh, Joanne comments:

> I dislike answering questions in class. Not all the time, sometimes I don't mind, but like if you do a lot of work in class people will sometimes make comments.

Isabel agrees, describing how visible hard work can lead to being called boffin. Online, *maths_genius2192* starts a thread with the question 'Do you ever get tired of being told you're smart?' and complains of the increased teacher attention and 'hype' that surround her early promotion from a Year 10 to Year 11 math class. *Gabriellamontez* responds:

> Yes I do to be honest but its more the pressure and sarcasm from the students that I get sick of. I get things like 'Gabriella you're smart whats the answer to this?' and 'Oh my god the boff doesn't know the answer'. I get tired of teachers asking me to do things for them because I have enough to do already, and they stop to talk to me and people take the michael and call me teacher's pet and things like that just because I get on with the teachers.

Similarly, at St Ursula's, Sally describes debating with her teachers on levels of equality as a source of pleasure. She apparently has no difficulty in participating in those classroom processes which cultivate rationality, as described by Le Doeuff (2003). It should be noted, however, that St Ursula's is a girls' school. Sally goes on to describe negative social outcomes outside the confines of the classroom, saying, 'I think it does make a difference on how other people in your group view you, even outside of school'.

The role of teacher interaction in the construction of identities that are both iterative and cumulative, and confirmed through reward and punishment, is indicated in this exchange at St Ursula's:

SALLY: Sometimes you're like ... I wanna hear someone else speak.

KIRSTY: Yeah. If you don't put your hand up they just pick you.

SHAMEEM: *Yeah, they pick you.*

KIRSTY: If no-one puts their hand up or if say a few people put their hand up they just go right, Kirsty, what did you put down? And everyone else is like, I had my hand up!

SALLY: And that's really mean on other kids because you sit there feeling like, why pick on me? It's not fair on everyone else sitting there, now hating you.

SHAMEEM: And then like, the person you are builds up to say, teacher's pet, and like, you get these labels. And it's like, you try not to.

SALLY: And you can't talk to the teacher 'cause like, 'you're her best friend'!

Thus, school and popular discourses invest the achieving identity with risks associated with recognition, and reinforce the need for caution and vigilance. Teachers themselves can be seen to participate in reinforcing discourses of acceptable and unacceptable achieving behaviours.

Classroom Participation and Endorsed Femininities

The above responses illustrate the ways in which competing discourses meet and compete in the smart girl subject position. They show difficulties girls have in coping with public affirmation which 'builds up' to create an ability-associated identity among peers. It is hard for them to reconcile the performances they must engage in to elicit teacher recognition with peer-endorsed, feminised behaviours. Kara (Maple Grove) explains:

> People from, like, lower sets, they think that you're like – neek – or they think you're really like, smart but you're a nerd and it makes you seem less of a ... cause you may think you're like, really girly and stuff but they think that makes you less girly.

The tension she describes between her sense of feminised self and the assignation of an unwelcome, de-feminised identity based on the behaviours in which she must engage to be recognised as smart recalls the naming processes described in Chapter 4. As Gonick (2003, 131) observes, making claims to space within the classroom is a risky undertaking precisely because the behaviour is deemed unfeminine.

I have discussed in Chapter 1 the historical association of rationality with masculinity. Walkerdine (1990) argues that for girls, engaging in debate, especially with teachers and in a public arena, implies the assumption of a kind of masculinised power (46). This is the power derived from the association of masculinity with rationality, identified by Battersby (1988) and Le Doeuff (2003) as underpinning the Western philosophical tradition particularly with regard to the origin and production of genius. Thus, while it can bestow a certain kind of enhanced status, the earning of teacher recognition through the rationalities of highly visible classroom discourse can mean girls have increased difficulty in negotiating feminised and social identities. Stella (Sir Walter Raleigh) describes how this must be managed through self-monitoring:

> If you know the answer to something you don't every five minutes put your hand up. Kind of ... so people don't make fun of you, saying you're a geek and things like that. You've got to kind of watch yourself and make sure you're not putting your hand up all the time.

Earlier, Sally describes her enjoyment in classroom interaction with teachers and the intellectual status it bestows. However, this is qualified by her understanding that it may have a negative impact on her peers. The source of this she identifies as not only the visibility it bestows on her and the nature of the interaction, but also her sense of fairness. She describes how

> I don't wanna be always making comments that someone else might wanna make, or like, it's always being me taking the stage because I don't feel like I'm an important part of the class. If I can understand what's going on, then someone else should have the chance to develop, like, their debating skills and stuff in front of everyone else.

Once again, the balancing of recognition and risk, of both ability and feminised identities with all their encultured assumptions, emerges as the core to the identity work involved in inhabiting the smart girl subject position. The conflict that sustaining a smart subject position can create with discourses of meritocracy and with girls' sense of fairness is also suggested. Ways in which the girls work hard narrative enables an ethical subjectivity are explored further below.

Girls Work Hard: Permitted and Precarious Identities

If smart girl status is achieved by dint of both hard work and teacher recognition, this renders it immediately less secure than identities based on innate models of ability. If the work stops or the performance is overlooked, the claims to the identity vanish. So firmly established is the narrative of girls' success produced by hard work that where behaviours deviate from the model, the ability/identity itself is thrown into doubt. This is visible in both girls' accounts and popular narratives. Sally describes such doubts regarding her entitlement to her 'gifted and talented' status not because she is not successful, but because she does not perform according to the hard-working girl script:

> It's really weird actually because I'm supposed to be 'gifted and talented' but if I like, sit back and think over the last couple of months I don't even know if I push myself that hard and apparently I did well and I feel like … I was talking to my dad about it and I didn't feel like I put like, my whole self into it because I don't really know what it's like to work really really hard.… I don't really know if I push myself hard enough. You begin to doubt yourself.

Sally's struggles to reconcile her need to perform 'working hard' to endorse her identity as smart are interesting. It offers evidence that an 'effortless achiever' identity is not available to girls (Jackson and Nyström 2015). Accounts from some participants suggest that investing in the hard-working girl identity is a way in which success can be rendered acceptable among peers, as a means of masking unacceptable desire and ambition and casting success in an appropriately feminised frame. This is in direct contrast to the 'disguised effort' predominant in boys described by Jackson (2006); here girls disguise effortlessness. At St Ursula's, Sally describes how

> sometimes, if you know you did well in something, you're quite proud of yourself, and well people start to point out the fact that you did well compared to them, you're kind of like, OK. [Justine looks away and shakes her head, indicating disapproval.] No need to make me feel bad!

This shows girls in the group policing each other's performance, indicating the necessity for masking behaviours – Justine disapproves of Sally's claim to pleasure in success. This kind of policing is also evoked by Sally's earlier comment, that she not really work very hard – both are treated as unacceptable display. This is interesting in a number of ways. It suggests that claims to the hard-working girl identity may be context-dependent performances. Hills (2005a) describes such performances as characteristic of claims to identity in specific contexts; he identifies generic structures and tropes as shaping claims to authority within both academic and fan communities. The hard-working girl identity can be seen as a generic, authorised subject position within school communities, a position from which a girl may speak as smart. Its endorsed status derives from its alignment with school-sanctioned models of feminised performance and with discourses of meritocracy. It also suggests that girls' take-up of the hard-working girl identity can be a conscious strategy for balancing academic success and femininity through avoiding those achievement models associated with masculinity, such as effortless success. This is supported online when *Jurda* describes her hard-working identity as a disguise which enables her to pursue her own interests, saying, 'Most people think i study a lot, but instead i love to read (fiction)'.

At Maple Grove, girls report that it is more acceptable to express pleasure in achieving something that has been a struggle than in something that comes more easily to them. Thus, girls themselves may be seen as active in circulating gendered discourses of achievement both as a peer approval device and as a threat reduction strategy under the terms of the new sexual contract (McRobbie 2009). If, however, such discourses become internalised, they can leave the achieving girl doubting her capacities. This may go some way toward explaining reported differences in girls' and boys' academic self-concept among students achieving the same grades, and the increasing anxieties regarding their intellectual abilities described by successful female students (Jackson 2003). As noted earlier, the discursive assignation of the hard-working model of achievement as female and the privileged, inspired model as male is, as observed earlier, a continuation of traditionally gendered discourses of ability. What also seems to persist is the way that this model continues to function in terms of 'the systematic inferiorization of women in their own minds', as Coquillat (2001, 224) describes the impact of gendered Enlightenment models of intelligence on women.

Anxiety regarding the precariousness of 'gifted' status attained through work and confirmed through academic groupings and teacher recognition was expressed by a range of group interview participants. It was particularly noticeable in Maple Grove, the inner-city comprehensive. The importance of school context in framing smart girl subjectivities and experiences has been noted by Pomerantz and Raby (2011) and Francis (2009). In this, the least privileged of the schools, participants seemed the least secure in their academic identities and groupings, and referred more often to feelings of inferiority and doubt. For example, Sonia, who has also expressed anxieties regarding her position within middle-class success narratives, describes how

> [the head teacher] scared me on the first day. That's what got me working. I was just petrified. I walked out of that assembly and I was like 'Oh my God! Oh my God!' Since then, I've worked. I started in [the middle set] and so I had to like, work up … so now I'm really struggling. Cause when I came into Year 9, they knew so much more. And I was like, what's going on? I was really confused.

Jess is tentative; her 'gifted' identity is also insecure, but she feels reassured by the school structures and the expectations created by them:

> I guess it feels like … you're clever sometimes. If you think, like you're stupid sometimes … you know, that you're not stupid because you're in the high band, so obviously they think, your teachers and everyone, think you're clever.

Kara describes how she 'was in the top set and then I moved back down and then moved back up'. For Dora too, her class grouping is the indicator of her academic identity, but one which is not stable and is undermined by competition and comparison:

> I think a lot of us feel like, a bit inferior to people in our class, but actually we're all in the top set so maybe we are all really good.

While Lydia admits, 'I don't think I'm very smart', Kara is clear that 'the set they put you in' determines whether you are clever. With circular logic, the girls see setting as providing key evidence of an ability which is produced by the hard work they put into getting there. Here we see at work what Gonick (2003, 139) describes as school hierarchies 'providing an explanation for difference which is based on the results of its own effects'. This is the same logic that Schlinger (2003) identifies as central to intelligence testing.

Girls Work Hard: Compliance and Commodity

If the smart girl is by definition hard-working, then a relationship between classroom compliance and constructions of ability is implied. Group interview participants described the way this functions within schools with a degree of cynicism and resentment. Suzanne (Sir Walter Raleigh) observes that 'if people hear that you are clever, they assume that you're like really well behaved as well'; Tina agrees, pointing out that they sometimes get labelled 'goody two-shoes'. Lydia (Maple Grove) describes similar expectations: 'They're a bit dismissive of you. They kind of just think, Oh well, you're top set, you're not fun or something', as does Lucy (Sir Walter Raleigh), who complains,

> Yeah, people think if you're this then you have to be this. If you're clever then you have to be quiet and good in lessons but it's not always true. It's a stereotype.

At St Ursula's, girls complain that they are not allowed the same leeway as other girls:

SALLY: Other girls in class, it's like, almost all right for them to not work.
OTHERS: *Yeah!*
SALLY: It's that they can have a bit of, um, a muck-about and if you muck about even a little bit …
SHAMEEM: It gets noticed straight away.
SALLY: … it's like, oh my god! She mucked about! It's supposedly like you're genetically programmed to never do anything wrong.

At Sir Walter Raleigh, Rachel's view was more cynical; while she didn't think her teachers really believed 'gifted' pupils were naturally more compliant, she felt that they 'use the excuse' to manipulate behaviour.

RACHEL: Like they say, you're in the top set, you shouldn't be talking. But just because you're intelligent or something doesn't mean …
JOANNE: You're not gonna talk.
RACHEL: I think it's a bit like … stereotyping. It doesn't mean you're gonna be really obedient.
ISABEL: Like a dog!
JOANNE: *Yes, like a dog!*

The ambivalence toward expectations of compliance in the girls work hard narrative, and a tension with more assertive and confident femininities are also found in screen contexts. Using a psychosocial approach, Walkerdine identifies 'splitting' as central to the achieving girl's experience. She argues that in the need to identify herself as good, the achieving girl projects her unacceptable desires onto a fantasy other (1990, 151). The 'bad twin' figure is a recurring trope in the teen TV shows watched by participants. This can be seen in the smart and sensible and sexy and irresponsible divide between the sisters in the sitcom *8 Simple Rules* (2002–2005) and in the cartoon alter ego of *Lizzie McGuire* (2003), while supernatural genres allow for more extreme manifestations. Both the *Vampire Diaries* (2009–2012) and *Buffy the Vampire Slayer* (1997–2003) feature vampire doppelgangers defined by their sexual appetites and their capacity for violence, and also by their power and charisma. In *Buffy*, the fact that Willow observes that her doppelganger is 'kinda gay' (3.16 'Doppelgangland') and the following season comes out as a lesbian herself supports the idea of the split self as the projection of unacceptable desires. The 'evil twin' has a function within achieving girl discourses that is in the end regulatory. As Gonick (2003) observes, the spaces for manoeuvre for smart girls are tight.

The ways in which such restricted spaces are defined and regulated in schools emerge in interviewee and forum accounts. How teachers deal with non-compliance, and the difficulty of divorcing behavioural from intellectual expectations, is discussed with enthusiasm by some participants. The difficulty is recognised and criticised by Kelly:

> I'm not an angel and that. I get sent out a bit and I talk a lot and stuff like that so people don't think I'm clever, but I am. In my maths lesson I get sent out nearly every lesson but I don't know why 'cause I'm still quite good at it.

Here a girl who seems secure in her own ability is nonetheless excluded, her achieving girl status effectively denied. She disrupts the hard-working girl narrative, which would have her sitting attentively with her hand up ready to be called on and playing what Jones and Myhill (2004, 553) call 'the classroom game' according to its gendered rules. She challenges the trope of the diligent achieving girl who does not 'make undue demands on teacher time/attention and who experience schooling as "naturally" compatible with their (feminine) gender identity' (Archer et al. 2007, 550). The desire to 'muck about' (see Sally's comment above) also suggests the compensatory performances described by Jackson (2006, 80) as undertaken by some girls to offset the negative identity effects of achievement – disruptive behaviour and enhanced femininity. In not conforming to the compliant model of the hard-working smart girl, Kelly's experiences also support Gonick's (2003, 167) observation of ways in which classed and gendered discourses underpin teachers' apprehension of smartness and are reinforced by them. Some girls observe such reinforcement operating within the structures of the school as well as within teacher–student interactions. Here the relationship between endorsed behaviours and academic identity is underscored by behavioural aspects of ability setting. Dora describes how 'a few people got moved down because they had bad behaviour but they were really smart. And it just seemed a bit unfair'.

The recognition or denial of ability – Kelly's 'so people don't think I'm clever, but I am' – based on compliance is central to critique of setting practices as reproducing structural disadvantage, since the links between compliance with school-sanctioned behaviours, class, gender and 'race' are well established (Archer et al. 2007). Kelly, as noted earlier, is also the participant who has regularly aligned herself with working-class discourses of femininity throughout the interview, for example, in claiming to be a 'chav' and expressing her ambition to be a footballer's wife.

At St Ursula's, Alison describes how compliance combined with the abject positioning of the smart girl can render her vulnerable, but also identifies her abilities as having some exchange value among her peers, one that she can trade for enhanced visibility via affirmation from more popular students. She asserts that smart girls are often

> ... taken advantage of, so, like, say if someone wants to cheat on a test or something, most of them are just useful ... sometimes they do notice it and they don't do anything about it because they might not get something back ... like they might get spoken to by somebody more popular ... something like that.

It is not just peer exploitation to which they are vulnerable; online, *Gabriellamontez* complains, 'I get tired of teachers asking me to do things for them because I have enough to do already'. While real-world and online participants also highlight the ways in which they can feel like a resource in classroom transactions, screen narratives from the US tend to feature a more systematic exploitation of the achieving girl through formalised peer tutoring. Participants identify a range of instances of the smart girl as school resource; for example, Hayley in *One Tree Hill* (2003–2012) has the semi-derogatory nickname 'Tutor Girl' and Joey in *Dawson's Creek* (1998–2003) organises revision marathons for her friends to prepare for tests. Even the glamorous Naomi of *90210* (2008–2012) takes on a tutoring role, while in *Buffy the Vampire Slayer* (1997–2003) Willow acts as a substitute computer teacher for a semester.

Such screen representations mirror the real-world 'quasi-teacher' role into which girls are directed by helpful/compliant girl discourses as a 'correct' gender position (Francis and Skelton 2005, 117). The hard-working girl discourse positions her as particularly vulnerable to such casting due to her abilities, and as particularly suited to the role itself due to their gendered nature; the talents of girls and women are constructed as best realised when devoted to the service of others – a narrative variant explored further below. In the tutoring role, not only does the smart girl's ability appear as an exploitable academic resource, but her compliance makes her an agent in the transmission of the values of the school and the wider discourses it promulgates, a means by which its authority is diffused and dispersed via the relationship between individuals after Foucault's (1979) disciplinary model.

'Girls Work Hard' and the Neoliberal Script

The girls work hard narrative aligns with the neoliberal script as both embodying the meritocratic ideal and positioning success as lying within the individual's capacity and responsibility to control. In conditions of economic uncertainty and social and technological change, the individual must demonstrate the flexibility and agency to construct her own career path and take responsibility for realising her own potential (Beck 1992; Furlong and Cartmel 1997). Women in particular are identified as the key bearers of new subjectivities as their participation in the workplace increases and the workplace itself becomes increasingly feminised (Wilkinson et al. 1997). Within these optimistic accounts girls are now expected to fulfil both their feminine and their economic potential, and are limited only by their own capacity to envision and pursue success (Harris 2004; Gill 2007b; McRobbie 2009; Gonick et al. 2010).

While the neoliberal project is restrictive in the kinds of opportunities actually made available, in its broad address it interpellates those without the cultural and other resources necessary for success in educational and economic terms as though opportunities were equally distributed. It does so through discourses of aspiration and self-management, and is thus deeply problematic in the ways it enables the less privileged to make sense of their lives. As Bradford and Hey (2007) observe, within such discourses the most significant form of capital is the very desire to improve the self. A failure to achieve implies a failure in desire or in implementation, not a failure in the structures or resources which support achievement. As Aapola, Gonick, and Harris (2005, 62) remark, 'Pressure on young people to become responsible for their own destiny is at the heart of the invention of the new girl'.

How achieving girls mobilise neoliberal discourses to make sense of their own achievement – and the failure of others – is a recurring theme in this study; it is therefore interesting to examine the ways participants' accounts show evidence of the situated production of such discourses, drawing on the vocabularies of TV dramas and school assemblies to produce narratives of their own successes, anxieties and projected futures.

Rose (1999) finds that linguistic, visual and narrative tropes associated with neoliberal self-improvement now circulate across different contexts and practices, especially with regard to the media. These tropes appear in popular texts and in everyday conversation, providing resources for defining the self as responsible, capable and ethical. In this study, girls show evidence of adopting and circulating such language tropes, and those associated with post-feminist discourses, through sound bites of self-management and identity coherence. These illustrate 'the emphasis upon self-surveillance, monitoring and discipline ... individualism, choice and empowerment' described by Gill (2007a, 150) as defining the address of post-feminist TV.

For example, Poppy (Maple Grove) asserts, 'I think you can be highly achieving and be, like, popular or socially, like, have loads of friends and ... you can be everything' encapsulating the achieving girl vision, while *scatter-brain* advises forum members: 'Don't be afraid to fulfil your potential and most importantly don't change who you are'. *Oipoodle* commends two of the *Doctor Who* companions for being 'intelligent and strong while still being feminine', and Tina (Sir Walter Raleigh) also admires Rose Tyler because 'she's had to fight to get what she wants'. Carrie (St Ursula's) admires Amy Pond, (the 11th Doctor's companion) because she 'has confidence in herself', and also the characters on the show *Glee* (2009–2012) because 'even if they like, fail and stuff, even if they're upset, they'll try again. I think that's important, to keep at what you wanna do'. Tanya, discussing *Grey's Anatomy* (2005–2012), says, 'If you're like [Christina Yang] in a way it's good because you kind of believe in yourself and believe you can do it'. At Sir Walter Raleigh, Lucy feels Hermione Granger 'shows that whatever you are like you can have a chance to shine', and Isobel describes *8 Simple Rules* (2002–2005) as showing that 'no matter what you are you can get what you want'.

At St Ursula's, Anna recognises the discourse of 'unleashed capacity for life planning' which characterises the neoliberal subject's freedom from traditional structural barriers (Baker 2010, 3) in the career plans of female TV characters she likes. Talking of the medical drama *House* (2004–2012), she relates how

> you can tell that these people are quite successful and they know what they're doing with their lives. You know, like, what their next move's gonna be. Even though there aren't that many female doctors in it, the ones that are there obviously know what they're trying to achieve.

As McRobbie (2009, 77) observes, 'Having a well-planned life emerges as a social norm of contemporary femininity'. These statements and claims illustrate the pervasiveness of popular linguistic tropes and the ways they provide the tools for smart girls' construction of their own identities and projected life narratives.

Such tropes abound in the hugely popular Disney made-for-TV film *High School Musical* (2006). In the interviews, every participant had seen the film, most more than once. Some girls were able to quote the dialogue verbatim and knew all the song lyrics by heart. Disney in fact made printouts of lyrics available on its website after the film's heavily advertised first broadcast, and then broadcast a further 'singalong' close-captioned version on the following night at the same time, as part of a multi-platform audience enticement strategy (Potter 2012, 124). Participants on the smartgirls.tv forum also shared links to *High School Musical* fan-created role-playing sites where they could act out their fantasy identifications with the films' characters. In this way, the marketing strategies and the audience's own convergence practices can be seen to work not just to secure viewing numbers, but also to disperse the language and subjectivities of the film widely. The film's content is framed within the aggressive unified global marketing strategy which made it an international phenomenon. Potter (2012) describes *High School Musical* as driven purely by an audience-pleasing entertainment aesthetic, as

> the kind of children's program which could only be spawned by America's television system – a commercialized model, driven by ratings, advertising revenues and profits.... It pays little heed to the Reithian view of children as a special audience entitled to high-quality educational programming. (122)

The film's chief character, Gabriella Montez, is the neoliberal, post-feminist smart girl par excellence. Of Hispanic heritage, but bearing no cultural markers beyond her name, she is the child of middle-class, supportive parents. She is characterised as a 'genius' but also performs a hyperfeminised 'niceness'. She prevails in competitive situations through this niceness, which is contrasted with the naked ambition of less successful girls. The film's overt pedagogy instructs young people that they can be anything they want. However, it constructs such possibility within a cultural landscape of bland homogenised privilege in which class does not exist and race is not relevant. In contrast with the tensions played out between the haves and have-nots of *Veronica Mars* (2004–2007), problems of self-actualisation in *High School Musical* (2006) concern a successful basketball player who really wants to be a cook, and a talented mathematician who prefers to sing. The neoliberal mandate is manifested in the closing number, the film's signature song, which includes verse after verse exhorting individuals to achieve their potential, take chances and refuse to recognise limitations, including those of 'difference'. The repeated refrain between these verses is also the song's title: 'We're all in this together'. While this may seem to cut across the individualising message of the rest of song, in fact the inclusion and unity it seems to celebrate provide a situating context for self-actualisation, in the affirmation that no one need be left behind. Aapola et al. (2005, 113) point out that this tension between autonomy and connection lies at the heart of a culture that 'incites us to remake ourselves', and that young people's friendship groups provide important contexts for their practices of self-making.

The song thus brings together many of the injunctions of neoliberal discourses: It positions the individual's possibilities as limitless, although she herself has to recognise her opportunities; it elides difference and suggests that all have the same opportunity for success; it positions aspiration as the chief determinant of success, and assumes an inner authentic self that the individual is responsible for actualising. The 'We're all in this together' chorus again suggests that old divisions are meaningless (interestingly, this phrase was also adopted by the UK's Conservative-led coalition government to promote its view of the self-managing, self-reliant society in times of austerity).

As well as popular culture and television, schools emerge in participant accounts as key sites of production of smart girl subjectivities. In a visible process of governmentality, discourses (re)produced in their schools appear and are circulated in girls' accounts. Participants at both St Ursula's and Maple Grove refer to their schools as hard working; they describe them as places where they are consistently enjoined to take responsibility for transforming themselves into successful subjects in competitive markets. The following exchange with Amina shows how the language of economic policy, competitiveness and individualism has permeated schools, down to communication between teachers and students and in students' self-narratives:

AMINA: You always, like, hear about how there's so many people competing for the same jobs, like all the time in assembly. And it just pushes you to try harder cause you know that there's gonna be more people out there in the workforce that want the same job.

MP: Is it motivating or does it worry you?

AMINA: It's kind of both. Because it makes you feel like, OK, what if I try so hard and do my best but I don't actually get where I want to be? And then it's just … yeah [*holds hands up in gesture of defeat*].

Bradford and Hey (2007, 597) argue that educational initiatives such as 'gifted and talented' work to reconcile ideologies of competitiveness with discourses of individual success, through aligning national economic and social goals with personal goals and fulfilment. They describe how, through a range of policy and organisational initiatives, schools are 'enjoined to encourage their students to think of themselves as ambitious and aspirational subjects, in charge of their own futures'. Amina's responses demonstrate the success with which this project has been accomplished in her framing of her experiences in the language of national education and economic policy.

Perpetuation of the ethical and meritocratic narrative is also evident in participants ascribing their success to hard work. In response to my question as to whether somebody could make themselves smart if they put enough work into it, the response is unqualified affirmation at St Ursula's. Adele says, 'I think some people in our year, they could be really smart if they pushed themselves', and Geri elaborates, 'If you have the right enthusiasm at St Ursula's, if you want to do it then I think, yeah, you are able to'. Nicki (Maple Grove) describes how

you came to a point and you wanted to try harder. To be like, where the high people were. Like for example if you was in a lower set in Year 7 and you look up to the people and you try and work harder to get to that point.

However, when I ask her if that was what she had done, she laughs and answers, 'No! I was already in top sets'. This is interesting in its suggestion that the discourse of limitless self-improvement is taken up and recirculated by girls even when it does not reflect their own experience. It suggests how far the workings of the meritocratic promise shape girls' accounts of success and failure while they are still in school, in providing an explanatory narrative for unequal outcomes that cast them as deserving (Skeggs 2005).

Success, Failure and Doing Right

In its alignment with neoliberal and post-feminist discourses, the 'girls work hard' narrative is one through which participants attempt to frame their own and others' success or failure. However widely circulated the linguistic tropes, they do not reflect an equally wide distribution of resources in the lives of the girls who mobilise them (Skeggs 2005). This leaves girls with experiences for which they cannot account and irresolvable binaries in their attempts to formulate a coherent narrative of self. While they demonstrate an easy familiarity with the language tropes of the achieving girl and have developed some strategies for managing tensions between academic success and doing girl (Skelton et al. 2010, 186), stresses emerge in the attempt to sustain the position.

Poppy's (St Ursula's) earlier statement, 'You can be everything', is later qualified by her admitting, 'It's really hard though, to try and be, sort of, everything'. Lucy (Sir Walter Raleigh) contemplates the expectations that a smart girl identity creates with mixed feelings, saying, 'Sort of like you would get further in life, so you'll have a career have like a perfect house, perfect life but if you're clever you have to work harder'. Anna (St Ursula's) shows awareness of how discourses of success have become individualised and internalised when she says, 'It's just kind of, I think girls put that on themselves sometimes'. Beyond the incitements to 'be anything you want' and 'be everything' message, such discourses offer little articulation of how success may be influenced by anything beyond self-belief and persistence, nor how a lack of resources may be overcome.

Other participant comments illuminate how girls struggle with the contradictions of a discourse that tells them that they are better than their peers, but also that anybody can be what they want if they work hard enough. On the forum, participants engage in discussion about the meaning of 'smart' for them. Tensions emerge with regard to the function as well as the meaning of such identities. *Jen.nzgirl* states:

> I don't believe in all the 'gifted and talented' crap where people are placed above others in certain subjects – even though I have been involved in these programs since year 6. I think that people are 'gifted' in different aspects of life, and every one on equal amounts.

She goes on to elaborate the exclusionary nature of labels and practices. *Jen.nzgirl* is clearly uncomfortable with the hierarchy at the top of which she has been placed, and insists on an alternative view of talent in which everybody has 'equal amounts' of potential.

It is thus difficult to accommodate individual narratives of failure, especially where girls have invested in the hard-working model but do not attain their goals. At Maple Grove, while the group has been discussing how hard they work, and how this leads to set promotion and increased expectations, Farida comments:

> I was thinking of, like, to be a lawyer, but it's really hard work. And my grades ain't up to what they have to be to do law and I don't think I have the ability to do it.

Neither the broader neoliberal script of self-improvement nor its particular manifestation in the 'girls work hard' narrative allow Farida to form an account in which she might understand being unable to achieve her ambitions as related to factors beyond her own 'ability'. As Gonick (2006, 17) points out, 'Neoliberal discourse, stressing success as a feature of individual effort, leaves these girls few other explanations for their lack of success except for their own individual failings'.

Furthermore, while enabling some participants to position their own success as deserved, aligning themselves with the neoliberal vision of success leaves them with few resources to account for the failure of others than those which imply individualisation and blame. For example, Nicki (Maple Grove) describes how 'there are some people who are like, really smart, but don't put enough effort, so like, they could be amazing but ...'. Like the discourses of jealousy noted by Francis (2009, 660), this reinforces the meritocratic narrative and allows the positioning of the less successful classmate to be justified as one of individual choice.

Within these restrictive frames, however, some girls do attempt to articulate diverse rationales for failure. Online, *jen.nzgirl* offers an explanation for some people's failure to realise talents which she claims are equally distributed, and demonstrates awareness of how 'gifted and talented' initiatives may create inequities. She describes how

> it's just that a lot of people's talents are denied by others or themselves, for reasons like fear of isolation from the mainstream, thinking that its not important and irrelevant in society, missed opportunities, or even being ashamed of what they're good at. When people are identified as gifted it leaves other people feeling that they are not, and those people may convince themselves that they are average or bad at something they actually have a talent for.

Her statement shows understanding that her identity as 'gifted' can only be produced against the identification of others as 'not gifted'; her explanations for their 'not giftedness' do not extend to structural inequality, but are framed in the individualised, therapeutic language described by Rose (1999).

Some girls attempt to give an account of failure framed within the individual's inability to withstand very local cultures of peer pressure, for example, in Adele's (St Ursula's) view:

> Cause of the people they're ... they hang around with, they don't want to push themselves because they're scared of what they might say to them.

Her comment is interesting in that it not only aligns with discourses of self-improvement, but also attempts to offer a view in which context plays a part. Such an awareness is also demonstrated by Holly, who struggles to account for her less achieving peers' lack of engagement thus:

> I'm not saying anything against them but there are some people who don't work as hard as each other ... they don't work as hard, like with that group of people.

At Maple Grove, Poppy has similar difficulties in trying to describe underachievers in both individual and social terms, saying, 'There are some girls I guess that don't ... that probably want to seem more cool than care about their, like, education'. Sally gets closer to a structural explanation of failure when she describes

> certain people who are really clever but they're of a certain social group where they're supposed to be the 'muck about' people, but they're clever.

Her description of a 'certain social group' who are 'supposed to' resist compliance again suggests an awareness of the relationship between social stratification and the take-up of certain subject positions in school, but the neoliberal account gives her no frame of reference or vocabulary within which such difference can be expressed, other than that of individual responsibility.

What is invoked instead is a vocabulary of morality and authenticity, of the duty to do one's best, and of the imperative to be oneself in the face of pressure to conform. In this enjoining of the smart girl to 'be herself' in the face of competing pressures, the girls work hard narrative aligns itself yet more closely with neoliberal post-feminism, and in doing so provides further space for accounts of difference that elide structural inequalities.

'Girls Work Hard' as Narrative of Authenticity

The splitting and duality inherent in the smart identity presents girls with a dilemma in terms of performance and perceived authenticity, because the element of the 'split' performed will be judged as authentic or inauthentic according to audience and context. This dilemma can be understood within terms of neoliberal self-reflexivity, in which the individual must be able to locate the authentic self and be true to it in the processes of decision making and self-actualisation (Giddens 1991).

Feminised and achieving identities are positioned as conflicting by a range of scholars, with the visible performances of achievement coded as competitive and masculinised (Renold and Allan 2006; Allan 2010), engagement in classroom debate as a masculinised form of rationality (Walkerdine 1990), and engagement in hyperfeminised identities as a characteristic of working-class girls' resistance to school cultures or as a compensatory strategy for achieving middle-class girls (Francis, Skelton, and Read 2010; Renold and Allan 2006).

Differently valued subject positions emerge along various axes of power, and the legitimation of those positions is dependent on their valuation within wider discursive matrices – the 'conditions in which one might recognise a self, and have that self recognised by others' (Gonick 2003, 11). For girls identifying with middle-class subjectivities in this study, investing in achieving and compliant identities can be (although is not consistently) less problematic. Where there is conflict, the smart rather than the girl is privileged as authentic, whereas for girls aligning with working-class discourses, their smart identity can be seen as the inauthentic 'graft' among class peers.

The 'girls work hard' script can be seen to offer a more unified sense of self for middle-class girls in the group interviews. Poppy in particular demonstrates an enthusiasm for can-do discourses and claims resilience with regard to the opinions of others:

> I think if you're outgoing and you just ... it's OK to be proud of doing well academically. If you don't care what people think, people see you as being, I dunno, I guess it's easier if you don't care what people think.

This 'not caring' is easier for those for whose smart identities are endorsed by both class and school discourses of femininity and meritocracy. However, the achieving–feminine identity split can be an issue for middle-class participants less confident in their social identity. For example, Anna (St Ursula's) describes how

> ... it's kind of like, I don't want to act smart in case a certain group of girls don't like this and will go back to the boys and tell them this ... it's kind of like, you alter yourself to fit in and then you're classed as fake. You can't really win either way.

Anna's account positions her 'authentic' self ambiguously – she is worried about being classed as 'fake' if she disguises her abilities, but her ability identity itself may be a matter of 'acting' smart, a performance she is unwilling to engage in when it is not endorsed. Authenticity in the end has to derive from 'the dialogic nature of identity' (Budgeon 2011, 150). The dependence on external affirmation and the conflict with perceived inner coherence is highlighted by Anna, as is the concern not to be seen as fake. Gonick draws our attention to the ways in which 'inside functions as a site of coherence in contexts that constantly challenge girls sense of unity' (2003, 158). This sense of inner coherence is central to the concept of authenticity as moral; as Budgeon (2011) argues,

> Authenticity as an ideal implies that each individual has an original way of being human, which requires that each of us discover what this inner weight of ourselves consist of. The moral weight of the ideal of authenticity resides in the right of every person to discover and express this inner feeling of what is right for them. (150)

The conflict that achieving identities can create with feminised, classed identities is illustrated by Kelly (Sir Walter Raleigh), who says she is called 'Malteser' (a sweet made of honeycomb covered in chocolate) by some of her friends. She explains this as meaning 'blonde on the inside', describing her friends' perception of her as somebody who bears external markers of being smart (she is in top sets and on the 'gifted and talented' register) which conflict with her authentic self (here the implication of 'blonde' can be read as 'dumb' and hyperfeminised). It is Kelly who earlier described herself as being sent out of lessons for non-compliant behaviour, who labels herself a chav and states her ambition to be a footballer's wife. Kelly, however, is also one of the few participants to describe herself as 'clever' and to contest the relational link between being smart and being good. For her, inhabiting a smart girl subject position involves a very visible form of splitting along the axes of both class and gender. Her claims to authenticity necessitate a frequent reiteration of her classed femininity among her 'gifted and talented' peers, while her claims to intellectual status need reaffirming to her teachers; her claims to class, gendered and ability identities are all repeatedly iterated within the context of this group. It is important to take the group context into account. Just as online forums have been found to elicit an expanded sense of audience and to lead to experimentation with ideal identities, as well as to affirmation seeking with regard to authenticity (boyd 2007; Manago et al. 2008), so the groups interviewed in schools provide specific audiences – in both the researcher and the groups convened – for the performance of identities.

Authenticity becomes more complex when, as noted earlier, the economics of smart identity production draw largely on institutional markers. This may mean for some girls that such an identity is dependent on the school context and is less intelligible beyond it. It may also mean that the smart identity is newly produced, and its affirmation dependent on contextual factors: the 'anchored' and 'transient' identities posited by Merchant (2006, 239). For Sally (St Ursula's), her achieving identity appears anchored both historically and in the context of her peers. She explains,

> But if like being quite clever has been your identity for a long time … like I used to be friends with, um like best friends, with two very popular people, one being very smart and one being average. But because it had been like our identity to be like, quite clever normally, it didn't matter that we pushed ourselves cause that's kind of expected of us … cause we were clever like, we pushed ourselves, but we were still like, relatively cool.… It's well, gifted and talented … if you've always been kind of able, you don't think Oh, I've kind of changed and now I've got a label. It's like, why did you give me a name for something I already do?

At Sir Walter Raleigh, Rachel maintains, 'It doesn't really mean that much. I don't really get called by it. It doesn't really affect the way I do anything'. At St Ursula's, for Geri too the process of formal identification is incorporated into her existing identity. She describes how 'I think I kind of knew, but when I got the letter it just kind of confirmed it'.

However, Kirsty describes the same process of getting the letter as a surprise, and one that needed her unexpectedly high SAT results to confirm it. Shameem's take-up of what seems a new subject position for her too is more cautious. She describes how

> you are put into classes based on your ability for some of the lessons but like, there are so many other people who are like, of the same ability as you. It's kind of like, not that well known that you are gifted and talented because there are other people in the same group and then like you can relate to them … you can be your own person as well as being gifted and talented.

Here the 'gifted and talented' label appears as a graft, and one which she fears may carry implications of change. Her emphasis on still being able to 'relate to' her classmates and on being her 'own person' suggests both a fear of the colonisation by ability suggested by Moreau, Mendick, and Epstein (2010), and the restrictions of the subject position in schools.

jen.nzgirl describes a context similar to Sally's in which she casts her ability identity as one which she feels morally obliged to fulfil, but that is also made easier by its established nature and her peer context:

> I don't really try to dumb down because I get disappointed in myself when I haven''t reached my potential. I think it's also because one of my best friends from all through primary and intermediate was pretty much equal to me in intelligence.

This again suggests that the smart subject position is constructed around a dual claim to morality based on both its invocation of the duty of the individual to achieve self-actualisation and its meritocratic appeal.

As we have seen, the girls work hard narrative positions the smart girl in a way that aligns her achievement with discourses of feminised compliance and also with those of neoliberal self-improvement. Such a positioning allows the reading of other's behaviours as inauthentic if they do not accord with this. For example, Tanya (St Ursula's) observes that

> just from the way like, some of the people in our class act ... some of them ... only care what people think of them. They think they're cool because they don't bring in homework and stuff.

Carrie (Maple Grove) describes the difference between in-class behaviours and personal interaction with some of her peers thus:

> I'm not saying anything against them but there are some people who don't work as hard as each other and its weird because when you're like, talking to them on their own and they're like really nice, and you can tell they're like smart and stuff. But when they're in a group of people I find that they're like, not as nice and they don't work as hard, like with that group of people.

The linking of being 'nice' with working hard, and of being cool and not working with being both 'not as nice' and acting again associates authenticity with middle-class identities in casting non-compliant behaviours as inauthentic. As discussed above, cool or non-compliant behaviours are likely to be associated with working-class and some minority students.

Poppy (Maple Grove) offers a similar view, saying, 'There are some girls I guess that don't ... that probably want to seem more cool than care about their, like, education', again investing the girls work hard script with an authority that is both authentic and moral, where 'seeming cool' is placed in opposition to 'caring'. This illustrates the insinuation of class into 'the intimate making of self and culture' through discourses of cultural value premised on morality, as described by Skeggs (2005, 969). Read, Francis, and Skelton (2011) describe 'girls own ambivalence and tension about succeeding in presenting to others a single, culturally legible authentic self' in their exploration of high-achieving pupils' constructions of authenticity with regard to popularity. While many of their participants focus on issues of cool and 'wannabe' social identities, in this study comments tend to focus on the performance of hard-working identities, describing those who could be smart as overinfluenced by peer cultures and failing to inhabit their 'true' identity. However, they too highlight the difficulties they themselves encounter in trying to occupy conflicting subject positions without being seen as, or feeling, fake. Tanya (St Ursula's), who like Kelly has previously aligned herself with working-class positions, recognises the dilemma and pressures created by different contexts differently valuing subject positions:

> I think it is sort of difficult to do, because of the people around you. You're worried about what they're gonna think of you and what they're gonna say ... so you find it difficult.

As Daisy (Sir Walter Raleigh) observes, 'I think all people act so that everyone likes them'.

While Shameem (St Ursula's) recognises her hard-working girl identity as performance, saying, 'Sometimes you just think, okay, I need to take a break from that role I play in class', Anna adds a further layer of complexity by recognising that others' responses to the performance of smart identity may themselves be performances – that is, that peers may respect the autonomous stance of the achiever but nonetheless mock it due to peer context:

> If you are able to stand up ... do what you need to do, not what someone else needs you to do, I think people kind of look up to you for that but because they're with a certain group of people they'll take the mick out of you for it.

This not only complicates issues of cultural legibility/authenticity, but also reinforces the class basis of morality attaching to the achieving identity.

Authenticity and Disclosure Online

Issues of authenticity and splitting in the achieving girl subject position emerge as important on the forum. *Teri-beri* starts a poll asking if participants feel the need to change who they are to fit in, while *Ikkin* focuses on the duality that such identification has created for her as she attempts to internalise oppositional discourses:

> Being smart is part of me because I want to achieve my best grades but I think I have split personality because when I'm in class I do all the work and get high levels but when I'm out of class I'm completely different.

Maths_genius2192 and *Gabriellamontez* also describe themselves as having 'two vocabularies' for friends and for teachers, while also claiming that their smart identities are an authentic part of their sense of self.

While there are claims to resilience and authenticity framed in terms of moral rectitude – for example, *scatter-brain* advises 'if you live your life to please someone else to seem cool then how are you ever gonna realise who you are?' – unlike the group interview members, online participants readily admit to engaging in a range of fake behaviours. For example, under the thread 'What do you do to fit in?' *Martha* describes her anxieties around retaining friends, 'I dumb myself down a lot, partly so as to fit in', and *Charlotte* describes keeping quiet in class for similar reasons. One of the key differences emerging between the web forum and the group interview participants is the degree to which they describe themselves as adapting their behaviour, including not working, in order to fit in with peers. This balance is interesting to observe in the light of work which suggests that girls both present an ideal, 'shinier' self and seek affirmation for their 'authentic self' in online spaces (Stern 2008, 106). This can be seen in *Gabriellamontez*, who in one thread claims resilience to peer pressure and states, 'People know I'm smart and frankly I don't care that they tease me … . I'm proud to be smart', but in another confesses to engaging in non-compliant behaviours as a means of securing peer approval, claiming:

> Sometimes I mouth at the teachers (although not so much I get in trouble) and have lessons where I don't do anything and just laugh with my mates.

In spite of acknowledgement of peer pressure within the interview groups, accounts of camouflaging and compensatory behaviours are far more common in the virtual discussions. This may be a feature of context; on the forum, girls do not know each other and everyone operates under a pseudonym. The forum is an elective space that is not regulated in the same way as the group interviews; it is asynchronous and participants can and do comment as and when they please. The fact that it is also an anonymised space away from school, where participants take up smart girl subject positions voluntarily, may encourage a culture of greater disclosure without fear of judgement – as we have seen, the morality attaching to both working hard and not being 'fake' is a powerful inducement to claiming resilience to peer pressure. Moreover, in classrooms and with teachers the performance of the right kind of visibility is, as discussed earlier, important in creating and sustaining a smart profile; the group interviews take place within schools, among school-identified ability peers and with an adult moderator who may present academic authority to the girls, all of which will shape their responses.

While the public nature of a web forum might be thought to militate against disclosure, boyd argues that on social sites the concept of 'public' is similar to that of 'audience' in that 'both refer to a group bounded by a shared text, whether that is a worldview or a performance' (2007, 125). Stern supports this, finding that online youth often communicate with a clear sense of who their likely audience will be (2008, 104), and that the Internet allows girls to share common anxieties with like-minded peers in a managed way (2002, 228). Of course with the smartgirls.tv forum, there is awareness that they are taking part in a research project, but the sense of this may not be as immediate and vivid as in the group interviews, for reasons associated with user autonomy and control, as described above. This, combined with anonymity, may indeed incite disclosure, or the performance of something resembling confession as a technology of self. Well before the communication practices associated with the Internet, Foucault observed that 'the obligation to confess is now relayed through so many different points ... that we no longer perceive it as the effect of a power that constrains us' (1978, 60).

This is not to suggest that online participant accounts are in some way more true than those produced in group interviews; indeed, as Stern observes, 'the strategy and intentionality behind self-presentation is illuminated in virtual settings, because communicators must consciously *re*-present themselves online' (2008, 106). Rather, it demonstrates that the different contexts call forth different kinds of discourse and performance for different audiences and purposes.

Authenticity and Essentialised Femininities

Discourses of authenticity with regard to feminised and achieving identities also circulate in popular representations, and are recognised and endorsed by participants. *Crazygirlx* admires *Doctor Who* (2005–2012) companions Rose Tyler and Martha Jones because 'they aren't influenced by those around them'. At Sir Walter Raleigh, Tina also endorses Rose because 'she doesn't change for anyone. She's not a fake', and Joanne agrees, saying, 'She's always, like, herself'. Anna (St Ursula's) identifies the film *Mean Girls* (2004) as exemplifying issues of peer pressure and autonomy, saying that in the film, 'you definitely alter yourself to try and fit in with certain people and everyone aspires to a certain image'. At Sir Walter Raleigh, when the film is raised as illustrating the dangers of inauthenticity, Isobel describes it as a story which shows that

> there is no point in being fake because then people get to know someone who isn't you. And then when you actually start being yourself you can't be. You have to keep up your act.

In *Mean Girls*, discourses of desire and shame associated with the make-over narrative trope are complicated by their intersection with discourses of authenticity. The central character, Cady Heron, is introduced into the American high school world having previously been educated at home by her parents. Her parents are anthropologists and Cady has grown up in Africa. This back story is significant in the film, as it is mobilised to present girls' aggressive and sexualised behaviour as naturalised and unregulated via fantasy sequences of animals around a water hole. However, when Cady is befriended by the popular coterie she comments via voiceover address to the audience, 'Having lunch with the Plastics was like leaving the actual world and entering girl world, and girl world had a lot of rules', thus constructing the girl world as artificial in opposition to the 'actual world'. As the film progresses, we see her sense of authentic selfhood being eroded as she increasingly assumes the habits and values of the group she originally judges as an outsider. Her attempts to justify her behaviour to her friends show the confusion between seeming and being: 'I know it may look like I was *being* like a bitch, but that's only because I was *acting* like a bitch'.

Cady is identified as smart from the outset with a particular liking for mathematics, and this identification is created as problematic in girl terms. She is enjoined to become part of the competitive 'mathletes' team, which her friends tell her would be 'social suicide'. The subject (math), the competitive nature of the activity and the costume worn by the mathletes (chinos and letter jackets) position the smart identity in opposition to the hyper-femininity of the Plastics. At one point, Cady attempts to shed her achieving identity to gain the interest of a boy. Her reward for such inauthenticity is academic failure. She recognises this when she tells him:

> I pretended to be bad at math so that you'd help me. But the thing is, I'm not really bad at math. I'm actually really good at math. You're kind of bad at math. Anyways, now I'm failing.

The geek–Plastic tension is resolved for the audience when Cady arrives at the school dance straight from a mathlete tournament which she has just helped win, and while still wearing her asexual mathlete uniform she is crowned 'Spring Fling Queen'. This crowning endorses her academic self as authentic, proper girlhood and subordinates her feminised Plasti' self as performed and inauthentic. The shame/desire discourses which usually operate to regulate the geek girl's behaviour in feminised ways are here turned against feminised behaviours themselves as in need of regulation.

Mean Girls thus supports discourses which locate authenticity in the academic self, which is put at risk through peer pressure. This casting of the authentic in opposition to the gendered self lies at the heart of the 'vulnerable girl' narratives identified by Gonick (2006). In *Reviving Ophelia*, for example, Pipher (1994) describes healthy 'authentic selves' of pre-adolescent girlhood as characterised by an inner unity, compared with adolescents who must learn to become 'female impersonators'. This same oppositional alignment, with the class overtones of what it means to be good, can be seen in the popular parenting guide *The Curse of the Good Girl: Raising Authentic Girls with Courage and Confidence* (Simmons 2010).

In *Mean Girls*, the authentic academic self is presented via the medium of mathematical ability, which is constructed as pure and discursively uncontaminated in terms of gender and other forms of difference. Cady perceives mathematics as a value-free, culture-free space in which the rules (unlike those of girlhood) are unvarying and easy to navigate.[1] She is 'so happy to get to math class', she explains via voiceover, because 'I'm good at math. I understand math. Nothing in math class could mess me up'. She justifies her liking to other students thus: 'Because it's the same in every country'.

However, this narrative of authenticity is complicated by the fact that the bullying and hyperfeminised behaviours which constitute nega-tive peer pressure are also constructed as essentialised and authentic girl behaviours. Kelly and Pomerantz (2009) describe *Mean Girls* as one of a range of popular films that constitutes girls as an object of knowledge in a way that

> naturalizes negative behaviors as a normal part of girlhood and works to limit access to feminist and other oppositional discourses that name girls' experiences and link their feelings to the ongoing quest for gen-der justice. (3)

Such behaviours must be overcome through individualised therapeutic edu-cative intervention rather than a critical address of the patriarchal cultures that produce them (Ringrose 2006). In the film, all the girls in the school are called to the gym for a kind of mass group therapy where they identify their failings and commit themselves to change.

Such a mobilisation of therapeutic discourse is also evident in participant accounts of inauthenticity. For example, *jadoremisique* asserts that 'people change who they are to fit in because they have a low self-esteem'. The rise of self-esteem as an issue in education is one of the ways in which is it possible to see such discourses harnessed to solve social problems through self-governance (Cruikshank 1996; Rose 1999).

While *Mean Girls* resolves the splitting inherent in the smart girl subjec-tivity through privileging an academic self as authentic and distinct from a feminised self, *The OC* (2003–2007) endorses as authentic a hybridised, feminised smart self. This resists the masculinising forces of rationality while adopting some masculinised behaviours such as competitiveness and ambition, yet makes coherence possible through a gendered model of intelligence itself. The model of girlhood offered is hard working, yet also motivated by connectedness and circumscribed by the limits of an essen-tialised femininity. When Summer Roberts is challenged by her boyfriend about her choice of Prada as her intellectual role model in her college selection interview, she defends her choice saying,

> If you wanna rehearse answers that you think they wanna hear that's fine. But I believe in being myself.... If I say something I don't believe in I could end up with the wrong life. How awful would that be? (3.9 'The Perfect Storm')

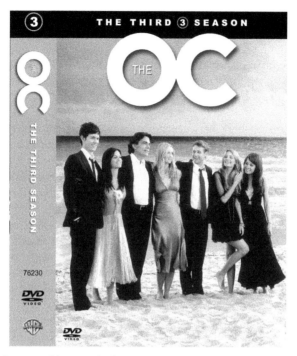

Figure 5.1 The ensemble cast of *The OC*.

The idea of authentic self as a determinant of destiny in personal narratives emerges among participants too, as in the following exchange:

KIRSTY: I don't really think I have role models. I just like … to be me. Like, I want to see what I can do. Not to try and do what somebody else has already done [St Ursula's].

DORA: I don't really have any role models. I kind of just plan to be my own self and … just kind of take life as it comes and … yeah [Maple Grove].

POPPY: I dunno. Just see what happens in life and just, yeah, I wanna like be, like, my own self. I don't wanna like, base my life looking at what someone else has done and then trying to recreate that myself.

SONIA: Like, um, a role model. … You can look at somebody and think, yeah, they're good at that, I'd like to be able to do that. But I don't think you should really, completely want to be that person. …

Here the girls reject the notion of a role model as possibly compromising their 'own self' and thus jeopardising their authentic trajectory. Online, however, *Buffy-Veronica* sees the liking of a role model as an incentive for self-improvement:

> Well, I think that all of us have to be "like" someone. When you have an idol, someone who you look up you will change in a better way.

At Maple Grove, Anna expresses a similar view on role models, describing her response to her favourite media figures thus:

> You see people and you think, yeah, I wanna be like that so I've gotta do this, to try and get to that. I think it's ambition as well. And celebrities, like, you can think, if I could be half as good as her.

There is a tension here between discourses of authenticity ('be yourself') and those of self-improvement ('change yourself'). Both, however, circulate within wider neoliberal and post-feminist discourses of the flexible, self-inventing subject. The anxieties and tensions evoke Giddens's (1991) fragmentation–unification dilemma, which he argues characterises the individual in late modernity. In this dilemma, the authentic self is at risk of being overwhelmed by the 'false selves' who are called into being by different contexts but cannot fill the vacuum left by the 'true self' (91). This is heightened in achieving girl discourses: Not only are girls already subject to gender discourses which require them to shape themselves as objects of desire and so involve them in a constant process of self-invention and subjective construction (Lucey, Melody, and Walkerdine 2003, 287; Skeggs 1997, 162), but also a further complexity is added through their requirement to adopt some qualities which have heretofore been associated with masculinised success (Reay 2001a, 163).

In this chapter, I have identified an overarching narrative in which girls' achievement is characterised as being produced by application. I argue that this narrative normalises middle-class identities, practices and values, and suggest that some girls claim to work harder than they do in order to manage the competing pressures of gendered and achieving identities, through characterising their success as produced in acceptably feminised ways. For other girls, I argue, the hard-working identity creates particular pressures in terms of precariousness and associated behavioural expectations. I have shown that the girls work hard narrative is closely aligned with discourses of individuation and aspiration, but provides few explanations for failure and occludes the role of advantage in producing success. I find that the alignment of achievement with discourses of authenticity privileges classed models of femininity. In Chapter 6, I explore statements and narratives which produce the smart girl as something less than successful; these I identity under a broader narrative of 'girls hang back'.

Note

1. See Walkerdine (1988) and Mendick (2005) for a critique of mathematics as affect/value-free.

6 'Girls Hang Back'
Choice, Complementarity and Collaboration

So far I have explored some popular variants of achieving girl discourses, and considered how these mobilise both historical discourses of gendered achievement and some contemporary neoliberal and post-feminist tropes of optimism and self-management. I have shown how girls are aware of some of the limitations of the subject positions offered, and also how those positions themselves are unequally available even to girls formally identified as achieving in their schools. In this chapter, I look at the statements and narratives coalescing around success and gender which at first appear to exist in tension with discourses of the achieving, autonomous self-actualising individual and which express ambivalence toward taking up fully the 'can-do girl' subject position. However, this does not imply simple rejection; I have labelled the overarching narrative 'girls hang back' because girls within these accounts do not take up stances of assertive refusal of achieving subject positions; rather, they demonstrate difficulties in engaging with some of the contradictions of the discourse itself, in reconciling individualism and ambition with feminised ethics of care and cooperation. 'Girls hang back' narratives also reveal strategies by which girls attempt to navigate some of the complexities and pressures created by contemporary social and educational contexts, in which they are faced with apparently limitless possibilities but also dilemmas of choice and heightened competition. The narratives also reveal ways in which 'cultural feminisation' works to disadvantage girls.

I identify variants which express a 'hanging back' from success and recognition in ways that shape the smart girl subject position itself. These variants represent girls' abilities and self-actualisation as best achieved via connection and self-abnegation. They reflect some entrenched historical discourses of femininity which continue to contain and direct girls' ambition, and to normalise a complementary and subordinated model of gendered intelligence. I find that discourses of collaboration and solidarity, now as in the past, are rare but where present sit low on the hierarchy of achievement. 'Girls hang back' narratives offer their own range of shifting, partial and temporary subject positionings that girls describe occupying as a means of managing the pressure to succeed, their social relations and the pressures of individuation. Like the 'girls work hard' narratives, these are located within wider discourses of power, inclusion and exclusion.

Girls Hang Back: The Difficulty of Choosing

The project that is reflexive selfhood is constructed on the individual as a skilled chooser. Giddens (1991) argues that while the range of possibilities for the individual has been opened up by diminished importance of traditional structures, institutions and barriers, at the same time, choosing itself has become a far more difficult business, as traditional sources of authority have also disappeared. Within this context, the individual experiences increasing uncertainty and a greater sense of risk in facing an apparently open future with reduced guidance, while her own identity and sense of selfhood depend on the success of the project. Furlong and Cartmel (1997, 4) identify a 'growing disjuncture between objective and subjective dimensions of life' in that while individuals are increasingly cast as responsible for their own life paths and success, traditional barriers to such success, such as class, 'race' and gender, persist. Thus, the possibilities open to the individual are no less constrained, even while the subject increasingly sees herself as responsible for her life story. This works to create 'a constant source of frustration and stress' (7).

McRobbie (2009) identifies the ways in which girls and young women are called upon increasingly to 'invent their own structures ... both internally and individualistically, so that self-monitoring practices ... replace reliance on set ways and structured pathways'. She states, 'Individuals must now choose the kind of life they want to live. Girls must have a life plan'; recognising the coercive nature of the choice discourse, she points out that it is 'within lifestyle culture, a modality of constraint. The individual is compelled to be the kind of subject capable of making the right choices'.

Such coercion creates a particular pressure on teenagers who are at the stage of making important, life planning choices. Giddens (1991, 113) identifies particular stress points, which include significant educational decisions, where the individual's sense of identity and security is threatened by uncertainty in the face of life-altering decisions. Gonick (2003) suggests that achieving girls in particular carry the weight of school, family and wider cultural expectations. The process of choosing is rendered manageable, Giddens (1991, 127) argues, by the familiarity and normality of local practices with regard to choices. The influence of such local practices can be seen in the choices described by girls, and in the degree to which they reproduce school, family and wider cultural discourses as sources of authority in choosing.

In all three sites, an identifiable affective trope is feeling constrained to choose, and an accompanying fear of making the wrong choice. The confidence with which choices are made and the resources deployed in doing so can be seen as closely allied to class and associated forms of cultural capital; the normalisation of middle-class aims and values in discourses of aspiration emerge particularly through those who turn away from the cultural dis-identifications implied in such choices.

Choice and the School Production of Subjectivities

If choices and success narratives for young women are made available primarily through their educational experiences and qualifications, this makes schools themselves prime sites of choice and therefore anxiety, but also sites of authority. Kelly (2009, 11) calls them 'institutionalized risk environments' which produce a kind of 'regulated freedom' for students where learning to make the right choices is a part of the process that shapes them into productive, self-reliant citizens. It is therefore unsurprising that difficulty in engaging in the processes of choice emerges as a regular feature in both participant accounts and the popular texts that engage them.

Anxiety surrounding the institutionalised choices that form part of the structure of schooling is evident in participant accounts. These focus on feeling unprepared for choice, feeling doubt as to their ability to choose correctly, and negotiating discourses of aspiration which may conflict with class identities. Hanging back emerges as a reluctance to engage in processes of choosing, or as a refusal of aspirational subjectivities. Participants describe their experience of pressure to make the right subject choices and career choices, both of which they see as central to their life plans, but for which they feel unprepared.

Lucy (Sir Walter Raleigh) and Nicki (Maple Grove) both express anxiety connected with making choices now for futures they cannot yet imagine:

LUCY: I haven't a clue really. And I'm quite worried because I've got like, two years and then I've gotta start, like thinking about it.

NICKI: We just chose our options, like for next year. And some of that involved our A levels. But I don't even know what I wanna do when I grow up so it's hard to choose.

At St Ursula's, girls have recently chosen their GCSE subjects. They describe the array of options as bewildering, and themselves as unsure about the choices they were making. Being positioned as highly able increases their options, but this also serves to exacerbate the problem. Sally's (St Ursula's) perception of the dilemma extends beyond school:

I kind of find it annoying that we have too many choices, because if I was only good at one or two things it would really restrict what I could do when I'm older. When people ask me, Oh, what do you want to be when you're older? I don't really want to be anything. I like a lot of the things that I'm good at, so it's a lot of pressure to find something you really wanna do, um, there's a lot of pressure to narrow everything down.

Adele describes how

> there are, like, so many chances to do different things, but kinda that you had to choose yourself, and it was really hard, because you wanted to do a lotta things … cause you're good at them.

Shameem agrees, saying:

> Yeah, it's like choose one thing when you can choose like so many, because you're like, you can do anything really and they tell you to choose, and you're just like, I don't really want to yet.

The very 'you can do anything' discourse in which the smart girl subject position is framed works to prevent her from taking it up fully, because of the overwhelming nature of the challenge it poses. Online participants describe similar dilemmas; *AlwaysTakeBackup* posts:

> I'm not even sure what I'll end up doing. Does anyone else have trouble choosing their A-levels or Degrees? It's a little daughnting for me, deciding what you will need as qualifications for your career later.

Jurda uses the forum as a resource and asks participants for their A-level recommendations; *hyperpinkdramaqueen* simply says, 'i have no clue', while *jadoremusique* states:

> i just want to get through school. My future will come later so why stress about it now. Advice to all those people stressing about their future and future jobs let your life flow you'll figure it out in the end.

Maths_genius2192's response to the pressure is defiant, as she claims, 'I don't know what I want to do with my life, and I don't care right now'.

Kelly (2009) argues that youth in particular are regulated in institutional ways to produce themselves as ideal subjects capable of making rational choices. We have seen earlier how neoliberal discourses and vocabularies associated with national policy are recirculated in schools and taken up by girls; discourses of choice are also built into the language and structures of school, particularly into educational transitions. At these perceived critical junctures, participants variously express, according to their own class positioning, either a dependence on or a lack of confidence in the structures and people that should support them in making the 'right' kinds of choices.

Girls at St Ursula's describe ways in which teacher advice works to produce them as aspirational subjects in the following exchange:

KIRSTY: Before the parents' evening I'd made up my own mind what I wanted to do and then all the teachers told me what I should do and by the end of it I'd changed all my options.

SHAMEEM: Yeah I was gonna choose ICT and then my uh, the head of Key Stage 4 came up to me and was like, you can't chose ICT, *it's not academic enough for you. And I was just like* ... Oh [*makes disappointed face*].

JUSTINE: Yeah I was doing ICT and then a teacher came up to me and they were like, oh, for you, it's not, like, academic enough and I'm expecting you to get into university.

GERI: I had a little bit of an idea but, um, when it came to parents' evening I kind of thought I was gonna do one subject and then the teacher came along and said no, you shouldn't, you should do a different subject because you're better than that and everything. You should be able to do more and that subject will really help you with whatever you want to do in the future, so I picked that one instead.

This process acts in a regulatory way not only in ensuring they are on the right kind of trajectory according to their ability identity, but also in shaping that identity itself; 'not academic enough' and 'you're better' work to reposition the girl not only in terms of her expectations, but also in her identity. Here again, some girls depend on their schools to provide them with the right choices and to support them in their identity work; this is indicative of the fact that some of them will be the first in their families to consider higher education. For these girls, aspirational discourses work as an intervention, redirecting their goals and rewriting their life narratives, in effect redefining their subjectivities.

The participation of some girls in discourses of success and aspiration depends in part on their teachers and schools recognising and creating their ability identity – and as we have seen, this can depend on girls' willingness and capacity to undertake certain kinds of visible classroom performance, and also on teachers' capacity to recognise as 'smart' those who do not display the right cultural cues. On the forum, *Dark Angel* complains that she was the only pupil from a council estate doing A levels at her school, and that she was overlooked and underestimated by teachers:

> i was just there to work but i dont think the teachers ever saw me as smart because i didn't dress or talk like the others or do the things they did. i think they were surprised that i did well – my predicted grades were always lower than what i came out with.

Not all participants are willing to engage in processes of self-reinvention. Lucey, Melody and Walkerdine (2003) describe how upward social mobility is taken for granted as an unquestioned good in education policy, but that it fails to take into account the implied identity transformations and the potential losses and compromises for the individual. They point out that not only are working-class girls who do well at school and go on to higher education moving into intellectual and occupational spheres traditionally seen to be masculine, they are also moving out of their class sphere. (297)

Combined with a kind of paralysis engendered by being confronted with a whole new terrain of choice but little in the way of a map, this may provide an explanation for some of the girls' reluctance to take up the achieving subject position in their planning for life beyond school. At Maple Grove, two participants, who have only partially aligned with middle-class discourses during the interview, describe careers and subject advice as presenting them with unwanted choices. Unlike the St Ursula's girls, they do not change their options:

KARA: I like, want to work with animals and I saw the Connexions person, the guidance counsellor. And he um, he was trying to, like, give me options that were like better for my grades. That were more ... that would be like better jobs than what I actually wanted, just cause I could get them ... cause I'm a high achiever But, like, I don't really wanna do that [*smiles apologetically*].

NICKI: [*Nods in agreement*] Yeah. I went to the connexions guy and I told him I wanted to do something with Art. And he gave me all these options. And it kind of put me off.

Here the increased range of choices available to girls identified as smart, and the discourse of self-betterment, is discomforting for them. Both Kara and Nicki appear embarrassed and apologetic about their unwillingness to take up the aspiring subject position. The alignment of notions of self-betterment with discourses of morality has been explored earlier, and provides a context for the girls' rejection of choice appearing as a source of shame. Their responses suggest that while they reject the discourse of self-improvement in terms of their plans, they have nonetheless internalised its value judgements. They illustrate the limitations of Giddens's (1991) model of the autonomous chooser, and illustrate the ways in which choosing is a processes embedded within wider power structures. Budgeon (2005, 75) describes how 'regimes of subjectification work to give meaning to what we think we should be – we then become that kind of subject'. The tension here is one inherent in discourses of (always upward) social mobility in that they act on subjects already interpellated by other, more familiar discourses by representing the kind of subject they are as the one they ought not to be.

A middle-class participant conversely rejects school advice regarding subject and other choices because her home provides resources in terms of life planning, knowledge of options and preparing her to make the right choices. Sally, assured of her intellectual status in the school and aware of her appeal to teachers, is suspicious of their advice and has more confidence in the guidance that she receives at home. She describes the parents' evening as a marketplace where teachers are all trying to 'sell' their subject area, saying:

> I don't take any teacher's opinions because they all go for their own subject, so I was like, I'll listen to you, but in the end I'll listen to my dad.

Here we again see the middle-class parent as expert as described in Chapter 5. It also shows how more privileged girls enter educational and self-improvement narratives at different starting points, yet still feel inadequately equipped to make the right choices.

Choosing as TV Trope

The university–careers choice dilemma is, unsurprisingly, a standard narrative trope in teen TV – we have already seen how positioning characters as college-bound works to address ideal commoditised audiences. Characters experience specific dilemmas of choice with regard to imagined futures in all these texts discussed by participants: *Buffy the Vampire Slayer* (1997–2003), *Dawson's Creek* (1998–2003), *Gilmore Girls* (2000–2007), *Legally Blonde* (2001), *The OC* (2003–2007), *Joan of Arcadia* (2004–2005), *Veronica Mars* (2004–2007), *Gossip Girl* (2007–2012), *90210* (2008–2013), the *Twilight* franchise (2008–2014) and *Pretty Little Liars* (2010–). These all construct dramatic narratives around the importance of choosing the right college in line with future ambitions, the pressures of getting grades and constructing the right sort of extra-curricular profile. The dilemmas experienced by the young characters are resolved in very specific ways that align with discourses of gender, class and authenticity. Where dilemmas are unresolved or unsatisfactorily resolved, the narratives act as cautionary tales in representing choosing wrongly as risking descent into the netherworld of the abject other.

An entire episode of *The OC's* third season (owned by one of the group at Sir Walter Raleigh and frequently rewatched with peers), tellingly titled 'The Game Plan' (3.8), is based around the difficulties and dilemmas young people face in their higher education choices; it constructs educational choice around class and gender. Such constructions of choice are also seen in other teen dramas, but *The OC* combines a range of the tropes within its ensemble in a single episode, and so provides a useful example. While Seth, the geeky, intellectually ambitious son of the wealthy Cohens, recognises that acceptance into a prestigious university is 'the opportunity of a lifetime', his girlfriend, Summer, bases her choice on wanting to be with him. While Seth's choice is rational and individualist, Summer's reflects gendered models of ambition in which women are constructed as having a 'primary priority of establishing and maintaining satisfying relationships' (Stiver 1982, in Wrye 2006).

This gendered choosing aligns with both historic and contemporary discourses of feminised achievement. The discourse of femininity mobilised here is essentially that of the complementary intelligence and a cooperative destiny as proposed by Enlightenment and Victorian theorists (Schiebinger 1989; Alaya 1977). As an ideal post-feminist subject, Summer can 'have it all' because she combines ambition suitably tempered by femininity and authenticity. Although she achieves highly, the threat is removed from her success. This same pattern of choosing can also be seen in *Legally Blonde* (2001) and *Joan of Arcadia* (2004–2005), in which following a boyfriend to college is a key motivator for the lead female characters.

The OC aligns choosing with class as well as gender. While privileged Seth has expectations of success and is well versed in the unwritten rules of the application process, Ryan (the working-class foster son) is unsure about his motives and whether he will belong. He is told by his foster mother, 'A lot of people go to college to find themselves, and maybe you're one of those people'. This accords with working-class narratives of motivation for entering higher education as described by Reay (2001b). A further variation on the college choice narrative in this episode in terms of anxiety, class and education is that of *The OC*'s troubled rich girl Marissa, who is nominated as a smart girl by Isobel at Sir Walter Raleigh on the grounds that she gets into a good college. Marissa earns a place at Stanford University, but feels ambivalent and increasingly pressured about it and eventually rejects it. Her distress and increasingly self-destructive behaviour are viewed by her friends and family in ways that evoke the stressed middle-class subjects of Walkerdine et al.'s (2001) study, whose parents, although anxious, never propose alternatives to educational success; within this narrative, dropping out is 'unthinkable'.

I was interested to see what would be done with the character as the season unfolded; in fact, within a few episodes she was killed off. Her death was the end of a downward spiral (involving drink, drugs and violent relationships) of which her stepping off the college track was an important part. This mobilisation of extreme forms of social exclusion echoes the ways in which class is raised as a threatening spectre of otherness in smart girl narratives, as noted above. Such images work to regulate the proper aspirations of middle-class youth and to position them as moral choices. The alternative to educational success is posed as unthinkable through constructing it as a threatening, violent world without rational boundaries. Marissa forgoes her status as recognised, rational, consuming citizen in her rejection of the inscribed life plan, and is expelled from the drama in the manner of the abject (Kristeva 1992). Hers is the fate of youth whose transgressions 'disturb the natural order of society, the system, thus the secured identities of those who can be considered to be full citizens' (Sharkey and Shields 2008, 243). As Hamann (2009, 45) observes, within neoliberalism 'an individual's failure to engage in the requisite processes' of self-management and choice 'is due to the moral failure of that individual'.

Choosing as Narrative Technology

In long-running TV dramas, reiteration as a technology of storytelling also works as a disciplinary technology in terms of normalising subjectivities in accordance with the economic expectations of the imagined audience. Foucault (1979, 182) describes processes of pupil classification in schools as those which distribute students according to the use that can be made of them later in life; in television shows, one can see this same distribution process at work in terms of not only the characters' narrative trajectories, but also the view of the alternatives that is conjured. In teen TV, the fate of the dropout is regularly and substantially dramatised and forms the focus of significant narrative arcs, both within episodes and across series arcs. The ways in which such narratives are constructed according to the conventions of television drama serve both regulative ends and commercial purposes, as I shall discuss with reference to Rose Tyler in *Doctor Who* (2005–), a character identified by participants in schools and on the forum in terms of her class and non-academic smartness.

In the much anticipated episode that relaunched *Doctor Who* in 2005, the shot that introduces Rose shows her from an angle directly above, in bed in a cramped and untidy room. We then see her go through her morning routine of saying goodbye to her mother, Jackie (who lounges in a dressing gown in their small council flat in a tower block), and then going to work to spend the day folding sweaters in a department store. The shots and sequences and performances are constructed to suggest claustrophobia and monotony. Not only is Rose's life shown to be constricting, but also it is shown to be socially undesirable; even the shop dummies appear to look down on her as if they are judging her and finding her wanting, visually evoking the makeover genre with all its classed associations (Gill 2007a; Ringrose and Walkerdine 2008).

The narrowness and pointlessness of her life is repeatedly emphasised. When she first meets the Doctor he tells her, 'You go home. Go on, go home and have your lovely beans on toast' and later, 'You lot, all you do is eat chips, watch the telly and go to bed'. Her mother expresses concern that she is getting 'airs and graces' from working in a big department store. After the store blows up she tells Rose, 'There's no point you getting up sweetheart. You've got no job to go to' and urges her to make a cash compensation claim against the shop – portrayed as a something-for-nothing lazy scrounger, Jackie is positioned as the moral opposite to and restraining force for Rose's aspiration.

Rose is positioned as unequivocally aspirational. She says she should be 'doing A levels', not serving chips. Her choice to go travelling with the Doctor is explicitly constructed as a rejection of her life with her mother and boyfriend; indeed, he challenges her to 'let go of the tiny little world you're clinging to'. A model neoliberal subject, she takes opportunity to make the best of what she has got. Just before she saves the Doctor by swinging across a fiery pit to his rescue, she says:

> Got no A levels. No job. No future. But I'll tell you what I have got. Jericho Street Junior School Under 7's gymnastic team. I got the Bronze. (1.1 'Rose')

Here within the establishing episode we can see the technologies of visual representation, plotting and dialogue work to create a value system which normalises Rose's choices and desires, and constructs the working-class world as one at best dull, constricted and lacking in hope and at worst peopled with lazy resentful scroungers.

In these ways, the technologies and poetics of TV representation work to reinforce neoliberal, classed discourses of success. They conjure and then reiterate the alternatives to producing oneself properly through making the right choices; not to do so is to risk descent into the hapless underclass in what Nayak (2006, 814) describes as the 'world filled with table-waiting jobs, public administration, bar work, call centres and humdrum service sector employment' that awaits those who 'stand out from their peers by not following "traditional" life course expectations' in post-industrial, risk-enhanced societies. Teen TV can thus be seen as part of a wider discourse that normalises middle-class anxieties and values through narrative trajectories. Like schools, these shows circulate wider discourses of the reflexive individual with a life plan, and discourses of anxiety and exclusion for those unable or unwilling to engage in such planning. Like ability identification tropes, the choice tropes work to secure shows' address to ideal imagined audiences.

Leaning In or Leaning Out? Ambition and Ambivalence

Closely aligned with narratives of choice are those of ambition. For participants, narratives of ambition proved to be among those where holding onto oppositional discourses of femininity and success proved most difficult. Their statements reveal some of the limits of neoliberal feminisms in their failure to reconcile a commitment to equalities with an acceptance of existing patriarchal structures. It is interesting that at the time of the study, Sheryl Sandberg's *Lean In: Women Work, and the Will to Lead* (2013) was published and quickly rose to prominence as a 'new' fashionable form of feminism which both drew attention to gendered workplace inequalities and put the onus for resolving them on the individual woman through modifying her own behaviour and expectations, and cast the motivation for doing so as individualised ambition (hooks 2013). Starting as a TED talk in 2011 which addressed problems women faced in gaining leadership roles at work, Sandberg enjoins women to address patriarchal cultures through making the right personal choices. McRobbie (2015) theorises that this brand of feminism works to regulate women yet more strictly through creating cultures of the 'perfect' of which competition, not solitary or equity, is the key component. This is a significant way in which feminism becomes folded into neoliberal discourses of individualism and self-responsibility. This book has spawned a movement aimed particularly at girls entitled 'Ban Bossy', which has attracted celebrity advocates such as Beyoncé.

Ambition and competition were among the most complex and ambivalent elements in the achieving girl discourse, in terms of both poplar manifestations and local reproduction by girls in the study. The recurring rift between success and feminised behaviours re-emerges: Investment in neoliberal success narratives leads them to claim they can do and be anything that they want; simultaneous investment in more traditional discourses of femininity leads them to locate this 'anything they want' within traditionally gendered caring roles, to deny a desire for power and to disavow competitiveness. At St Ursula's, the following exchange took place in response to my question 'Where do you think being smart comes from?'

ANNA: I think it's ambition as well.

TANYA: If you're smart then you're probably more likely to get a better job and things … more likely to, um, be more successful when you're older. But then, that's … it's good stuff but then, I dunno it's just like … the people who, like what Monica was saying about like, the people in your workplace will be like the same as you, kinda like, will want the same things as you. But then there's other people who are like, might be above you. Who will be like, kind of looking down on you and then … so it's like … I dunno.

ALISON: I dunno. I think that, um, smart women are looked up to in the workplace, like, people … try use them like to try and do better as well. But then like they're kind of like despised as well because … you don't want them … because they have the same ambitions in the same job. You don't want them to get the better job because that's a disadvantage against you because is kind of like dog-eat-dog, so if you don't get it you kind of miss out so you despise them sometimes.

CARRIE: It's not just fitting in. It's like sexism in the workplace, like women not being as able as men to do certain jobs.

Anna's statement acknowledges the element of desire in becoming smart – the group have already identified enjoying praise when they were young as a motivating factor – and Tanya frames this within a discourse of deferred gratification. However, Tanya is also concerned about the competition implied in ambition. She refers to an earlier statement by Monica that being smart in the workplace will be easier because she expects to be in a context where she is surrounded by people of similar abilities and ambitions. Tanya fears that the workplace may not be the supportive environment that Monica anticipates; her fear is that hierarchies and competitiveness are intensified rather than resolved in life beyond school. Alison expresses further concern that she may be exploited and looked down on. These anxieties suggest that girls' school experiences shape their visions of their futures with regard to ambition and competiveness. Any original desire is written out of the discourse as risk laden, in a 'dog-eat-dog' world lacking in solidarity, and in which these girls feel they will not cope.

Hey (2003) describes how the drivers for success for working-class women entering academia leave them particularly vulnerable in ways similar to the anxieties expressed by Tanya and Alison:

> This wanting, of course, is only equalled by a fear and anxiety of shame lest this desire and/or its fulfilment, or worse (perhaps?), its non-fulfilment, leave us vulnerable, stranded between the dream and the endgame which never ends, now of course, since we have to keep up the performance. (328)

It is the muffling of a discourse of 'wanting' in terms of ambition that I wish to explore further. In popular representations, as I have suggested earlier, success is tempered with femininity in ways that fulfil the post-feminist contract (McRobbie 2009). The double bind this creates is illustrated by Carrie's comment, in which she fears that femininity is equally problematic to ambition in the workplace. This is interesting in its indication that girls do not necessarily accept the post-feminist proposition that equality can be taken as achieved.

An illustrative example from television discussed by participants at both St Ursula's and Maple Grove is that of Dr Christina Yang, a surgeon in the hospital drama *Grey's Anatomy* (2005–2016). It is the risk of failure that accompanies ambition that Tanya (St Ursula's) identifies as problematic in the character, saying,

> If you're like her [Christina] in a way it's good because you kind of believe in yourself and believe you can do it, but then, if things are like, too ambitious then you kind of know you're not gonna get there so, it's like, there's kind of not much point in thinking about it.

This comment reveals fissures in the relentless optimism of post-feminist and neoliberal discourses. Tanya's doubts as to whether self-belief is realisable result in a turning away from ambition; in Christina, however, we have a character who instead abjures the performance of femininities.

Christina is characterised from the outset by both her ambition and her refusal to participate in feminised behaviours, to 'do girl'. In the very first episode, surgery is established as a masculinised, heterosexualised and competitive field – a male intern who shows nervousness is called a 'pansy-ass idiot' by a surgeon. Christina stakes her claim there, saying,

> Surgery is hot. It's the marines. It's macho. It's hostile. It's hardcore. Geriatrics is for freaks who live with their mothers and never have sex. (1.1 'A Hard Day's Night')

She asserts, 'I didn't like teenage girls when I was a teenage girl' (2.7 'Losing My Religion'), and her rare attempts to perform 'girl' in order to demonstrate to superiors that she has qualities necessary for promotion are played for humour. The following extract, labelled 'Christina Talks Girl' as a YouTube clip, features on *Grey's Anatomy* fan sites:

CHRISTINA: [*To a group of her fellow interns around lunch table*] I would like us to talk today. I would like us to talk cause I ... care ... and I, er, wanna know ... things, and I ... I [*checks her watch*] I have fifteen minutes to hear about your feelings. So, er, Alex! Alex, you look very thoughtful. I'm very interested to hear, I mean ... what are your thoughts? [*Alex sucks noisily at his milkshake while looking askance at her.*] Does it hurt that she's married? Is it hurt, your er, heart?
MEREDITH: What's the matter with you?
CHRISTINA: I'm trying to talk girl. But you know what? I can't talk girl and I shouldn't have to talk girl because *I* diagnosed the patient.

(4.13 'Piece of My Heart')

The stilted, elliptical and inarticulate performance here is written and enacted to demonstrate a woman who does not have the appropriate resources to offer a convincing performance of femininity. Instead, she offers an imitation which borders on parody, picking up on key linguistic tropes which circulate in 'girl talk', such as 'care', 'feelings', 'hurt', heart' and 'talk' itself. The verbal performance is further undermined by the visual: Christina's inability to maintain eye contact, the checking of the watch, the noisy slurping of milkshake and her best friend construing her desire to discuss emotions as a sign that something is 'the matter'. This not only plays to comic effect, but also serves to emphasise the subordination of perceived feminised behaviours in the 'hostile' and 'macho' world of surgery.

Within this world, however, male characters are lauded for displaying empathic and caring qualities – for example, the boorish Alex Karev is rewarded both professionally and personally when he displays a particular talent for healing newborn babies. This vision of a 'caring masculinity' is closely aligned to the ideal neoliberal subjectivity (Walkerdine 2003). There is not an equally valorised discourse of 'competitive femininity' and, as Francis and Archer (2005, 126) observe, the ideal neoliberal subject 'must also be invested in independence, competition and risk'; this disadvantages girls whose success must be defined and contained within gendered models of acceptability and subordination. The alternative – the masculinised, individualised forms of success of *Lean In* (Sandberg 2013) are presented as risky and undesirable.

Despite Christina's embracing and apparent naturalisation of behaviours suitable for a highly competitive environment, she is consistently punished for her ambition and failure to 'do girl'. This is not just in terms of hostility from many of her peers; the character is punished at the narrative level. She is frequently passed over in terms of professional opportunity; she is shown to be incapable of sustaining romantic relationships; she is jilted at the alter in Season 2; in Season 3, she is literally impaled by an icicle in a deliberate invoking of the snow queen fairy tale narrative. The icicle is removed by a soldier-surgeon against whose hypermasculinity her femininity can be redefined, and they marry. However, the marriage flounders when she terminates a pregnancy.

The character's very desire for professional recognition is shown to be dangerous, when she is taken hostage and made to perform surgery. It is this event that Amina (Maple Grove) identifies to try to explain why Christina is a problematic character for her:

> I think she's too ambitious. She, but then in the end, in the episode that then came on like last, she quit her job. She's working in a bar so, cause of like, trauma, a man came into the hospital and he was like, he had a gun to her head and he was like trying to make her operate at the same time cause his wife got killed or something.

Amina's analysis mirrors the character's own reflection, that if she had acted within the confines of appropriate femininity she would never have been in danger. In response to that danger, Christina quits surgery, takes a job in a bar and plans the perfect wedding. Her 'escape', however, is tinged with desire, regret and the privileged superiority that is a reward of ambition, as suggested in the following monologue:

CHRISTINA: [*Looking through a bridal magazine*] It's like the only thing in the world that matters is that they find the perfect shoes to match that dress. God, you know, I knew these girls, I went to school with them. It's funny. I used to feel sorry for them. They're simple girls. They just wanna find the guy and get married, you know? Live. I don't know, I think you're either born simple or you're born ... me. I wanna be the person who gets happy over finding the perfect dress. I wanna be simple, 'cause no one holds a gun to the head of a simple girl.

(7.1 'With You I'm Born Again')

This dialogue positions the ambitious woman as caught between a nostalgic yearning for a simplified traditional femininity and a desire for power and success. The smiling bride and the ambitious surgeon are emblematic of the two routes to visibility which Gonick (2003) proposes are available to girls: respect or recognition, popularity or smartness. These routes are juxtaposed in a dualism which subordinates the feminised and suggests it cannot coexist with reason or ambition. Tanya's and Amina's comments on the show, together with the workplace anxieties expressed by Anna and Alison above, suggest that girls struggle to reconcile the dualism inherent in the achieving girl position.

Ambition and Cultural Feminisation

Adkins (2002) has explored the supposed feminisation of culture with regard to hybridised gender identities in the workplace. Such feminisation she defines as sociological in terms of de-industrialisation and the decline in traditionally male fields of work, the growth of the service sector and the increased participation of women in the workplace. However, she argues that it is also cultural in the flexibility and self-reflexivity demanded of workers (61). She describes how

> while male professional workers may 'take on' the aesthetics of femininity, perform 'reversals' and gender hybrids, woman professional workers not only find it difficult to 'take on' masculinity, but performances of masculine aesthetics often have negative workplace consequences. (75)

Adkins's thesis aligns with Battersby's (1998) argument regarding the appropriation of cultural femininities in the construction of the male genius, in which women's demonstration of qualities associated with genius, such as sensibility and passion, were merely seen as evidence of female gender. Similarly, Adkins argues, the deliberate adoption of appropriate workplace femininities by professional women is not recognised as professional strategy, but rather as evidence of sex, and therefore has no workplace value (79). Both would support Halberstam's (1998, 269) assertion that gender is 'reversible only in one direction'. This one-way reversibility, Adkins (2002) finds, creates new and less visible barriers to success for women.

In both popular and participant accounts, 'workplace feminisation' as performed by and rewarded in women is largely absent; instead, sexual and domestic feminisations are evoked to balance the potential negative sanctioning of workplace success. When I ask Amina's group (Maple Grove) if they can think of any examples of women in medical dramas whom they think are better role models than Christina in terms of ambition, they respond:

NICKI: *Scrubs!*
KARA: She [Elliot] always gets picked on and she's blonde. But she does her job well [*referring to a* Scrubs *character who is an underconfident, pretty and scatty intern nicknamed 'Barbie' by her superior*].
NICKI: Yeah but she's quite beautiful and she's good at what she's doing.
AMINA: Karla in Scrubs. She's a good nurse and has to juggle between her family and like, when she has her children she gets ... she's a good nurse. And in Grey's Anatomy there's ... I forget her name. She's really short. Yeah, Dr Bailey. She's like, a dominant character and she's got a family.

In discussing the same show, participants at Sir Walter Raleigh make similar observations. Isobel describes Elliot as 'really clever' but also 'quite dippy', and Karla is 'very strong minded and also really clever'. She describes Karla as having 'achieved more I think because she has a long-term boyfriend'. In each of their examples, ambition, power and professional success are tempered and qualified by extra-professional heterofeminised codings. One can see the same balancing of ambition with feminised signifiers in participants' own ambitions in a range of fields:

ALISON: I do admire people who like, go to big lengths to help others, like doctors cause they work really long hours.
CARRIE: I wanna be a GP. I just wanna, like, help people. Out of all the health services, that's the one I want.
AMINA: Yeah, same for me. I wanna do something working with young children, but I know that, I just don't know exactly. Like, do I wanna work with child psychology, or teaching?
ANNA: It's kind of out there but ... I wanna be a tattoo artist. I've already got some of my work done on people ... because how you can interpret different things ... how tattoos can be symbolic and how you can help people and I just thought, yeah, I wanna do that, I wanna make people feel happy about themselves.
MONICA: I wanna do like, zoology or marine biology ... I always liked animals. I had this idea of like being a vet, then kinda lost focus. Operating on animals, I didn't really wanna do.

This orientation toward caring roles is also characteristic of popular discourses of girls' and women's achievement, particularly in teen shows. Bavidge (2004) argues that the contemporary American teen TV heroine draws on older discourses to construct girls as figures of social redemption and salvation. Examples in which the central girl characters perform this function, frequently sacrificing their own feelings, wishes and ambitions to do so, include *Buffy the Vampire Slayer* (1997–2003), *Charmed* (1998–2006), *Dark Angel* (2000–2002), *Joan of Arcadia* (2004–2005), *Tru Calling* (2003–2005), *Wonderfalls* (2004–2005), *Veronica Mars* (2004–2007), *Ugly Betty* (2006–2010) and *Doctor Who* (2005–). In *Joan of Arcadia*, for example, while creative talents are evenly distributed between male and female characters, the show consistently constructs male creative troubles concerned with artistic integrity and the ability to maintain conditions which promote creativity, while the female characters' concerns are social and their talents repeatedly directed to serve those around them.

Such narratives of girls' cultural mission and complementary destiny can be seen as a contemporary update of those circulated in historical discourses of gender and talent, as discussed in Chapter 1. The 'complementarity' discourse continues to function as a means of justifying binaries and hierarchies while appearing to acknowledge equality, through casting gendered differences as essentialised, and mobilising discourses of authenticity and self-fulfilment. It is a visible strand in the greater discursive network which positions women as fulfilling their nature in caring roles, and its persistence remains a focus of concern in academic and professional fields.

Girls' orientation toward 'caring' careers has been explored by a range of scholars, most notably Skeggs (1997), who looks at the role of class, gender and institutional discourses within wider economic contexts and the ways in which they work to frame imaginable futures for young women. While Skeggs examines working-class subjects in the north of England whose employment prospects are bleak, the same regulative principles can be seen in young women who are differently positioned; achieving girls opting for a career in medicine are choosing the 'helpful' and caring roles. Concern regarding the orientation toward lower-status, people-orientated careers of women doctors is evident in a report prepared for the Royal College of Physicians (Elston 2009) which finds that not only will women soon comprise the majority of general practitioner positions (GPs sit low in doctor hierarchies), but also women GPs are increasingly likely to be employed on a salaried rather than a partnership basis, removing them a stage farther from leadership and higher-status roles. The report observes that

> it seems likely that at the very top of the different leadership domains in the profession – clinical, academic, managerial and representational – the proportion of women may remain comparatively low. (Elston 2009, ix)

The difficulty of simultaneously investing in discourses of care and discourses of ambition emerges in some of the girls' accounts. At St Ursula's, Alison expresses apprehension about the possibility of combining a career in caring, for which she has expressed a preference, with being ambitious. She frames this within anxieties surrounding authenticity – this has been a focus for discussion earlier in the interview, and adds to the tensions and complexities for the achieving girl of holding together oppositional discourses and constructing a coherent sense of selfhood:

> I think it's possible but I think its like ... you have to think about it carefully and think about the ways in which you're gonna go about it without kind of changing who you are or without seeming like ... two different people. Like when you're around someone else, seeming different like, so you have to think about how you go about doing it see.

Other group interview participants express ambitions which allow them to resolve some of the tensions through opting for caring roles within a field that are nonetheless high status or creative. However, as the Royal College of Physicians (2009) report suggests, such a resolution can hold girls and women back from leadership roles, for example, in medicine.

Some accounts of problematic ambition in women mobilise therapeutic strategies to resolve them. For example, while Wrye (2006) explores popular narratives surrounding publicly successful women such as Hilary Clinton and Tina Turner, as a psychoanalyst her conclusions and recommendations are inevitably rooted in the individual's capacity to initiate change and recovery. Her study identifies the causes in patriarchal culture's 'abrogation of female capability and the denigration of ambition as unfeminine' (76), and in male fears that ambitious women have appropriated masculine qualities. In this analysis, there are clear parallels with Battersby's (1988) analysis of historical concepts of genius, in which feminine qualities are assigned to successful men, and in which women's abilities are a locus of anxiety and denial. Wrye maintains that ambition in women appears as 'deformed' because it is always subordinate to relationship management. She finds that women have internalised patriarchal anxieties; this works to self-sabotage ambition as women prioritise their social relationships. Wrye concludes that

> we need to take responsibility for our own ambition, stilling the disabling voices of the characters in our own intrapsychic dramas while maintaining consciousness of the deformative voices in the culture at large and attunement to voices of support for ambition integrated with nurturance and aggression. (79)

This enjoining of women to 'take responsibility' for the disabling impact of patriarchal structures aligns such analysis with discourses in which individuals must themselves make good the effects of inequality through fashioning themselves as the right kind of aspiring subject. Such individualised explanations are core to the therapeutic, individualised ethos characterising contemporary educational approaches to addressing unequal achievement. Although this is more usually focused on male 'underachievement' at policy level (Francis and Skelton 2005, 52), it also characterises 'vulnerable girl' discourses and interventions (Aapola, Gonick, and Harris 2005, 54) and the corporate feminism of Sandberg's (2013) *Lean In*.

In the light of the anxieties, hybridisations and compromises evident in group interview participants' and popular accounts, it is interesting to see ambition appear in different ways on the forum boards. While online participants express interest in careers in medicine, working with animals and the arts, as do the girls in the group interviews, they are not usually expressed in terms of helping people, but in terms of fulfilling interest or creativity.

When I started a thread with the question 'What are your ambitions?' *Jurda* responded, 'I want to be a brain surgeon because I like the things you have to take e.g. biology and am not a bit squeamish'. Her view of a medical career and her recognition of its morbid aspects contrasts strongly with Carrie's desire to be a GP to 'help people'. **Scatter-brain** says, 'I wanna b either A) a surgeon or B) I want to work in the EU or UN', suggesting that it is the power and status of surgery that appeals. *Charlotte*'s ambitions are to 'build my own eco home with straw bales. I would also quite like to have a breakfast radio show'. *AlwaysTakeBackup* would like to 'direct or produce hard-hitting films (like Crash) or films with strong female characters', and *jen.nzgirl*'s 'biggest dream is to become an established author but I also want to sell my art as well and become involved in the art world'.

These responses differ markedly from those in the group interviews; the ambitions are more various, more success orientated, more lofty and more openly expressed. The creative responses contrast with Anna's casting of tattoo artistry as a means of helping others. As noted above regarding authenticity, this may be a feature of the particular communicative context created by the forum, which provides a less restrictive space for expression. The same phenomenon is also apparent in girls' expression of competitiveness online, as discussed below.

Girls Hang Back: Competition and Cooperation

Competition in girls is constructed differently from that conventionally attributed to boys. Popular discourses of female competition are those of relational aggression focusing on peer hierarchies and are constructed around currencies of heterosexualised attractiveness and conspicuous consumption (Gonick 2004; Ringrose 2006). This is the competitiveness of *Mean Girls*, and it is a discourse that circulates in academic as well as popular texts: Merton (1997, 175) describes popular girls as 'brazenly heterosexually competitive' and as characterised by 'relentless public narcissism' in a study of peer group relationships; Hughes (1998) describes girls' competitiveness as fundamentally different from that found in boys, both in motivation and in the behaviours that stem from it. Competition in girls then is unhealthy, yet essentially feminine, and thus in need of restraint and intervention (Duncan 2004), as opposed to the 'healthy' motivating competitiveness of boys (Fennema et al. 1990; Flood 2001; Neall 2002).

It is, however, the masculinised form of competitiveness that is valued in school cultures, and this can limit girls in the conflicts it creates with middle-class identities of 'niceness', as well as with broader discourses of meritocracy and equality (Jiwani, Steenbergen, and Mitchell 2006). Masculinised models create particular difficulties for achieving girls, who must manage their success in highly competitive and hierarchised school environments at the same time as preserving feminised identities. In this way, the achieving girl is not advantaged as the 'ideal neoliberal subject' within feminised education contexts, but rather experiences particular tensions in attempting to reconcile subjectivities created by oppositional discourses (Francis and Archer 2005, 125).

Group interview and forum participants indicate that while participating in discourses of niceness, girls develop strategies for the management of identity and relationships in competitive school contexts, and also find alternative contexts in which the expression of competiveness is more acceptable – these include sports, hobbies and peer alliances.

Modesty as Relationship Management

In terms of management strategies, the importance of caution in expressing pleasure in achievement and not appearing to boast emerges as key. This enables girls to address the tension between both being successful and being a considerate friend, as the following exchange at Maple Grove suggests:

NICKI: It's like, you're happy with your grades but you don't wanna like, boast about it, tell people who like, got lower grades.

DORA: I think, on many occasions you can't kind of portray that as in like the physical way [punches the air]. You kind of secretly are proud of your achievements but you kind of have to take into consideration everyone else around you.

For some girls, public knowledge of their 'gifted and talented' status makes them subject to comparison among their peers, which makes them feel uncomfortable in terms of their relative success. At St Ursula's, participants describe feeling vulnerable to being treated as a sort of high water mark by which peers judge their own success, as well as feeling unable to express disappointment if their grade is lower than expected:

ADELE: [They call me] like, really smart and then they always ask me what I got in tests and it's really annoying.

SHAMEEM: And then, if they get higher they're just like, ah-hah!

GERI: They just go over the top!

SHAMEEM: They're just like, oh my gosh, how did you not get that?

SALLY: Then it's rubbed in your face.

SHAMEEM: Yeah! It just gets, like, really over the top sometimes.

GERI: When you get your exam results and, like, you're a bit disappointed with getting a level, and some of your friends are a bit like, well, if I got that I'd be really happy and you're just you're just kind of thinking, yes, but I would have thought I'd done a bit better than that, and you're just hoping you'd have done better, but you can't say it.

Girls at all three schools describe their friendship groups as not aligned with their ability groupings/status; this implies a need for careful management of their relative success. Emerging in their statements is a range of relationship management strategies, which means they have to eschew displays of pride or competitiveness in their friendship groups, even while being subjected to such displays from peers. At Maple Grove, some of the girls describe not feeling able to celebrate their own achievements:

FARIDA: If you have friends in lower sets and you talk about what you do in class and you say, Oh, I'm so happy that I can do that, they'll be like, 'Oh!', you know, 'she's talking about herself too much' or 'she thinks she's too good'.

ELAINE: It's like, you're happy with your grades but you don't wanna like, boast about it, tell people who like, got lower grades.

POPPY: I guess some people see it as being boastful or not cool to be like, smart.

Online, *Gabriellamontez* describes how

> I can vary, depends who I'm with realy, my mates know how good I am but sometimes I joke that I'm fabulous to make them laugh but some people I downgrade my abilities a lot because I'm scared of what they'll think.

whereas *jadoremusique* offers a gendered explanation in which girls

> are modest or shy about things they do and looks because their worried about what people will think whereas guys want to show off to get attention, to look and manly and to hope fully get a girlfriend.

There is also evidence of a qualified sense of success even among the highest attainers that the tying of achievement to finely differentiated marks schemes engenders, leaving those getting an A-grade feeling as if they are only comparatively successful; for example, Farida says:

> Because like, in grades, even if you get the lowest A, it's like the highest A, so people can like, criticise you for thinking you're like, great, cause it's the same grade overall.

As Francis, Skelton, and Read (2010, 321) observe:

> The current preoccupation with achievement and delineation of 'giftedness' in schools has manifested in an acute and detailed awareness among pupils of their positioning in hierarchies of achievement.

Enculturated models of development by which girls achieve maturity through developing successful social relationships as posited by Gilligan (1982) can make competitive school cultures and grading systems particularly difficult as girls strive to manage the competing demands of individuated success and successful relationships. Shameem describes an ideal in which her friends support her in her achievements, which at the same time evokes the discourses of female competition of *Mean Girls*:

> I think that if they do put pressure on you not to achieve your best then it's kind of like they're not the kind of friends you want. Because they're not like supporting you to do your best. And if they like, bring you down so they can make themselves be as good as you then [*shrugs*] it's not really worth it.

These findings would seem to suggest that competitiveness, or at least claims to competiveness, are suppressed in achieving girls despite the pressures toward individuation and competition. They indicate a conflict with feminised identities and with the empathy and connectedness which Gilligan (1982) proposes characterise the ethical maturation of girls. Such findings seem to challenge the essentialising tendencies of discourses of complementarity, indicating that girls can be competitive but repress this in favour of relationship and identity management in school contexts. It is a further example of the 'splitting' which has been identified as central to the smart girl subject position.

Competition and Achievement as Pleasure

It is interesting to observe that claims to pride in achievement and pleasure in competition emerge in other contexts. One of the most notable is in sport. At St Ursula's, when I asked if there is anything they have done that they are proud of, the following exchange ensued:

ALISON: I think it's like, some of the competitions I've been to, cause some of them have been like really big ones, bigger actually than I've ever been to before. *So it* kinda felt like, I could, I did believe in myself, that I could do it.

TANYA: [*Proudly*] Um, like in year 6 or something I got chosen to represent [names borough] in a competition thing at Crystal Palace.

Rina: I do karate and I went to a karate competition and I did quite well in that. I kind of felt proud because I did one of the best in the group.

TANYA: That was the 2nd one.

RINA: You weren't in it!

MP: You compete against each other?

TANYA: Yeah – we've gone for two competitions and the first one she won and in the second one I got two medals so I beat her there.

RINA: [*Enthusiastically*] Yeah! She's a better fighter but I'm better at kicking her and things.

TANYA: I beat her at other things!

Pleasure and pride in their achievements and in the external recognition is described by both Alison and Tanya. Similarly, Rina and Tanya both appear to enjoy their openly competitive exchange, of which the focus is not only sport but a martial sport. It is interesting that Tanya, who here is described as the 'better fighter', expresses particular anxiety about competiveness in the workplace elsewhere in the interview.

The same question provokes similar responses at Maple Grove, where Dora replies,

> Um, my personal favourite is sport. I've always enjoyed it from a young age. In primary school I've always kind of competed in competitions and I think, it just, kind of, grew my passion for it.

Dora says she likes the competitive element; in the same discussion, May expresses discomfort with academic grades being made public in the same way as sports results, saying that 'the grades go up for everyone to see like football. But I thought that football is just, like, a hobby'.

Here it is not the visible success that is the problem, but rather the field in which success is achieved. Such differences between the discussion of sporting and academic prowess could be attributed to a range of factors already noted. For Dora and May, expressing pride in grades would create conflict with school discourses of meritocracy and fairness. The linking of grades to the placing of students on particular success trajectories has already been noted above; expressing pride in school achievement or grades seems to be equated to celebrating one's better life prospects among less advantaged peers. May's comment suggests that competiveness and pride are, however, permissible and enjoyable in lower-stakes activities that can be considered hobbies. The sports the girls enjoy are competitive in nature, but winning has little significance for them beyond the sport itself. At St Ursula's, for example, girls describe being good at sport as bringing no enhanced status, compared with being in a school R&B group. This contrasts with the experiences of boys, for whom sporting prowess can be a means of offsetting the potential social risks of high achievement (Jackson 2006; Francis et al. 2010). Rina and Tanya's exchange also centres on extra-curricular sport and further indicates that competition can be openly expressed if it is felt to be fair – they are clearly taking part at similar levels, and can boast of beating each other without breaching peer consideration rules.

The smartgirls.tv forum seems to provide a different sort of context for claims to success, for competiveness and pride in achievement, and here this includes the academic. *Andrea* starts a thread called 'Tell the world you are smart', asking, 'Do you have a skill that you keep from others? Why do you keep it to yourself? Or do you tell everyone you know?' In response, participants describe pride in a range of achievements, including hobbies, school subjects they do well at and reading they enjoy. *Jurda* states, 'i get good grades in most subjects but fantastic in science' and gets into a competitive exchange with *hyperpinkdramaqueen* about achievement levels. *Hyperpinkdramaqueen* also starts a thread on the 'Anything/everything' else board about chess. She leads with the claim that she beat her teacher in three moves and likes the fact that it 'improves your logic' and boasts about the number of tricks she knows. *Jurda* and *Gabriellamontez* describe with some relish playing and beating, or getting beaten by, family members.

Like Rina and Tanya's discussion of karate, these exchanges express pleasure in competition and pride in demonstrating expertise in traditionally masculinised fields – information and communications technology (ICT), science, and chess/logic. As with Rina and Tanya, the same disinhibiting factors seem to apply: context for expression and perceived equality in peers. These conditions suggest that girls are more likely to participate in competitive discourses if they can align these with perceived fairness and without risk of gendered stigma. They may also, as with the ambitions expressed earlier, demonstrate the ways online contexts can foster a benign kind of disinhibition because of perceived flatness of hierarchy combined with anonymity (Suler 2004).

Discourses of girls' pleasure in competition and pride in success are rare in the shows discussed by participants beyond the heterofeminised rivalry in such films as *Mean Girls* (2004) and *Legally Blonde* (2001); where they do exist, they are negatively sanctioned – for example, in Christina Yang and in the overly competitive Paris in *Gilmore Girls* (2001–2007).

Teen TV texts model the same modesty and relationship management strategies displayed by group interview participants with regard to ambition and competition. One of the more interesting examples is in a globally successful TV show (2001–2004) and film (2003) popular with both groups of participants at Sir Walter Raleigh and Maple Grove and online, *Lizzie McGuire*. This show appeared daily on the Disney Channel and was the subject of similar successful marketing strategies as another Disney production, the film *High School Musical* (see above). The show's success has been identified as originating in Disney's realisation that 'tweens' (preteenage girls) wanted to think of themselves as teenagers, and so developing a show centring on a young teenager whose identity draws on her school friendship group more than her family (Dammler, Barlovic, and Clausnitzer 2005). Designed as a figure for identification, this character models successful consumer femininities and is a vehicle by which a range of spin-off products, such as jewellery, accessories, school stationery and other such branded memorabilia, can be marketed (Tally 2005). The Sir Walter Raleigh girls in particular described watching the film frequently as the DVD is owned by one of the group, and it is to this film text specifically that I refer.

This film focuses on school and social life of the eponymous 14-year-old schoolgirl heroine. Designed to interpellate mass girl audiences, Lizzie is described as both smart and 'typical' by participants, as neither particularly 'geeky' nor fashionable, and as being 'nice' and also friendly, including to unpopular characters. Stella describes the film as showing that 'if your heart is good and you believe in yourself then it doesn't matter if you're popular or not'. Other participants describe her as a character that is easy to relate to. Online, *jadoremusique* says she feels like Lizzie 'because we're both clumsy, shy and "goodietooshoes", and loyal to our friends'. Like that of *High School Musical*, the interior world of the film is largely white and privileged. The limitations of Lizzie as an interpellative figure are explored by Skinner (2004), who finds the association of class, race and 'goodness' in the character creates tensions for her students, one of whom describes her as 'a little angel … like a white girl'. Although no such issues were raised by participants in this study, the group interview participants who claimed identification with her were all white themselves.

Lizzie McGuire is unusual within the high school drama genre in that it mixes live drama with animation. Superimposed onto the screen at key dramatic moments is a cartoon mini-Lizzie who acts as a commentator on events and gives voice to the character's innermost feelings. As her authentic inner self, this cartoon expresses the responses and desires that Lizzie as a nice girl cannot: Cartoon Lizzie accepts praise like a diva, while the flesh-and-blood character demurs; she has smart, biting comebacks toward the school's bullies where Lizzie has no defences; she makes flirty comments to attractive boys with whom Lizzie is blushing and shy; she jumps at the chance to perform in public (giving a school speech, singing on stage) where the 'real' Lizzie says, 'I'm not good in front of crowds' and 'I could never do that'. The film involves Lizzie being called on, despite her protests, to sing in a huge concert thanks to her uncanny resemblance to a missing pop star. She is thus allowed to enjoy the pleasures of performance, attention and celebrity while at the same time disavowing the desire for any of these except that which is revealed by her cartoon alter ego (Figure 6.1). This enables her to retain her 'nice girl' status. This film thus illustrates some of the complexities involved for girls in navigating the competing discourses of girlhood, success and desire while preserving both their own sense of authenticity and their claims to endorsed nice and feminised identities.

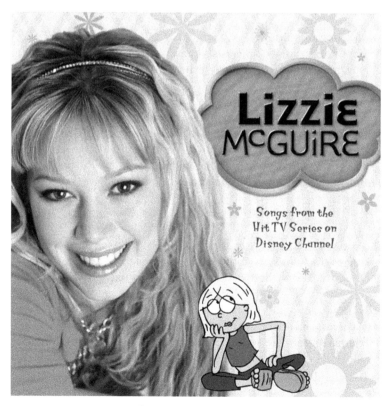

Figure 6.1 Lizzie McGuire with cartoon alter ego.

Collaboration, Feminisation and Achieving Identities

One of the key discourses identified in Chapter 1 was that of the collaborative genius. In exploring this discourse, I argued that it was an historically repressed account because it characterised the achievements of subordinated groups and ran counter to hegemonic discourses of individualised, masculinised achievement. I suggested that it was feminist and critical revisionist work in particular that had contributed to revealing the collaborative elements in exceptional production. Foster (2015, 210) points out that what is notably lacking in Sandberg's *Lean In* capitalist feminism is solidarity – if, she argues, 'emancipation is won on an individual basis for you and your hardworking family', then fighting for structural and legal changes for all women is a 'pointless distraction'. hooks (2013) too finds Sandberg's (2013) neoliberalised vision of women's ambition is devoid of context and purpose other than personal gain; her vision of corporate structure merely seeks to accommodate a few privileged women more comfortably. Yet it is working for local and community change that is most likely to provide contexts for women and other underrepresented populations to take up leadership roles (Cassell and Huffaker 2006). This is not to suggest that women and girls should only aspire to community leadership – although their absence from local politics is a factor in women's exclusion from national leadership, and the patriarchal nature of formal politics has long existed as a barrier to political activity in girls and women (Harris 2008). It does, however, point to the continued absence of available discourses other than that of individual achievements; this absence might be particularly significant for marginalised groups.

It was interesting therefore in girls' accounts to see collaborative working practices described both as something that supported their attainment and as something to be concealed. One of the strategies girls describe adopting to cope with the pressure to perform in competitive school environments involves the exploitation of social media, engaging in quasi-clandestine communication and work online, and adults' relative ignorance of its possibilities.

This was particularly the case at St Ursula's, where girls describe their homework habits.

The group had been discussing some of the issues created by digital technologies, including the potential for distraction and negotiating with parents whose lack of understanding leads to what girls feel are arbitrary and overly anxious limitations on use. While doing homework, participants describe how they will also have their phones on and next to them, their instant messaging service open, and Facebook and music streaming. While Geri, Shameem and Kirsty say it can be a distraction if the homework is 'really boring', the following exchange reveals ways in which girls use unrestricted Internet access to collaborate on work, share resources and compete.

SHAMEEM: There's always people online doing the same thing as you, so you could be doing the same homework as someone who you were talking to, and it's like, oh, let's do our homework together.

KIRSTY: Yeah, like on webcam, you like show each other what we've written ...

SALLY: [*Interrupts*] ... this is how much I've done. Don't bother trying to write more!

MP: So you use it to help each other?

ALL: Yeah.

MP: Do your teachers and your parents know you do that?

GERI: No.

SHAMEEM: I think my Mum kind of figured it out when I was holding my book up to the screen. She was like, what are you doing? I was like, me and Adele are doing our English homework.

MP: So have any of you ever been helped by someone else doing the same work at the same time?

ALL: Yeah!

SHAMEEM: Me and Adele, we do it all the time.

SALLY: You get inboxes or like wall posts: Are you doing homework? I haven't done it yet. Can you help?

SHAMEEM: Yeah, there's always someone online.

JUSTINE: I was stuck on science homework a few nights before ... you go on Facebook and you ask someone what they've put for it or something.

JUSTINE: Or if you like need a sheet and stuff you can, like, email them to each other.

SALLY: Yeah, there's always someone online.

KIRSTY: And then like, if you've forgotten something at school, and they have them, you can just like make a copy.

JUSTINE: Scan them in.

ADELE: If my parents took my laptop away I'd be kind of relieved for a certain amount of time but then if I got to a homework that I didn't understand, cause sometimes teachers just set homework that is nothing to do with what you're doing ...

SHAMEEM: Yeah, it kills.

ADELE: ... then I get really kind of worried about what the teacher will say. And the teachers say, why didn't you come ... because if you don't finish your homework, the teachers say, what didn't you come to me for help? Well you don't do homework as soon as you get it because I know I've been working hard at school and then I just don't wanna do anything at home. So I just leave it for a bit. But then I get in trouble because I didn't finish it.

This suggests that access to the Internet and autonomous access to hardware do more than promote ICT skills (Chen and Wellman 2004; Livingstone 2007; Moyo 2008). They also allow girls to mitigate the pressures created by school work, to reinforce social bonds, and it seems, to achieve better as individuals through sharing resources, approaches and examples of good work. Online, *Gabriellamontez* also uses the focus of the smartgirls.tv forum itself as a resource for a school project on media portrayals of men and women, and posts a specific request for ideas. This would support revisionist challenges to discourses of 'lone genius', which argue that historical repression of the role of communities of practice in producing high achievers has enabled the individualist myth to flourish.

Girls' use of social networking sites such as Facebook and video call/ conferencing platforms such as Skype to work together while they chat seems to contradict Drotner's (2008) observation that young people tend to avoid blending school learning activities with online leisure practices; it suggests that there is not only a blurring of on- and offline worlds in young people's lives, as suggested by Thomas (2006), but also a blurring of educational and social worlds online, as noted in the offline behaviours of achieving girls by Renold and Allan (2006).

However, it is important to note that such collective practices here take place within a highly achieving group, dominated by participants who have good ICT access and are encouraged to use it autonomously – all factors that facilitate the development of capital-enhancing ICT practices (van Deursen and van Dijk 2011). Engagement with new technologies is shaped by a complex mixture of social, psychological, economic and pragmatic factors. These ways of working may not be available to all students, and such practices may thus work to increase division between groups of students even as they work to lessen that between individuals within highly achieving groups.

Furthermore, while Drotner (2008) argues convincingly for greater attention to be paid to the development of digital competencies and collaborative processes in schools, there may be difficulties in doing so beyond access. When I ask girls at Maple Grove whether they engage in the same kinds of collaboration online as described by the St Ursula's participants, they all say that they do not. A reason given by Sonia and Poppy is that teachers seem to actively encourage it. Sonia also says her teachers 'spam' her with advice: 'I was like, stop sending me emails'. This is interesting in two ways: It suggests some ways in which the Internet is under negotiation as a teen space and also as a learning space (Stern 2004b; boyd 2007). While the St Ursula's girls use social networks and digital platforms to create their own circles of practice and collaboration as a covert means of dealing with pressure and supporting each other, Maple Grove girls see the incitement to do the same as an intrusion of the school into their social domain. As Kelly, Pomerantz, and Currie (2006) advise, it is important to recognise that part of the pleasures girls experience in online engagements lies in their removal from extensive adult monitoring and formal pedagogy, and to consider carefully therefore attempts to formalise learning in this way.

The role of the Internet in not only enabling collaborative work but also concealing such collaboration is interesting. Adopting, concealing or rejecting collaborative working models can be seen as a conscious discursive positioning by students with regard to the dominant and individualised learning patterns they perceive to be most highly valued. Allan (2010) has shown how girls whose achievement invoked feminised discourses of care and collaboration were seen as inferior by teachers to those whose performance aligned with more masculinised rational, competitive models. The collaboration model is thus seen to align with the 'diligent plodder' or girls work hard narrative. The covert nature of the St Ursula's girls' collaboration and the refusal of Maple Grove girls to follow teacher advice to do likewise, and their refusal of extra teacher help, endorse low status of collaborative learning in competitive school environments. This suggests that visible performances of collaboration may be subject to some of the same restrictions and management strategies as, for example, classroom participation. The status of collaborative working has to be understood in wider contexts which locate power, authority, authenticity and ownership 'in an autonomous, masculine self' (Lunsford and Ede 1990, 235). In either covertly adopting or rejecting collaboration, girls appear to be investing in being 'the good student' in masculinised terms (Belenky et al. 1997, 134).

The status of collaboration on screen can be seen to align with the gendered individualist–collaborative dualism, and its gendered casting. It is interesting that in all the texts featuring a teen TV heroine cited by participants, the central figure without exception operates most effectively with the support of peers. Whatever is achieved is achieved by group effort. Furthermore, going it alone is specifically negatively sanctioned and shown as leading to disaster, for example, in *Buffy the Vampire Slayer* (1997–2003), *Dead Like Me* (2003–2004), *Veronica Mars* (2004–2007) and *The Vampire Diaries* (2009–).

Collaboration in participants' statements and that circulated in more popular texts suggests an ongoing ambivalence toward the collaborative model. While it is characterised as effective, enjoyable and indeed at times necessary, it is nonetheless subordinated to individual, masculinised means of production and ways of knowing. Given that formal assessment in schools is based on what the individual can do and competition is ingrained, within cultures where test scores carry high stakes, it is perhaps understandable that collaborative models should be either devalued by girls or clandestinely practiced.

This reveals a further layer of complexity to achieving girl discourses in schools. Tensions emerge with regard to the need to manage peer impressions against the need to sustain a visibly hard-working profile. Girls' academic identities are in themselves acceptably feminised through their characterisation as diligent and compliant. However, this diligence needs careful management as a subjugated model of achievement; girls must impress the same teachers with their individuality at the same time as pleasing them with their cooperation. As Belenky et al. (1997, 137) observe, women who manage both individualistic-rational and connected-empathic ways of knowing recognise and have a high tolerance as learners for the inevitability of contradiction, conflict and ambiguity. It is through such recognition, they suggest, that women come to perceive the constructed nature of knowledge and experience.

While I would not suggest that their claims to identity management and visible learning strategies constitute evidence that the girls in this study are fully knowing constructivists, their statements with regard to a range of aspects of achieving girlhood suggest that they are aware of some aspects of its performative and constructed nature. Such awareness, however, does not necessarily engender agency; there is a lack of space for manoeuvre as identified by Gonick (2003), a restriction in endorsed femininities as discussed by McRobbie (2009) and an internalised neoliberal discourse which tells them that they alone are responsible for producing themselves as successful within its restrictions.

Conclusions

This study set out to explore the nature of achieving girl discourses within educational and popular culture settings, and to examine the ways in which girls themselves are taking them up and recirculating them in their own statements and claims to identity. It sought to discover how screen and school narratives make sense of achieving girlhood within wider cultures which that simultaneously promote heightened and consumer forms of femininity and competitive individualisation. It examined how girls draw on such narratives to make sense of themselves in contexts that celebrate the possibilities open to girls while eliding the limitations constructed along traditional axes of class and gender. A further aim was to explore the usefulness of an approach drawing on Foucault's (1969) *Archaeology of Knowledge* in addressing some current concerns within audience and girlhood studies, and in conducting research in new conditions of media convergence and teen engagement.

I found that recognisable tropes of language, performance and narrative circulate within and between schools, online and teen TV texts. As described in Chapter 4, these tropes constitute a discourse of girls' achievement which reproduces some historical binaries of traditionally feminised or masculinised success, and which normalises middle-class identities and aspirations. These tropes are reproduced within peer group dynamics in processes which claim, assign and negotiate identities, drawing on local and wider discourses of femininity and success. These processes work to reinforce existing power hierarchies (in which class and successful femininities are already strongly implicated) and to promote heterofeminine behaviours.

While I found evidence of an at times sophisticated awareness of the nature and regulative function of the 'smart girl' stereotype, such awareness does not necessarily 'empower' girls to resist its interpellation. Rather, they are simultaneously alert to the problems of labelling and to the limitations of achieving girl stereotypes even while participating in their circulation.

Class and Normativity

While I found that discourses of middle-class femininity can create tensions with school incitements to competitiveness and visible performance, for working-class girls the tensions are greater. There is a lack of narratives of the achieving working-class girl. The working-class characters that do exist in the teen shows discussed are defined through markers of abjection and exclusion, such as the council estate 'chav' or the young single mother described. Working-class girls who demonstrate the 'right' sort of potential are themselves marked as aspirational subjects, and this creates particular tensions and dilemmas for them. Aspiration implies dis-identification with home culture for working-class girls; participants show awareness of this and it results in either attempts to erase the markers of class (e.g. through elocution lessons) or a rejection of the success narratives on offer (e.g. refusing to follow career advice). The turning away from the aspirational discourse is not, however, complete; there is evidence of the internalisation of such discourses even while they are rejected, that is, in those girls who describe rejecting career advice for 'better' futures than those they had been considering, but doing so with embarrassment, as if confessing personal failings.

Althusser (1997, 130) famously describes interpellation using the metaphor of a discourse 'hailing' an individual through the scenario of a police officer calling, 'Hey, you!' and the individual responding in recognition that he or she is being called. This rather alarming image of apprehension by a powerful figure does not, I find, fully account for the ways in which interpellation works as an act of entreaty as well as of compulsion: Both school and popular narratives hail the achieving girl subject through a combination of gratification and anxiety.

While the pleasures of consuming, middle-class feminised identities are privileged, those associated with working-class identities, with the failure to pursue the right kinds of success (dropouts and slackers) or with the right kinds of femininity (transgressive or recalcitrant geeks) are, with few exceptions, cast as 'unthinkable'. This works to normalise middle-class narratives, creating anxiety in middle-class and aspirational girls, and shame in working-class girls. My findings also confirm ways in which middle-class values are deeply embedded in smart girl discourses. This is evident in the alignment of the diligent hard-working girl with middle-class 'niceness' in terms of modesty, compliance and authenticity. It is also evident in the consumer femininities of the privileged 'alpha' girls, and in the valorisation of middle-class parenting practices in accounts of developmental ability. Accompanying these alignments is an elision of the role of class in producing apparently individuated success.

While there was a range of cultural and racialised identities represented in the sample that was broadly representative of school cohorts, there was a marked absence of considerations of 'race' in the statements produced. Indeed, there was some evidence of dis-identification with racism with regard to media consumption and majority identities. Among the majority white participants, especially online, there was evidence of the elision of race as a significant category, as participants claimed serial identities across boundaries of race and nationality. These findings should, however, be regarded with caution; the nature of the activity in school and my whiteness as researcher may have inhibited girls from expressing critique. Online, no participant defined herself as non-white; while this may constitute further evidence of dis-identification, it may simply be the case that the website was unsuccessful in attracting non-white participants. As boyd (2011) has found, youth use of online sites can follow patterns of raced identification.

This study reinforced the role of privilege in terms of class in the production of the smart subject position, both in spite and because of its marginalisation as an explanatory framework for success. However, the marginalisation of race is more complete; there was an absence of discussion of the raced casting of the smart subject position even where I tried to prompt it; despite the diverse membership of some interview groups, whiteness persisted as a default identity. The neutralisation of race in popular discourses and the apparent dis-identification with racism among some participants suggest that racialised discourses of achieving girlhood are deserving of specific attention in further study.

It would have extended the scope of the study to have included girls from more privileged groups. Group interviews were all conducted in state comprehensive schools, and participants appeared largely to align with or aspire to middle- and lower middle-class identities. It would be interesting to see what perspectives girls from more elite backgrounds would have contributed, particularly with regard to discourses of ambition and meritocracy. Some work in this area is being conducted by Allan (2010) and Maxwell and Aggleton (2014).

Industry, Convergence and Critique

I have shown that in television representations of achieving girlhood the traditional, marginal 'geek' has been largely superseded by the alpha girl lead. I argue that the alpha girl, as the on-screen representation of the 'future girl' (Harris 2004), has emerged within contexts of media deregulation and as such can be viewed as a product of the broader workings of neoliberal free market policies. As well as appearing in a regulative role in terms of female desire and acceptable success, this figure has a function with regard to the political economy of audiences in ensuring an address to the most desirable consumer populations. Such an address is ensured through a reinforcement of classed narratives of educational successes combined with consumer femininities. I find that while the alpha girl has emerged most visibly within high school dramas, other hybrid genres with a stronger tradition of social critique, such as noir and sci-fi, can offer less restrictive models of achieving girlhood, and indeed a critique of the nature and limits of the geek and alpha figures themselves. That such critique should take place within conditions of challenge to generic conventions is interesting in terms of the wider episteme.

Taking a conventional figure from one genre and placing it in another would tend to reveal as constructs its taken-for-granted conventions because the context is no longer one in which they make sense. Thus, a hybrid of noir and high school can mobilise the conventions of noir to draw attention to the unquestioned context of privilege of the high school genre, and to the gendered restrictions within which its characters operate. Such a disturbing of accepted truths is an identifiable feature of the postmodern aesthetic of television (Strinati 1995), as it is of the post-structural research endeavour. Further, as the convergence and hybridisation of genre can enable critique within texts, so the convergence of media platforms and forms of engagement can enable critique among audiences, as alternative, resistant and parodic readings can be circulated as widely as the original texts themselves.

Subject Positions, Identification and Success

While the screen alpha girl models the successful blending of feminised, consumer and achieving identities, in the real world this position is harder to sustain. I argue that the technologies of ability identification – all those practices encompassed by the Foucauldian (1979) 'examination' – are dependent on girls' ability and willingness to undertake highly visible classed performances. The difficulty in managing such performances in terms of compromising feminised identities and risking both peer and teacher derision is described; I find that these can act as a barrier and a disincentive to the taking up of the smart girl subject position. The exclusion of girls who cannot successfully demonstrate the language displays necessary for teacher recognition is evident. This finding has implications for such girls since identification practices in schools serve purposes similar to those on screen, in that they work to create the smart identity itself and to establish girls on particular success trajectories.

The statements and claims to achieving identities do not carry equal authority. I find that security of girls' pronouncements and their placement on success trajectories are also dependent on family and wider cultural resources. While being identified as an achieving girl in school can open up new opportunities, it does not put all girls so identified on an equal footing; indeed, there is evidence that girls themselves are not only aware of the variety within success narratives, but also draw on such narratives in their creation of competitive peer hierarchies. These hierarchies can be seen as the product of both middle-class anxieties regarding the reproduction of privilege, and anxieties induced by school and wider policy discourses of competition.

Within the complex layering of classed and gendered positions emerges a concern for fairness which exists in tension with the smart girl identity. It is difficult for girls to access vocabularies and narratives associated with 'fairness' outside of the meritocratic discourse; there is an absence of a language of class or of exclusion except in its most abject manifestations, such as the chav and the lone teenage mother. However, the discomfort that participants describe with regard to some of the benefits they enjoy as a result of their 'smart' identification in school suggests that there are limits to girls' take-up of the meritocratic narrative.

Relationship to Historical Discourses

At the start of this work, I identified three key discourses of genius emerging from Western philosophical, artistic and scientific thought: the innate, the hard working and the collaborative. I argued that these discourses privileged masculinised models of achievement, personified in the lone male genius, and subordinated those cast as feminised – the hard working and the collaborative. I contended that perpetuation of hierarchies through 'new' sciences demonstrates cultural investment in binary models of gendered complementarity. One of the most interesting and disturbing patterns to emerge from all data sites was the persistence of these old models – in teen TV and classroom talk, as well as in popular accounts of neuroscientific findings. Claims to gender equality continue to be superseded by discourses of gendered difference and complementarity. In popular texts and in subjects' accounts, a subordinate, often caring, role is presented as enabling girls to fulfil their essential gendered natures, and to experience greater pleasure and fulfilment in doing so than they would in competing in masculinised terms. In this way, feminism continues to be taken into account by discourses of complementarity, as it was in philosophies associated with the Enlightenment (Schiebinger 1989) and the Romantics (Battersby 1988), and the science of the Victorians (Alaya 1977). Such complementarity is now framed within two overarching narratives that restrict and direct girls' desire to succeed and cast their achievements as secondary: 'girls work hard' and 'girls hang back'. In these narratives, I find that traditional discourses of feminised achievement are updated and recirculated in the terms of the post-feminist contract, as described by McRobbie (2009). In schools and in teen TV shows, this can be seen to work not only in terms of behaviours associated with success – complementarity rather than competitiveness, application rather than inspiration – but also in terms of the nature of ability itself, which is characterised by empathic, connected ways of working and knowing. These features coalesce to form the intelligibly female successful subject. However, such a subject is produced as achieving within explanatory frameworks which undercut her very achievement as secondary by positioning it as inferior to masculinised success.

Alignment with Neoliberal Discourses

The concept of individual genius as integral to the advancement of civilisation was a central tenet of neoliberal thought (Friedman 1962). My exploration of narratives of girlhood and ability reveals close alignment with neoliberal discourses, particularly those of meritocracy and self-management. A contribution of this study is the demonstration of the ways in which such pervasive discourses are circulated within and across diverse contexts, and between subjects and institutions. I have shown how achieving girls adopt the language tropes of economic policy as circulated within schools to understand themselves as human capital, and how they adopt the tropes of popular post-feminist texts to construct themselves as aspirational and self-reflexive subjects.

I have illustrated ways in which popular and school choice discourses operate to create the aspirational subject and shape life narratives. These choice discourses are closely related to school identification practices in which girls are placed within certain success trajectories, as discussed above. Family, school and popular narratives can provide resources and sources of authority, but also can be sources of anxiety as girls are constrained to make the right kinds of choices at a young age. Risk and anxiety are defining characteristics of girls' accounts of engagement with choice, and in their constructions of possible life plans. These anxieties are more marked in those whose class identities are less privileged and who have fewer cultural resources on which to draw when making choices. Such girls rely on schools as sources of authority for their sense of self as achieving and for support in constructing the choice narrative. However, such advice may not be taken up; aspirational narratives may be rejected where anxieties surrounding dis-identification are stronger than those surrounding the production of the successful self.

While the achieving girl is constructed as having limitless opportunities, the girls in the group interviews tend to express choices that align with traditional gender roles. This reveals ongoing tensions between femininity and success which penalise ambition and competitiveness in girls and women. Some girls express ambivalence and anxiety with regard to workplace ambition, and while still in school adopt a range of strategies to manage competition. However, as observed above, this was not true of the online forum, suggesting the role of context in girls' adoption of certain achieving subject positions.

Contexts and Conditions of Production

The relationship between discourses and the conditions of production has been central to this study. In schools, in considering the relationship between the object of knowledge (the achieving girl), the context in which it appears and the role and authority of the source, I have shown how the technologies of identification, teacher interaction and pupil grouping work in competitive and hierarchised environments to produce achieving girl subject positions, and have highlighted the instability of the identities produced in such contexts.

I have also shown how the conventions and technologies of screen representations are mobilised to produce versions of successful femininity which align with commercial industry priorities. As well as a consideration of the regularities and restrictions of genre, this has enabled a positioning of the alpha girl as part of an address to privileged audiences within contexts of industry deregulation and niche audiences. I have drawn attention to the narrative structures of serial TV and the ways these are mobilised to reinforce cultural anxieties surrounding aspirational identities, choice and life course narratives.

Consideration of the contexts of production has also enabled recognition of the degree to which popular narratives are shaped by the operations of wider neoliberal economic policy. The multi-site nature of this enquiry has allowed me to demonstrate the rise of the achieving girl in popular as well as educational contexts as a part of a wider discursive milieu, and to link this to specific contexts of broadcast deregulation and education marketisation. Through linking narratives to the contexts of production, I have also been able to demonstrate how wider discourses permeate down to individual levels. I have shown how girls draw on educational and media narratives as resources in negotiating their own identities as achieving girls within peer and classroom contexts, and in producing accounts of others as less successful. Such narratives provide a cultural lexicon of gendered ability performances drawn from school, wider policy, family and popular sources.

Girls' take-up and reproduction of the discourses is also contextual; there is evidence of the 'policing' of appropriate claims to success among participants, and also of self-monitoring in the management of their academic success among friends. This means that claims to 'working hard', for example, may be made because this is an acceptable success behaviour, whereas a claim to achieving without hard work is not an endorsed model for girls, even while apparently more highly valued by teachers.

Other discourses, such as competitiveness, appear differently according to context even within the group interviews; the regulations which govern their pronouncability seem to be closely aligned with those of 'niceness', as well as those of fairness. Claims to pleasure in competition are allowable for girls when the stakes are low and the sides are equal. Claims to authenticity also appear as central; I argue that girls' positioning of the hard-working, academic self as 'authentic' allows them both to adopt positions of moral superiority and to account for their own success within discourses of meritocracy. However, such claims can create tensions with classed and feminised identities.

Online, the regulations appear more relaxed and claims to pleasure in academic competiveness also appear, as well as disclosure with regard to 'inauthentic' behaviours. This contrast suggests a conscious management of achieving behaviours and of claims to authenticity according to context. These and other marked differences in the accounts produced by online and group interview participants I account for within the different contexts of production. The conditions of anonymity and the conventions of forum communications appear conducive to producing ideal identities and inciting disclosure.

However, I do not argue that forum contributions should be considered as somehow more authentic; within this space, participants communicate according to the conventions of fan communities and online socialising – just as within schools, their contributions are shaped by that context and its conventions. Rather, I suggest that the website provides a space where alternative subject positions can be inhabited to those that are possible in schools, especially those expressing proscribed masculinised desires – for power, for success, for winning – as well as spaces for the confessional and mutual support.

Further, across both virtual and school contexts, the take-up of some aspects of the smart girl subject position appears more internalised than strategically performed, especially those associated with self-improvement and autonomy; it is interesting that these discourses are less gendered in themselves, as all neoliberal subjects are enjoined to be self-managing and independent. This suggests that discourses associated specifically with the gendering of success are more likely to be recognised as constructs and challenged by girls, while those associated with class appear more natural and inevitable. However, any such challenges to gendered discourses are expressed in terms of autonomy and independence which characterise the successful, neoliberal self-producing individual.

Implications for Educational and Media Policy and Professionals

In researching media texts, there is often the temptation to conflate the desirability of a text's perceived ideology and address with its demonstrable impact on audiences (Durkin 1985), particularly those audiences perceived as vulnerable (Gauntlett 1998). The design of this study, in considering participant accounts alongside television texts and its epistemological stance in treating such accounts as discursive instances, in some ways guards against this. That is, the responses to texts and personal accounts given here are not offered as evidence of direct media effects. Indeed, as I hope this study has demonstrated, media texts and audiences, like educational discourses and students, work in a complex relationship with myriad other factors, and accounts are shaped by the context in which they are produced in such a way that they cannot be treated as verifiable 'truths'. Further, within Foucault's (1969) archaeological approach, it is not the scholar's task to comment on the desirability of discourses, but merely to describe their manifestations. Here there is tension with the feminist's critical concerns to expose the workings of gendered power relations, but this, I argue, is an allowable tension, given both Foucault's direct injunction to borrow from his toolkit and his own manifest departures from the principle of non-hermeneutic description in exploring the discursive workings of power.

Having said as much, this study has focused on the nature and circulation of discourses and narratives, and it is to these that I turn in considering implications and recommendations. I summarise the key implication from this study as 'girls need better stories'. By 'better' I mean those that are more closely aligned with a greater range of their subjectivities and experiences, and those which offer a broader array of possibilities in terms of gender and success. These implications are drawn not only from the researcher's perspective in identifying gaps and tensions in prevailing discourses, but also from the statements and preferences of the girls themselves, and also from broader national concerns which indicate a perceived need to intervene in the kinds of media narratives available to young people.

Rather than reiterating the issues which emerge in the findings and conclusions with regard to available narratives, I consider two popular examples. The first is *Doctor Who*'s Rose Tyler. In considering Rose earlier in this study, I have drawn attention to the ways in which she is constructed as working class. Also noted was the companion's role in the show as providing accessibility to the 'Who-niverse' for the viewer; Rose's very 'ordinariness' has deliberate working-class associations (Skeggs 2009) designed to render her as broadly appealing. I have also drawn attention to the ways in which narrative technologies in the pilot episode of *Doctor Who* (2005) are deployed to regulate the choices and aspirations of girls. Rose, as my Maple Grove and Sir Walter Raleigh participants point out, gets away.

However, this is only half the story: Rose also comes back. As Hoskin (2006, 88) observes, unlike previous companions, 'Rose was missed. She had a life before the advent of the Tardis and there are consequences to her leaving it'. The impact on her mother and boyfriend is dramatised, and they are both given regular roles on the show due to Rose's frequent returns. What the audience is offered in Rose is a working-class girl whose 'escape' is not final and does not constitute a breach with her family. Despite the opening episode's construction of Rose as a willing escapee from a life of monotony and dependence, there is also a divergence from normative middle-class identities and aspirations. Rose's defining feature for forum and group interview participants is her non-traditional 'smartness'; she is variously described as having 'common-sense', 'quick thinking' and 'non-academic', emphasising her difference from middle-class achieving identities. It is interesting to note that Rose is the most frequently discussed and admired character across group interviews and the online forum.

A key recommendation then is for the provision of more narratives and examples of girls for whom education and other forms of success can be accomplished without the necessary sacrifice of classed identities and the familiar. Such examples might go some way toward wider discursive dis-identification of class with certain kinds of success.

The second example is provided in another character whose identity is firmly established as outside privilege: the smartgirls.tv forum favourite, Veronica Mars. While I have already considered this show's critical representation of privilege as producing educational success and its genre-based transgressive femininities, its popularity with participants is due to more than this. In contexts in which making the right choices is crucial and girls are constrained to get things right and stay on track, Veronica is popular because she makes mistakes. She is described by participants as 'flawed' but able to 'pick herself up', and as getting things wrong. She puts personal issues before school, she fails tests and loses scholarships, and she refuses advice from authority figures. Despite all this, she is successful. My second recommendation therefore is for more narratives in which making mistakes – including educational choices – is something from which girls can recover to pursue meaningful and fulfilling lives with self-respect intact. Such narratives would provide an alternative to the prevailing discourses of anxiety and cautionary representations of 'the mismanaged life' (Hamann 2009, 44).

Schools, teachers and career services could collaborate to generate ways of introducing more of the above kinds of narrative possibilities in curricular, extra-curricular and life planning activities with girls. In terms of popular narratives, a more profound commitment may be needed at the national level. The conditions of commercial TV production and their primary concern with producing and packaging audiences for advertisers and sponsors (Meehan 2005) have been described at various points during this thesis, particularly with regard to niche broadcasting and the rise of consumer femininities in the characterisation of achieving girls.

It is important not to slip into the easy position of viewing young audiences as incapable of recognising and resisting commercial intent in broadcasting, nor of simplifying the complex relationship between commercialised gender categories and audiences because they appear undesirable to the adult eye. Indeed, the DCSF (2009b) recognizes, and this study has affirmed, 'girls themselves can be reflexive and aware of their ambivalent relationship with commercial culture' (121). Nonetheless, in its report into the future of children's television programming, Ofcom (2007) notes with some concern the fragmentation and commercialisation of children's television in particular, and makes a unique case for public intervention and additional funds to be directed specifically to the creation of original content for children – this is in the context of the bulk of the rest of Ofcom's recommendations for the withdrawal of public financial support for content creation, leaving market forces to prevail. It is surrounding funding for provision of children's media, therefore, that we see commitment to neoliberal free market principles break down at the government policy level. Ofcom acknowledges that commercial broadcasting is increasingly shaped by media conglomerates unwilling to invest in quality original broadcasting where revenues may be low. In this context, the argument for the production of narratives in which successful consuming femininities are not the primary identities on offer can be seen as part of a broader call for investment in public service broadcasting for young people in the face of free market policies operating elsewhere in the industry. This is an interesting disruption to the neoliberal metanarrative in that such an intervention draws attention to the shaky ethical premises – those of holding market goals above all others, of the moral imperative of acting to produce the entrepreneurial self, and of consumerism as the governing principle of good choices – of the discourse itself.

Note

Chapter 1: The Future Girl's Problem Past was previously published in slightly amended form as: Dinosaur discourses: taking stock of gendered learning myths. *Gender and Education* Volume 27, Issue 7 pp. 744–758.

Bibliography

Aapola, S., Gonick, M., & Harris, A. (2005). *Young femininity: Girlhood, power and social change*. Basingstoke: Palgrave Macmillan.

Adda, J., & Ottaviani, M. (2005). The transition to digital television. *Economic Policy*, 20, 159–209.

Adkins, L. (2002). *Revisions: Gender and sexuality in late modernity*. Buckingham: Open University Press.

Adorno, T. (1991). *The culture industry: Selected essays on mass culture*. London: Routledge.

Adorno, T., & Horkheimer, M. (2002). *Dialectic of enlightenment* (Trans. E. Jephcott). Palo Alto, CA: Stanford University Press.

Ajzenberg-Selove, F. (1994). *A matter of choices: Memoirs of a female physicist*. Brunswick, NJ: Rutgers University Press.

Aladjem, T. (1991). The philosopher's prism: Foucault, feminism and critique. *Political Theory*, 19:2, 277–291.

Alaya, F. (1977). Victorian science and the "genius" of woman. *Journal of the History of Ideas*, 38:2, 261–280.

Albert, R. (1969). Genius: Present-day status of the concept and its implications for the study of creativity and giftedness. *American Psychologist*, 24:8, 743–753.

Albert, R. (1992). *Genius and eminence* (2nd ed.). New York: Routledge.

Alcoff, L. (1988). Cultural feminism versus post-structuralism: The identity crisis in feminist theory. *Signs: Journal of Women in Culture and Society*, 13:1, 405–436.

Alcoff, L. (2005). Foucault's philosophy of science: Structures of truth/structures of power. In G. Gutting (Ed.), *Blackwell companion to continental philosophies of science* (pp. 211–223). Oxford: Blackwell.

Allan, A. (2010). Picturing success: Young femininities and the (im)possibilities of academic achievement in selective, single-sex schooling. *International Studies in Sociology of Education*, 20:1, 39–54.

Allan, A. J. (2006). Using photographic diaries to research the gender and academic identities of young girls. In G. Walford, B. Jeffrey, & G. Troman (Eds.), *Methodological issues and practices in ethnography* (pp. 19–36). Oxford: Elsevier.

Allen, A. (1996). Foucault on power: A theory for feminists. In S. Hekman (Ed.), *Feminist interpretations of Michel Foucault* (pp. 265–282). University Park: Penn State Press.

Allen, K. (2008). *Young women and the performing arts: Creative education, new labour and the remaking of the young female self*. Unpublished PhD thesis, accessed from British Library.

Allen, K. (2015). Top girls navigating austere times: Interrogating youth transitions since the 'crisis'. *Journal of Youth Studies*, 19:5, 629–645.

Allington, D. (2005). "How come most people don't see it?" Slashing the Lord of the Rings. *Social Semiotics*, 17:1, 43–62.

Allington, D. (2007). How come most people don't see it? Slashing the *Lord of the Rings*. *Social Semiotics*, 17:1, 43–62.

Althusser, L. (1997). Ideology and ideological state apparatuses: Notes toward an investigation. In S. Zizek (Ed.), *Mapping ideology* (pp. 100–140). London: Verso. (First published 1969).

Amatriain, X. (2013). Big & personal: Data and models behind Netflix recommendations. In *Proceedings of the 2nd International Workshop on Big Data, Streams and Heterogeneous Source Mining: Algorithms, Systems, Programming Models and Applications* (BigMine '13) (pp. 1–6). New York: Association for Computing Machinery.

Ambrose, D. (2002). Socioeconomic stratification and its influences on talent development: Some interdisciplinary perspectives. *Gifted Child Quarterly*, 46, 170–180.

Andersen, N. (2003). *Discursive analytic strategies: Understanding Foucault, Koselleck, Laclau, Luhmann*. Bristol: Policy Press.

Ang, I. (1996). *Living room wars: Rethinking media audiences for a postmodern world*. London: Routledge.

AoIR (Association of Internet Researchers). (2012). *Ethical decision-making and Internet research 2.0: Recommendations from the AoIR ethics working committee*. Retrieved May 10, 2016, from http://aoir.org/reports/ethics2.pdf.

Archer, L. (2005). *The impossibility of girls' educational 'success': Entanglements of gender, 'race', class and sexuality in the production and problematisation of educational femininities*. Working paper for ESRC Seminar Series Girls in Education 3–16, Cardiff, November 24. Retrieved February 12, 2009, from http://www.lancs.ac.uk/fass/events/girlsandeducation/docs/sem1/The%20impossibility%20of%20success%20ESRC%20Seminar.doc.

Archer, L., & Francis, B. (2006). Challenging classes? Exploring the role of social class within the identities and achievement of British Chinese pupils. *Sociology*, 40, 29–49.

Archer, L., Halsall, A., & Hollingworth, S. (2007). Inner-city femininities and education: 'race', class, gender and schooling in young women's lives. *Gender and Education*, 19:5, 549–568.

Archer, L., Halsall, A., & Hollingworth, S. (2012). Working-class girls' education and post-16 aspirations. *British Journal of Sociology of Education*, 28:2, 165–180.

Archer, L., & Hutchings, M. (2000). Bettering yourself? Discourses of risk, cost and benefit in ethnically diverse, young working-class non-participants' constructions of higher education. *British Journal of Sociology of Education*, 21:4, 555–574.

Arnett, J. (1995). Adolescents' uses of media for self-socialization. *Journal of Youth and Adolescence*, 24:5, 519–533.

Arnold, J., & Miller, H. (1999). *Gender and web home pages*. Paper presented at the CAL99 Virtuality in Education Conference, London, March 28–31. Retrieved November 12, 2010, from http://ess.ntu.ac.uk/miller/cyberpsych/cal99.htm.

AIoR (Association of Internet Researchers) and C. Ess. (2002). *Ethical decision-making and Internet research: Recommendations from the AoIR ethics working committee*. Retrieved August 12, 2007, from aoir.org/reports/ethics.pdf.

Atkinson, P., & Delamont, S. (2006). Rescuing narrative from qualitative research. *Narrative Enquiry*, 16:1, 164–172.

Atkinson, S., & Nixon, H. (2005). Locating the subject: Teens online @ ninemsn. *Discourse: Studies in the Cultural Politics of Education*, 26:3, 387–409.

Austin, J. (1976). *How to do things with words*. Oxford: Oxford University Press.

Austin, J. (2005). Youth, neoliberalism, ethics: Some questions. *Rhizomes*, 10:8. Retrieved May 2, 2011, from http://www.rhizomes.net/issue10/austin. htm#_edn11.

Baker, J. (2010). Great expectations and feminist accountability: Young women living up to 'successful girls' discourse. *Gender and Education*, 22:1, 1–16.

Banks, J. (Ed.). (2007). *Diversity and citizenship education*. San Francisco: Jossey-Bass.

Barbour, R. (2007). *Doing focus groups*. London: Sage.

Barker, C. (1999). *Television, globalization and cultural identities*. Buckingham: Open University Press.

Bartky, S. (1988). Foucault, femininity, and the modernization of patriarchal power. In I. Diamond & L. Quinby (Eds.), *Feminism and Foucault: Reflections on resistance* (pp. 61–86). Boston: Northeastern University Press.

Battersby, C. (1988). *Gender and genius: Towards a feminist aesthetic*. London: Women's Press.

Baumgardner, J., & Richards, A. (2000). *Manifesta: Young women, feminism and the future*. New York: Farrar, Straus & Giroux.

Bavidge, J. (2004). In *Chosen ones: Reading the contemporary teen heroine*. In G. Davies & K. Dickinson (Eds.), *Teen TV: Genre, consumption and identity*. London: British Film Institute.

BBC News. (2002). *Girls beating boys in almost all GCSE subjects*. Retrieved October 13, 2009, from http://news.bbc.co.uk/cbbcnews/hi/uk/newsid_2209000/2209179.stm.

BBC News. (2015). *Having Hermione look like me is amazing*. Retrieved December 28, 2015, from http://www.bbc.co.uk/news/world-us-canada-35156893.

Beck, U. (1992). *Risk society: Towards a new modernity*. London: Sage.

Beck, U., & Beck-Gernsheim, E. (2002). *Individualization: Institutionalized individualism and its social and political consequences*. London: Sage.

Becta. (2010). *Broadband for schools*. Retrieved January 11, 2011, from www. e-learningcentre.co.uk/../Broadband_for_schools_march_2010_summary_report. doc.

Beery, A. K., & Zucker, I. (2011). Sex bias in neuroscience and biomedical research. *Neuroscience & Biobehavioral Review*, 5:3, 565–572.

Belenky, M., Clinchy, B. M., Goldberger, N. R., & Tarule, J. M. (1997). *Women's ways of knowing: The development of self, voice, and mind*. New York, Basic Books.

Bell, K. (2005). www.Backstage.com. Retrieved November 4, 2010, from http://forums.televisionwithoutpity.com/index.php?showtopic=3119829&st=375.

Bellafante, G. (2007). Mother and daughter, each coming into her own. *New York Times*, May 17. Retrieved March 24, 2010, from http://www.nytimes.com/2007/05/17/arts/television/17gilm.html.

Benjamin, S., Nind, M., Hall, K., Collins, J., & Sheehy, K. (2003). Moments of inclusion and exclusion: Pupils negotiating classroom contexts. *British Journal of Sociology of Education* 24:5, 547–558.

Bennett, A. (2015). What a "racebent" Hermione Granger really represents: The beauty of the Harry Potter character as a woman of color. Retrieved December 28, 2015, from http://www.buzzfeed.com/alannabennett/what-a-racebent-hermione-granger-really-represen-d2yp#.xivJzXY91e.

Bennett, T., & Woollacott, J. (1987). *Bond and beyond: The political career of a popular hero*. Hampshire: Macmillan Education Ltd.

Bernstein, B. (1977). *Class, codes and control* (Vol. 3). London: Routledge.

Besley A. (2002). Fess up or else! Truth-telling, confession and care of the self in secondary schools. In T. Kvernbekk & B. Nordtug (Eds.), *The many faces of philosophy of education: Traditions, problems and challenges* (pp. 26–36). Oslo: International Network of Philosophers of Education.

Bilton, T., Bonnett, K., Jones, P., Skinner, D., Stanworth, M., & Sheard, K. (2004). *Sociology* (4th ed.). Basingstoke: Palgrave Macmillan.

Bizzari, J. (1998). An intergenerational study of three gifted women: Obstacles and challenges confronting women of high potential. *Roeper Review*, 21:2, 110–116.

Blair, T. (1996). Speech to Labour Party conference. October 1.

Blumenreich, M. (2004). Avoiding the pitfalls of 'conventional' narrative research: Using poststructural theory to guide the creation of narratives of children with HIV. *Qualitative Research*, 4, 77–90.

Bodek, E. (1976). Salonières and bluestockings: Educated obsolescence and germinating feminism. *Feminist Studies*, 3:3/4, 185–199.

Bolt, C. (2008). 'Normal is the watchword': Exiling cultural anxieties and redefining desire from the margins. In S. Ross & L. Stein. (Eds.), *Teen television: Essays on Programming and Fandom* (pp. 93–113). Jefferson, NC: McFarland.

Bombardieri, M. (2005). Summers' remarks on women draw fire. *Boston Globe*, January 17. Retrieved November 18, 2009, from http://www.boston.com/news/local/articles/2005/01/17/summers_remarks_on_women_draw_fire/.

Borland, J. (2004). *Rethinking gifted education*. London: Teachers' College Press.

Bociurkiw, M. (2008). Commentary: Put on your bunny ears, take your TV around the block: Old and new discourses of gender and nation in mobile, digital, and HDTV. *Canadian Journal of Communication*, 33:3.

Bovill, M., & Livingstone, S. (2001). Bedroom culture: The privatization of media use. In S. Livingstone & M. Bovill (Eds.), *Children and their changing media environment: A European comparative study* (pp. 179–200). Mahwah, NJ: Lawrence Erlbaum Associates.

Boyce-Tilman, J. (2005). Unconventional wisdom: Theologising the margins. *Feminist Theology*, 13:3, 317–341.

boyd, d. (2007). Why youth (heart). Social network sites: The role of networked publics in teenage social life. In D. Buckingham (Ed.), *MacArthur Foundation series on digital learning – Youth, identity, and digital media* (Vol. 9, pp. 119–142). Cambridge, MA: MIT Press.

boyd, d. (2009). Defining project boundaries: A response to Christine Hine. In A. Markham & N. Baym (Eds.), *Internet Enquiry: Conversations about Method* (pp. 26–32). London: Sage.

boyd, d. (2011). White flight in networked publics? How race and class shaped American teen engagement with MySpace and Facebook. In L. Nakamura & P. Chow-White (Eds.), *Race After the Internet* (pp. 203–222). New York: Routledge.

Brabazon, T. (2008). Review of *Geek chic: Smart women in popular culture* (Ed. S. Inness). *Times Higher Education*, May 29. Retrieved February 10, 2010, from http://www.timeshighereducation.co.uk/story.asp?storyCode=402178&sectioncode=26.

Bradford, S., & Hey, V. (2007). Successful subjectivities? The successification of class, ethnic and gender positions. *Journal of Education Policy*, 22:6, 595–614.

Braidotti, R. (1994). *Nomadic subjects. Embodiment and sexual difference in contemporary feminist theory*. Cambridge: Columbia University Press.

Braithwaite, A. (2008). 'That girl of yours, she's pretty hardboiled, huh?' Detecting feminism in *Veronica Mars*. In S. Ross & L. Stein (Eds.), *Teen Television: Essays in Programming and Fandom* (pp. 132–149). London: Macfarland & Co.

Brandels, D. (2008). The case of Gertrude Stein and the genius of collaboration. *Women's Studies: An Interdisciplinary Journal*, 37:4, 371–392.

Brannen, J., & Pattman, R. (2005). Work-family matters in the workplace: The use of focus groups in a study of a UK social services department. *Qualitative Research*, 5:4, 523–542.

Briggs, M. (2009). BBC children's television, parentcraft and pedagogy: Towards the ethicalization of existence. *Media, Culture & Society*, 31, 23–39.

Bringer, J. D., Johnston, L. H., & Brackenridge, C. H. (2006). Using computer-assisted qualitative data analysis software to develop a grounded theory project. *Field Methods*, 18:3, 245–266.

Brizendine L. (2008). *The Female Brain*. New York: Morgan Road Books.

Brocklesby, J., & Cummings, S. (1996). Foucault plays Habermas: An alternative philosophical underpinning for critical systems thinking. *Journal of the Operational Research Society*, 47:6, 741–754.

Brooks, D. (2009). Genius: The modern view. *New York Times*, April 30. Retrieved April 30, 2009, from http://www.nytimes.com/2009/05/01/opinion/01brooks.html?sq=talent%20code&st=cse&adxnnl=1&scp=1&adxnlx=1288346867-EecFaYlbPFvILa2JlUwvLw.

Broude, N., & Garrard M. (1982). *Feminism and art history*. New York: Harper & Row.

Brougere, G. (2006). Toy houses: A socio-anthropological approach to analysing objects. *Visual Communication*, 5:1, 5–24.

Brown, J. (1992). *The definition of a profession: The authority of metaphor in the history of intelligence testing 1890–1930*. Princeton, NJ: Princeton University Press.

Brown, J., & Pardun, C. (2004). Little in common: Racial and gender differences in adolescents' television diets. *Journal of Broadcasting & Electronic Media*, 48, 266–278.

Brown, P. (1990). The 'third wave': Education and the ideology of parentocracy. *British Journal of Sociology of Education*, 11:1, 65–85.

Buckingham, D. (Ed.). (2008). *Youth, identity, and digital media*. John D. & Catherine T. MacArthur Foundation Series on Digital Media and Learning. Cambridge, MA: MIT Press.

Buckingham, D., & Bragg, S. (2004). *Young people, sex and the media: The facts of life?* Basingstoke: Palgrave Macmillan.

Buckle, H. T. (1872). The influence of women on the progress of knowledge. In T. Heller (Ed.), *The miscellaneous and posthumous works of Henry Thomas Buckle*. Retrieved August 2, 2010, from http://www.public.coe.edu/~theller/soj/u-rel/buckle.html (Reprinted from *Fraser's Magazine*, April 1858).

Budgeon, S. (2001). Emergent feminist(?) identities: Young women and the practice of micropolitics. *European Journal of Women's Studies*, 8:1, 7–28.

Budgeon, S. (2003). *Choosing a self: Young women and the individualisation of identity*. Westport, CT: Praegar.

Budgeon, S. (2011). *Third wave feminism and the politics of gender in late modernity*. Basingstoke: Palgrave Macmillan.

Bullen, E. (2015). Disgusting subjects: Consumer–class distinction and the affective regulation of girl desire. In C. Bradford & M. Reimer (Eds.), *Girls, texts, cultures* (pp. 53–74). Winnipeg: Wilfrid Laurier.

Bunting, B., & Mooney, E. (2001). The effects of practice and coaching on test results for educational selection at eleven years of age. *Educational Psychology*, 21:3, 243–253.

Burman, E. (1994). *Deconstructing developmental psychology*. New York: Routledge.

Bury, R. (2005). *Cyberspaces of their own: Female fandoms online*. New York: Peter Lang.

Busetta, L., & Coladonato, L. (2015). Be your selfie: Identity, aesthetics and power in digital self-representation. *Networking Knowledge, Special Issue: Be Your Selfie* 8:6.

Butler, J. (1990). *Gender trouble: Feminism and the subversion of identity*. London: Routledge.

Butler, J. (1993). *Bodies that matter: On the discursive limits of 'sex'*. London: Routledge.

Butler, J. (1997). *A politics of the performative*. London: Routledge.

Calás, M., & Smircich, L. (2006). From the 'woman's point of view' ten years later: Towards a feminist organization studies. In S. Clegg, C. Hardy, & W. Nord (Eds.), *Sage handbook of organization studies* (pp. 218–258). London: Sage.

Callahan, C., Cunningham, C., & Plucker, J. (1994). Foundations for the future: The socio-emotional development of gifted, adolescent women. *Roeper Review*, 17, 99–105.

Calvert, S. (2002). Identity construction on the Internet. In S. Calvert, A. Jordan, & R. Cocking (Eds.), *Children in the digital age: Influences of electronic media on development* (pp. 57–70). Westport, CT: Praeger.

Cammaerts, B. (2007). Jamming the political: Beyond counter-hegemonic practices. *Continuum: Journal of Media and Cultural Studies*, 21:1, 71–90.

Canaan, J. (2001). *Haunting assumptions of ability: How working class and ethnic minority students signal academic failure*. Paper presented at Higher Education Close Up2 Conference, Lancaster, July. Retrieved July 9, 2007, from www.leeds.ac.uk/educol.

Cannella, G. (1999). The scientific discourse of education: Predetermining the lives of others – Foucault, education, and children. *Contemporary Issues in Early Childhood*, 1:1, 36–34.

Carey, M. (1993). The group effect in focus groups: Planning, implementing and interpreting focus group research. In J. Morse (Ed.), *Critical issues in qualitative research methods* (pp. 225–251). London: Sage.

Cassell, J., & Huffaker, D. (2006). The language of online leadership: Gender and youth engagement on the Internet. *Developmental Psychology*, 42:3, 436–449.

Center for Social Media. (2001). *TeenSites.com: A field guide to the new digital landscape*. Retrieved February 11, 2011, from http://www.centerforsocialmedia.org/future-public-media/documents/articles/teensitescom-field-guide-new-digital-landscape.

Center for Social Media. (2009). *Public media 2.0: Dynamic, engaged publics*. Retrieved February 11, 2011, from http://www.cmsimpact.org/future-public-media/documents/white-papers/public-media-20-dynamic-engaged-publics.

Chalfin, M., Murphy, E. R., & Karkazis, K. A. (2008). Women's neuroethics? Why sex matters for neuroethics. *American Journal of Bioethics*, 8:2, 1–2.

Chen, W., & Wellman, B. (2004). The global digital divide – Within and between countries. *IT & Society*, 1:7, 39–45.

Cheseboro, J., & Bertelsen, D. (1999). *Analyzing media: Computer technologies as symbolic and cognitive systems*. New York: Guilford.

Citron, M. (1986). Women and the lied, 1775–1850. In J. Bowers & J. Tick (Eds.), *Women making music: The Western art tradition 1150–1950* (pp. 224–248). London: MacMillan.

Clack, B. (1999). *Misogyny in the Western philosophical tradition*. Basingstoke: MacMillan.

Cleary Committee of the American Psychological Association, Board of Scientific Affairs. Quoted in Kamin, L. J. (1981). *Intelligence: The battle for the mind* (p. 94). London: Pan Books.

Click, M., Aubrey, J., & Behm-Morawitz, E. (2010). *Bitten by Twilight: Youth culture, media, and the vampire franchise*. New York: Peter Lang.

Cohen, M. (1998). 'A habit of healthy idleness': Boys' underachievement in historical perspective. In D. Epstein, J. Elwood, V. Hey, and J. Maw (Eds.), *Failing boys? Issues in gender and achievement* (pp. 19–34). Buckingham: Open University Press.

Coldron, J., Cripps, C., & Shipton, L. (2010). Why are English secondary schools socially segregated? *Journal of Education Policy*, 25:1, 19–35.

Coleman, R. (2008). The becoming of bodies: Girls, media effects, and body image. *Feminist Media Studies*, 8:2, 163–179.

Collins, G. (1978). Reflections on the head of Medusa. *Studies in Art Education*, 19:2, 10–18.

Colvin, G. (2008). *Talent is overrated: What really separates world-class performers from everybody else*. New York: Portfolio.

Common Sense. (2015). *The common sense census: Media use by tweens and teens*. Retrieved November 20, 2015, from https://www.commonsensemedia.org/research/the-common-sense-census-media-use-by-tweens-and-teens.

Conner, C. D. (2005). *A people's history of science: Miners, midwives and "low meckanics"*. New York: Nation Books.

Cook, D. T., & Kaiser, S. B. (2004). Betwixt and between: Age ambiguity and the sexualization of the female consuming subject. *Journal of Consumer Culture*, 4, 203–227.

Cookson Jr., P. W., & Persell, C. H. (1985). English and American residential secondary schools: A comparative study of the reproduction of social elites. *Comparative Education Review* 29:3, 283–298.

Coquillat, M. (2001). A male poetics (Trans. N. Birch). *Women: A Cultural Review*, 11:3, 223–237.

Corden, A., & Sainsbury, R. (2006). Exploring 'quality': Research participants' perspectives on verbatim quotations. *International Journal of Social Research Methodology*, 9:2, 97–110.

Cordes, H. (2000). *Girl power in the classroom*. Minneapolis: Lerner.

Costello, V., & Moore, B. (2007). Cultural outlaws: An examination of audience activity and online television fandom. *Television & New Media*, 8, 124–143.

Cottle, S. (2003). *Media organisation and production*. London: Sage.

Covay, E., & Carbonaro, W. (2010). After the bell: Participation in extracurricular activities, classroom behavior, and academic achievement. *Sociology of Education*, 83:1, 20–45.

Covington, M. (1998). *The will to learn: A guide for motivating young people*. Cambridge: Cambridge University Press.

Cox, C. (1926). *Early mental traits of three hundred geniuses*. Genetic Studies of Genius Series. Palo Alto, CA: Stanford University Press.

Coyle, D. (2009). *The talent code: Talent isn't born; it's grown*. London: Nicholas Brealey.

Cross, T., Cook, R., & Dixon, D. (1996). Psychological autopsies of three academically talented adolescents who committed suicide. *Journal of Secondary Gifted Education*, 7, 403–409.

Cross, T., Gust-Brey, K., & Ball, B. (2002). A psychological autopsy of the suicide of an academically gifted student: Researchers' and parents' perspectives. *Gifted Child Quarterly*, 46:4, 247–264.

Cruikshank, B. (1996). Revolutions within: Self-government and self-esteem. In A. Barry, T. Osborne, & N. Rose (Eds.), *Foucault and political reason: Liberalism, neo-liberalism and rationalities of government* (pp. 231–51). London: UCL Press.

Currie, D., Kelly, D., & Pomerantz, S. (2006). 'The geeks shall inherit the earth': Girls' agency, subjectivity and empowerment. *Journal of Youth Studies*, 9:4, 419–436.

Currie, D., Kelly, D., & Pomerantz, S. (2009). *Girl power: Girls reinventing girlhood*. New York: Peter Lang.

Currie, M. (1998). *Postmodern narrative theory*. New York: St. Martin's Press.

Curtin, M. (2009). Matrix media. In G. Turner & J. Tay (Eds.), *Television studies after TV: Understanding television in the post-broadcast era* (pp. 9–19). Abingdon: Routledge.

Daily Mail. (2007). University gender gap: Women outnumber men in all subjects and make up 57 per cent of first-time graduates. Retrieved October 14, 2010, from http://goliath.ecnext.com/coms2/gi_0199–9352862/University-gender-gap-Women-outnumber.html.

Daily Mail. (2009). Supergirl meltdown: How middle-class girls today are under unprecedented pressure to succeed. Retrieved October 13, 2010, from http://www.dailymail.co.uk/femail/article-1221344/Supergirl-meltdown-How-middle-class-girls-today-unprecedented-pressure-succeed.html#ixzz1QgOXHEY1.

Dammler, A., Barlovic, I., & Clausnitzer, C. (2005). What are brands for? *Young Consumers: Insight and Ideas for Responsible Marketers*, 6:2, 11–16.

Davies, J. (2002). Weaving magic webs: Internet identities and teen Wiccan subcultures. A consideration of one particular on line community and their web based interactions. Paper presented at the University of Sheffield for the ESRC funded seminar series Children's Literacy and Popular Culture. Retrieved October 13, 2010, from http://darkbooks.org/pp.php?v=1179301941#book_description.

Davis, G., & Dickinson, K. (2004). *Teen TV: Genre, consumption & identity*. London: British Film Institute.

DCFS (Department for Children, Families and Schools). (2009a). *Mythbusters: Addressing gender and achievement myths and realities*. Retrieved February 10, 2010, from http://webarchive.nationalarchives.gov.uk/20130401151715/http://www.education.gov.uk/publications/eOrderingDownload/00599-2009BKT-EN.pdf.

DCSF (Department for Children, Families and Schools). (2009b). *The impact of the commercial world on children's wellbeing.* Nottingham: DCSF.

de Certeau, M. (1984). *The practice of everyday life* (Trans. S. Rendall). Berkeley: University of California Press.

de Freitas, E. (2008). Mathematics and its other: (Dis)locating the feminine. *Gender and Education,* 20:3, 281–290.

De Haan, R., & Havighurst, R. (1961). *Educating gifted children.* Chicago: University of Chicago Press.

Delamont, S. (1994). Accentuating the positive: Refocusing research on girls and science. *Studies in Science Education,* 23, 59–74.

Delamont, S. (1999). Gender and the discourse of derision. *Research Papers in Education,* 14:1, 3–21.

Delap, L. (2004). The superwoman: Theories of gender and genius in Edwardian Britain. *Historical Journal,* 47:1, 101–126.

DeNora, T. (1995). *Beethoven and the construction of genius.* Berkeley: University of California Press.

Deveaux, M. (1994). Feminism and empowerment: A critical reading of Foucault. *Feminist Studies,* 20:2, 233–247.

DfEE (Department for Employment and Education). (1997). *Excellence in schools.* London: Stationery Office.

DfEE (Department for Employment and Education). (1999). *Excellence in cities.* London: Stationery Office.

DfES (Department for Education and Skills). (2002). *Excellence in cities.* Retrieved February 2, 2005, from http://www.standards.dfes.gov.uk/local/excellence/.

DfES (Department for Education and Skills). (2005). *Higher standards: Better schools for all.* London: Stationery Office.

DfES (Department for Education and Skills). (2006). *Identifying gifted and talented pupils: Getting started.* Retrieved November 10, 2007, from http://webarchive.nationalarchives.gov.uk/20130401151715/http://www.education.gov.uk/publications/eOrderingDownload/Getting%20StartedWR.pdf.

DfES (Department for Education and Skills). (2007). *Gender and education: The evidence on pupils in England.* Retrieved October 21, 2007, from http://webarchive.nationalarchives.gov.uk/20130401151715/http://www.education.gov.uk/publications/eOrderingDownload/00389-2007BKT-EN.pdf.

DfES (Department for Education and Skills). (2009). *The national strategies: Gifted and talented guidance.* Retrieved July 6, 2009, from http://webarchive.nationalarchives.gov.uk/20130401151715/http://www.education.gov.uk/publications/eOrderingDownload/00378-2009BKT-EN.pdf.

Dillabough, J., & Arnot, M. (2002). Feminist perspectives in sociology of education: Continuity and transformation in the field. In D. Levinson, R. Sadovnik, & P. Cookson (Eds.), *Sociology of education: An encyclopedia* (pp. 571–586). London: Taylor & Francis.

Dillabough, J.-A. (2001). Gender theory and research in education: Modernist traditions and emerging contemporary themes. In B. Francis & C. Skelton (Eds.), *Investigating gender: Contemporary perspectives in education* (pp. 11–26). Buckingham: Open University Press.

Dobson, A. S. (2014). Performative shamelessness on young women's social network sites: Shielding the self and resisting gender melancholia. *Feminism & Psychology,* 24:1, 97–144.

Dresner, E., & Herring, S. C. (2010). Functions of the nonverbal in CMC: Emoticons and illocutionary force. *Communication Theory*, 20, 249–268.

Driscoll, C. (2002). *Girls: Feminine adolescence in popular culture and cultural theory*. New York: Columbia University Press.

Driscoll, C. (2007). Girls today: Girls, girl culture and girlhood studies. *Girlhood Studies: An Interdisciplinary Journal*, 1:1, 13–32.

Drotner, K. (2008). Leisure is hard work: Digital practices and future competencies. In D. Buckingham (Ed.), *Youth, identity and digital media* (pp. 167–184). John D. & Catherine T. MacArthur Foundation Series on Digital Media and Learning. Cambridge, MA: MIT Press.Duchin, M. (2004). *The sexual politics of genius*. Retrieved March 11, 2009, from http://mduchin.math.tufts.edu/genius.pdf.

Duits, L. (2010). The importance of popular media in everyday girl culture. *European Journal of Women's Studies*, 25:3, 244–257.

Duits, L., & Van Zoonen, L. (2006). Headscarves and porno-chic: Disciplining girls' dress in the European multicultural society. *European Journal of Women's Studies*, 13:2, 103–117.

Duke, L. (2000). Black in a blonde world: Race and girls' interpretations of the feminine ideal in teen magazines. *Journalism and Mass Communication Quarterly*, 77:2, 367–392.

Duke, L. (2002). Get real! Cultural relevance and resistance to the mediated feminine ideal. *Psychology & Marketing*, 19:2, 211–233.

Duncan, N. (2004). It's important to be nice, but it's nicer to be important: Girls, popularity and sexual competition. *Sex Education*, 4:2, 137–152.

Dunn, H. (2005). The genres of television. In H. Fulton (Ed.), *Narrative and media*. Cambridge: Cambridge University Press.

Durham, M. (2001). Adolescents, the Internet and the politics of gender: A feminist case analysis. *Race, Gender & Class*, 8:4, 20–41.

Durkin, K. (1985). *Television, sex roles and children: A developmental social psychological account*. Philadelphia: Open University Press.

Dyson, A., Goldrick, S., Jones, L., & Kerr, K. (2010). *Equity in education: Creating a fairer education system*. Manchester: Centre for Equity in Education, University of Manchester.

Ecclestone, K. (2004). Learning or therapy? The demoralisation of education. *British Journal of Educational Research*, 52, 112–137.

Eco, U. (1983). Guide to neo-television. In Z. Baranski & R. Lumley (Eds.), *Culture and conflict in postwar Italy* (pp. 245–255). London: Macmillan.

Eggermont, S. (2006). Developmental changes in adolescents' television viewing habits: Longitudinal trajectories in a three-wave panel study. *Journal of Broadcasting & Electronic Media*, 50:4, 742–761.

Elfenbein, A. (1996). Lesbianism and Romantic genius: The poetry of Anne Bannerman. *English Literary History*, 63:4, 929–957.

Ellis, H. (1904). *A study of British genius*. London: Hurst & Blackett.

Elston, M. A. (2009). *Women in medicine: The future*. London: Royal College of Physicians.

Elwood. J. (2010). Exploring girls' relationship to and with achievement: Linking assessment, learning, mind and gender. In C. Jackson, C. Paechter, & E. Renold (Eds.), *Girls and education 3–16: Continuing concerns, new agendas* (pp. 38–49). London: Open University Press.

Epstein, D. (1993). Sexual subjects: Some methodological problems in research-ing sexuality in schools. Paper presented at the AARE Conference, November. Retrieved May 10, 2010, from www.aare.edu.au.

Epstein, D. (1997). Are you a girl or are you a teacher? The 'least adult' role in research about gender and sexuality in a primary school. In G. Walford (Ed.), *Doing research about education* (pp. 27–42). London: Routledge.

Epstein, D., Elwood, J., Hey, V., & Maw, J. (1998). *Failing boys? Issues in gender and achievement*. Buckingham: Open University Press.

Epstein, D., & Johnson, R. (1998). *Schooling sexualities*. Philadelphia: Open University Press.

Epstein, D., Mendick, H., & Moreau, M.-P. (2010). Imagining the mathematician: Young people talking about popular representations of maths. *Discourse: Studies in the Cultural Politics of Education*, 31:1, 45–60.

Ericsson, K., & Charness, N. (1994). Expert performance: Its structure and acquisi-tion. *American Psychologist*, 49:8, 725–747.

Erikson, E. (1968). *Identity, youth and crisis*. New York: Norton.

European Parliament and Council. (1995). Directive 95/46/EC on the pro-tection of individuals with regard to the processing of personal data and on the free movement of such data. *Official Journal*, 281, 0031–0050. Retrieved June 7, 2007, from http://eur-lex.europa.eu/LexUriServ/LexUriServ.do?uri=CELEX:31995L0046:EN:HTML.

Eynon, R., Fry, J., & Schroeder, R. (2008). The ethics of Internet research. In N. Fielding, R. Lee, & G. Blank (Eds.), *The Sage handbook of online research methods* (pp. 23–41). London: Sage.

Eysenck, H. (1995). *Genius: The natural history of creativity*. Cambridge: Cambridge University Press.

Fancher, R. (No date). *The examined life: Competitive examinations in the thought of Francis Galton*. Retrieved June 26, 2010, from http://htpprints.yorku.ca/archive/00000130/00/THE_EXAMINED_LIFE.html.

Feasey, R. (2006). Why teen television? *Journal of Popular Film & Television*, 34:1, 2–9.

Feasey, R. (2009). Anxiety, helplessness and 'adultescence': Examining the appeal of teen drama for the young adult audience. *European Journal of Cultural Studies*, 12:4, 431–446.

Featherstone, B., Scourfield, J., & Hooper, C. A. (2010). *Gender and child welfare in society*. Oxford: Wiley Blackwell.

Feldhusen, J. F. (2004). Beyond general giftedness: New ways to identify and educate gifted, talented and precocious youth. In J. Borland (Ed.), *Rethinking gifted edu-cation* (pp. 10–34). London: Teachers' College Press.

Feldman, D. (2004). A developmental, evolutionary perspective on giftedness. In J. Borland (Ed.), *Rethinking gifted education* (pp. 9–33). London: Teachers' College Press.

Fennema, E., Peterson, P., Carpenter, T., & Lubinski, C. (1990). Teachers' attri-butions and beliefs about girls, boys, and mathematics. *Educational Studies in Mathematics*, 21:1, 55–69.

Finders, M. J. (1997). *Just girls: Hidden literacies and life in junior high*. New York: Teachers College Press.

Fine, C. (2008). Will working mothers' brains explode? The popular new genre of neurosexism. *Neuroethics*, 1:1, 69–72.

Fine, C. (2010). *Delusions of gender: The real science behind sex differences.* New York: Norton.

Fine, M., Burns, A., Torre, M., & Payne, Y. (2008). How class matters. In L. Weis (Ed.), *The way class works.* New York: Routledge.

Fischer, M., Lyon, S., & Zeitler, D. (2008). The Internet and the future of social science research. In N. Fielding, R. M. Lee, & G. Blank (Eds.), *The Sage handbook of online research methods* (pp. 519–537). London: Sage.

Fish, S. (1980). *Is there a text in this class? The authority of interpretive communities.* Cambridge, MA: Harvard University Press.

Fisherkeller, J. (1999). Learning about power and success: Young urban adolescents interpret TV culture. *Communication Review*, 3:3, 187–212.

Fisherkeller, J. (2002). *Growing up with television: Everyday learning among young adolescents.* Philadelphia: Temple University Press.

Fiske, J. (1987). *Television culture.* London: Methuen.

Fiske, J. (1992). The cultural economy of fandom. In L. Lewis (Ed.), *The adoring audience* (pp. 30–49). London: Routledge.

Flood, C. (2001). Schools fail boys too: Exposing the con of traditional masculinity. In H. Rousso & M. Wehmeyer (Eds.), *Double jeopardy: Addressing gender equity in special education* (pp. 207–236). New York: State University of Albany Press.

Florin, D., Callen, B., Mullen, S., & Kropp, J. (2007). Profiting from mega-trends. *Journal of Product & Brand Management*, 16:4, 220–225.

Foehr, U. (2006). *Media multitasking among American youth: Prevalence, predictors and pairings.* Menlo Park, CA: Kaiser Family Foundation.

Ford, D., Grantham, T., & Whiting G. (2008). Culturally and linguistically diverse students in gifted education: Recruitment and retention issues. *Exceptional Children*, 74:3, 289–306.

Foster, D. (2015). *Lean out.* London: Repeater.

Foucault, M. (1969). *The archaeology of knowledge* (Trans. A. Sheridan). London: Routledge.

Foucault, M. (1970). *The order of things* (Trans. Tavistock). London: Routledge.

Foucault, M. (1977). The fantasia of the library. In D. F. Bouchard & S. Simon (Eds.), *Michel Foucault: Language, counter-memory, practice: Selected essays and interviews.* Ithaca, NY: Cornell University Press.

Foucault, M. (1978). *The history of sexuality: An introduction* (Vol. 1). New York: Vintage Books.

Foucault, M. (1979). *Discipline and punish: The birth of the prison* (Trans. A. Sheridan). New York: Vintage.

Foucault, M. (1980). *Power/knowledge.* Brighton: Harvester Press.

Foucault, M. (1981). Questions of method. *I&C*, 8, 3–14.

Foucault, M. (1991). Politics and the study of discourse. In G. Burchell, C. Gordon, & P. Miller (Eds.), *The Foucault effect, studies in governmentality* (pp. 53–72). London: Harvester.

Foucault, M. (1993). About the beginning of the hermeneutics of the self. Transcription of two lectures in Dartmouth on November 17 and 24, 1980 (Ed. M. Blasius). *Political Theory*, 21:2, 198–227.

Foucault, M. (1994). An interview with Michel Foucault. In J. D. Faubion (Ed.), *Michel Foucault power* (Vol. 3, pp. 223–238). New York: New Press.

Foucault, M. (1997a). Friendship as a way of life. In P. Rabinow (Ed.), *Ethics, subjectivity and truth: Essential works of Foucault 1954–1984* (Vol. 1). Chicago: University of Chicago Press.

Foucault, M. (1997b). The birth of biopolitics. In P. Rabinow (Ed.), *Michel Foucault, ethics: Subjectivity and truth* (pp. 73–79). New York: New Press.

Foucault, M. (2003). *Abnormal. Lectures at the College de France 1974–1975* (Trans. Graham Burchell). London: Verso.

Francis, B. (2009). The role of the Boffin as abject other in gendered performances of school achievement. *The Sociological Review*, 57:4, 645–669.

Francis B., & Hey, V. (2009). Talking back to power: Snowballs in hell and the imperative of insisting on structural explanations. *Gender & Education*, 21:2, 225–232.

Francis, B., & Paechter, C. (2015). The problem of gender categorisation: Addressing dilemmas past and present in gender and education research. *Gender and Education*, 27:7, 776–790.

Francis, B., & Skelton, C. (2001). *Investigating gender: Contemporary perspectives in education*. Buckingham: Open University Press.

Francis, B., & Skelton, C. (2005). *Reassessing gender and achievement: Questioning contemporary key debates*. Abingdon: Routledge.

Francis, B., Skelton, C., & Read, B. (2010). The simultaneous production of educational achievement and popularity: How do some pupils accomplish it? *British Educational Research Journal*, 36:2, 317–340.

Frankenberg, R. (1993). *White women, race matters: The social construction of whiteness*. Minneapolis: University of Minnesota Press.

Fraser N. (1989). *Unruly practices: Power, discourse, and gender in contemporary social theory*. Minneapolis: University of Minnesota Press.

Freeman, J. (1974). *Gifted children*. London: David Fulton.

Freeman, J. (1991). *Gifted children growing up*. London: David Fulton.

Freeman, J. (1998). *Educating the very able*: *Current international research*. London: Stationery Office.

Freeman, J. (2001). *Gifted children grown up*. London: David Fulton.

Freeman, J. (2004). Cultural influences on gifted gender achievement. *High Ability Studies*, 15, 7–23.

Freeman, M., de Marrais, K., Preissle, J., Roulston, K., & St. Pierre, E. (2007). Standards of evidence in qualitative research: An incitement to discourse. *Educational Researcher*, 36:1, 25–32.

Friedman, M. (1962). *Capitalism and freedom* (40th anniv. ed., 2002). London: University of Chicago Press.

Furlong, A., & Cartmel, F. (1997). *Young people and social change*. Buckingham: Open University Press.

Gaiser, T. J. (2008). Online focus groups. In N. Fielding, R. M. Lee, & G. Blank (Eds.), *The Sage handbook of online research methods* (pp. 290–306). London: Sage.

Gallagher, J. (2005). Commentary on national security and educational excellence. *Education Week*, May 25.

Galton, F. (1869). *Hereditary genius: An inquiry into its laws and consequences* (2005 ed.). London: Adamant Media Corporation.

Galton, F., & Schuster, E. (1906). *Noteworthy families (modern science): An index to kinships in near degrees between persons whose achievements are honourable, and have been publicly recorded.* London: John Murray.

Gamber, F. (2009). Riding the third wave: The multiple feminisms of *Gilmore Girls*. In S. M. Ross & L. E. Stein (Eds.), *Teen television: Essays on programming and fandom* (pp. 114–131). London: McFarland.

Gauntlett, D. (1998). Ten things wrong with the 'effects' model. In R. Dickinson, R. Harindranath, & O. Linné (Eds.), *Approaches to audiences – A reader.* London: Arnold.

Gay, J. (2009). Dirty pretty things. *Rolling Stone.* Retrieved November 6, 2011, from http://www.rollingstone.com/tv/features/dirty-pretty-things-20090402.

Gemant, A. (1961). *The nature of the genius.* Springfield, IL: Charles C. Thomas. Ebook downloaded May 18, 2016, from https://archive.org/details/natureofgenius00gema.

Georgakopoulou, A. (2014). 'Girlpower or girl (in) trouble?' Identities and discourses in the (new) media engagements of adolescents' school-based interaction. In J. Androutsopoulos (Ed.), *Mediatization and sociolinguistic change* (Linguae & Litterae 36, pp. 217–236). Berlin: Mouton de Gruyter.

George, R. P. (2007). *Girls in a goldfish bowl: Moral regulation, ritual and the use of power amongst inner city girls.* Rotterdam: Sense Publishers.

Gerbner, G., Gross, L., Morgan, M., & Signoielli, N. (1994). Growing up with television: The cultivation perspective. In B. Jennings & D. Zillman (Eds.), *Media effects: Advances in theory and research* (pp. 17–41). Hilldale, NJ: Lawrence Erlbaum.

Giddens, A. (1991). *Modernity and self-identity: Self and society in the late modern age.* Cambridge, UK: Polity Press.

Gilbert, L. S. (2002). Going the distance: 'Closeness' in qualitative data analysis software. *International Journal of Social Research Methodology,* 5:3, 215–228.

Gilbert, S., & Gubar, S. (1979). *The madwoman in the attic.* New Haven, CT: Yale University Press.

Gill, R. (2007a). Postfeminist media culture: Elements of a sensibility. *European Journal of Cultural Studies,* 10:2, 147–166.

Gill, R. (2007b). Critical respect: The difficulties and dilemmas of agency and 'choice' for feminism. *European Journal of Women's Studies,* 14:1, 69–80.

Gill, R. (2008). Empowerment/sexism: Figuring female sexual agency in contemporary advertising. *Feminism & Psychology,* 18, 35–60.

Gillborn, D. (2005). Education policy as an act of white supremacy: Whiteness, critical race theory & education reform. *Journal of Education Policy,* 20:4, 485–505.

Gillborn, D. (2006). Memorandum submitted to the House of Commons Select Committee on Education and Skills. Retrieved June 22, 2010, from http://www.publications.parliament.uk/pa/cm200506/cmselect/cmeduski/633/633we09.htm.

Gillborn, D. (2008). *Racism and education: Coincidence or conspiracy?* Abingdon: Routledge.

Gillborn, D., & Mirza, H. (2000). *Educational inequality: Mapping race, class and gender.* London: Office for Standards in Education, Children's Services and Skills.

Gillborn, D., & Youdell, D. (2000). *Rationing education: Policy, practice, reform and equity.* Buckingham: Open University Press.

Gilligan, C. (1982). *In a different voice: Psychological theory and women's development*. London: Harvard.

Giroux, H. (1994). Slacking off: Border youth and postmodern education. *Journal of Advanced Composition*, 14:2, 347–366.

Giroux, H. (2002). The war on the young: Corporate culture, schooling, and the politics of 'zero tolerance'. In R. Strickland (Ed.), *Growing up postmodern: Neoliberalism and the war on the young* (pp. 35–46) Lanham, MD: Rowman & Littlefield.

Giroux, H. (2005). Youth, higher education, and the crisis of public time: Educated hope and the possibility of a democratic future. *Social Identities*, 23, 89–101.

Giroux, H. (2009). *Youth in a suspect society: Democracy or disposability?* New York: Palgrave Macmillan.

Goertzel, V., & Goertzel, M. (1962). *Cradles of eminence*. Boston: Little Brown & Co.

Goldberg, D. (1993). *Racist culture: Philosophy and the politics of meaning*. Oxford: Blackwell.

Golden, S. (1998). *Slaying the mermaid: Women and the culture of sacrifice*. New York: Harmony Books.

Golden, S. (2001). *The benefits and challenges of excellence in cities: Teachers' views*. National Foundation for Educational Research. Retrieved May 18, 2016, from http://webarchive.nationalarchives.gov.uk/20130401151715/http://www.education.gov.uk/publications/eOrderingDownload/022001.pdf.

Goldthorpe, J., & Jackson, M. (2008). Education-based meritocracy: The barriers to its realisation. In A. Lareau & D. Conley (Eds.), *Social class: How does it work?* (pp. 93–117). New York: Russell Sage Foundation.

Goldthorpe, J. H. (1996). Class analysis and the reorientation of class theory: The case of persisting differentials in educational attainment. *British Journal of Sociology*, 47:3, 481–505.

Gonick, M. (2003). *Between femininities: Ambivalence, identity, and the education of girls*. New York: State University of New York.

Gonick, M. (2004). The mean girl crisis: Problematizing representations of girls' friendships. *Feminism & Psychology*, 14, 395–400.

Gonick, M. (2005). From nerd to popular? Re-figuring school identities and transformation stories. In C. Mitchell & J. Reid-Walsh (Eds.), *Seven going on seventeen: Tween studies in the culture of girlhood* (pp. 46–62). New York: Peter Lang.

Gonick, M. (2006). Between girl power and reviving Ophelia: Constituting the neo-liberal girl subject. *National Women's Studies Association Journal*, 18:2, 1–23.

Gonick, M., Renold, E., Ringrose, J., & Weems. L. (2010). "Brains before 'beauty'?" High achieving girls, school and gender identities. *Educational Studies*, 36:2, 185–194.

Graham, L. (2005). Discourse analysis and the critical use of Foucault. Paper presented at Australian Association for Research in Education 2005 Annual Conference, Sydney, November 27–December 1.

Greer, G. (1979). *The obstacle race: The fortunes of women painters and their work*. London: Secker & Warburg.

Grunewald, D. (2003). The best of both worlds: A critical pedagogy of place. *Educational Researcher*, 32:4, 3–12. Retrieved September 12, 2010, from http://faculty.washington.edu/joyann/EDLSP549Beadie_Williamson/gruenewald.pdf.

Gurak, L. (1997). *Persuasion and privacy in cyberspace: The online protests over Lotus MarketPlace and the Clipper chip*. New Haven, CT: Yale University Press.

Gust-Brey, K., & Cross, T. (1999). An examination of the literature base on the suicidal behaviors of gifted students. *Roeper Review*, 22, 28–35.

Gutting, G. (1989). *Michel Foucault's archaeology of scientific reason: Science and the history of reason*. Cambridge: Cambridge University Press.

Guzzetti, B. (2006). Cybergirls: Negotiating social identities on cybersites. *E-Learning*, 3:2, 158–169.

Ha, L. (2002). Enhanced television strategy models: A study of TV web sites. *Internet Research*, 12:3, 235–247.

Hagaman, S. (1990). Feminist inquiry in art history, art criticism, and aesthetics: An overview for art education. *Studies in Art Education*, 32:1, 27–35.

Halberstam, J. (1998). *Female masculinities*. Durham, NC: Duke University Press.

Hall, S. (1990). Cultural identity and diaspora. In J. Rutherford (Ed.), *Identity, community, culture, difference* (pp. 222–38). London: Lawrence & Wishart.

Hall, S. (2011). The neoliberal revolution. *Cultural Studies*, 25:6, 705–728.

Halsey, A., Lauder, H., Brown, P., & Wells, A. (2004). *Education: Culture, economy, and society*. Oxford: Oxford University Press.

Hamachek, D. (1978). Psychodynamics of normal and neurotic perfectionism. *Psychology: A Journal of Human Behavior*, 15, 27–33.

Hamann, T. (2009). Neoliberalism governmentality, and ethics. *Foucault Studies*, 6, 37–59.

Hargittai, E. (2010). Digital Na(t)ives? Variation in Internet skills and uses among members of the "net generation". *Sociological Inquiry*, 80:1, 92–113.

Hargittai, H., & Hinnant, A. (2008). Digital inequality: Differences in young adults' use of the Internet. *Communication Research*, 35, 602–621.

Harris, A. (2004). *Future girl: Young women in the twenty-first century*. Abingdon: Routledge.

Harris, A. (2008). Young women, late modern politics, and the participatory possibilities of online cultures. *Journal of Youth Studies*, 11:5, 481–495.

Harris, A. (2015). Discourses of desire as governmentality: Young women, sexuality and the significance of safe spaces. *Feminism and Psychology*, 15:1, 39–43.

Hart, K., & Kenny, M. (1997). Adherence to the super woman ideal and eating disorder symptoms among college women. *Sex Roles Journal*, 36:7/8, 461–478.

Hartley, J. (2009). Less popular but more democratic? Corrie, Clarkson and the Dancing Cru. In G. Turner & J. Tay (Eds.), *Television studies after TV: Understanding television in the post- broadcast era* (pp. 20–30). Abingdon: Routledge.

Harvey, D. (2005). *A brief history of neoliberalism*. Oxford: Oxford University Press.

Hasinoff, A. (2009). It's sociobiology, hon! Genetic gender determinism in *Cosmopolitan* magazine. *Feminist Media Studies*, 9:3, 267–283.

Hayes, C. (2006). Veronica Mars, class warrior. *In These Times*. Retrieved February 7, 2012, from http://www.inthesetimes.com/article/2671/.

Hayward, K., & Yar, M. (2006). The 'chav' phenomenon: Consumption, media and the construction of a new underclass. *Crime, Media, Culture*, 2, 9–28.

Heath, S. (2007). Widening the gap: Pre-university gap years and the 'economy of experience'. *British Journal of Sociology of Education*, 28:1, 89–103.

Hebdige, D. (1979). *Subculture: The meaning of style*. London: Routledge.

Helford, E. (2000). *Fantasy girls: Gender in the new universe of science fiction and fantasy television*. New York: Rowan & Littlefield.

Helsper, E. (2010). Gendered Internet use across generations and life stages. *Communication Research*, 37:3, 352–374.

Hemingway, A. (1992). Genius, gender and progress: Benthamism and the arts in the 1820s. *Art History*, 16, 619–646.

Herring, S. C. (2004). Slouching toward the ordinary: Current trends in computer-mediated communication. *New Media & Society*, 6:1, 26–36.

Herring, S. C., & Martinson, A. (2004). Assessing gender authenticity in computer-mediated language use. *Journal of Language and Social Psychology*, 23:4, 424–446.

HESA (Higher Education Statistics Agency). Higher education statistics for the UK 1996–97. Retrieved December 4, 2010, from http://www.hesa.ac.uk/dox/pubs_archive/student_1996–97_table_1b.pdf.

Hey, V. (1997). *The company she keeps: An ethnography of girls' friendships.* Buckingham: Open University Press.

Hey, V. (2003). Joining the club? Academia and working-class femininities. *Gender and Education*, 15:3, 319–335.

Hey, V. (2010). Framing girls in girlhood studies: Gender/class/ifications in contemporary feminist representations. In C. Jackson, C. Paechter, & E. Renold (Eds.), *Girls and education 3–16: Continuing concerns, new agendas* (pp. 210–222). Maidenhead: Open University Press.

Hill, D. (2003). Global neo-liberalism, the deformation of education and resistance. *Journal for Critical Education Policy Studies*, 1:1, 1–29.

Hill, D. (2006). Class, neoliberal global capital, education and resistance. *Social Change*, 36:3.

Hills, M. (2005a). *The pleasures of horror.* London: Continuum.

Hills, M. (2005b). Cult TV, quality and the role of the episode/programme guide. In M. Hammond & L. Mazdon (Eds.), *The contemporary television series* (pp. 190–206). Edinburgh: Edinburgh University Press.

Hine, C. (2000). *Virtual ethnography.* London: Sage.

Hine, C. (2008). *Virtual ethnography: Modes, varieties, affordances.* In N. Fielding, R. M. Lee, & G. Blank (Eds.), *The Sage handbook of online research methods* (pp. 257–270). London: Sage.

Hine, C. (2009). Defining the boundaries. In A. Markham & N. Baym (Eds.), *Internet enquiry: Conversations about method* (pp. 1–20). London: Sage.

Hollows, J., & Moseley, R. (2006). Popularity contests: The meaning of popular feminism. In J. Hollows & R. Moseley (Eds.), *Feminism in popular culture.* Oxford: Berg.

hooks, b. (2013). Dig deep: Beyond *Lean In. The Feminist Wire.* Retrieved February 8, 2015, from http://.thefeministwire.com/2013/10/17973/.

Hoskins, D. (2006). Roses, doctors, lovers and gods: Russell T Davies' year on Australian TV. *Metro Magazine*, 148, 85–90.

House of Commons. (1999). *Select committee report on highly able children 1998–9.* London: Her Majesty's Stationery Office.

House of Commons. (2006). *Select Committee on Education and Skills First Report* (personalised learning). Retrieved May 18, 2007, from http://www.publications.parliament.uk/pa/cm200506/cmselect/cmeduski/633/63306.htm#n32.

House of Commons. (2010). *Children, Schools and Families Committee: Gifted and talented programme oral and written evidence.* February 1, Q.10. London: Her Majesty's Stationery Office.

Howe, M. (1982). Biographical evidence and the development of outstanding individuals. *American Psychologist*, 37, 1071–1081.

Huffaker, D., & Calvert, S. (2005). Gender, identity, and language use in teenage blogs. *Journal of Computer-Mediated Communication*, 10:2, Article 1. Retrieved November 16, 2010, from http://jcmc.indiana.edu/vol10/issue2/huffaker.html.

Hughes, L. A. (1988). "But that's not really mean": Competing in a cooperative mode. *Sex Roles*, 19, 669–687.

Hughes, S. (2009). Supergirl meltdown: How middle-class girls today are under unprecedented pressure to succeed. *Daily Mail*, October 19. Retrieved June 10, 2010, from http://www.dailymail.co.uk/femail/article-1221344/Supergirl-meltdown-How-middle-class-girls-today-unprecedented-pressure-succeed.html#ixzz2JY2k7tSE.

Hutchings, M., & Archer, L. (2001). 'Higher than Einstein': Constructions of going to university among working-class non-participants. *Research Papers in Education*, 16:1, 69–91.

Independent. (1996). Girls leave the boys trailing in GCSEs. Retrieved July 13, 2009, from http://www.independent.co.uk/news/girls-leave-the-boys-trailing-in-gcses-1312224.html.

Independent. (2015). J K Rowling, we all know you didn't write Hermione as black in the Harry Potter books – but it doesn't matter. Retrieved May 24, 2016, from http://www.independent.co.uk/voices/j-k-rowling-we-all-know-you-didnt-write-hermione-as-black-in-the-harry-potter-books-but-it-doesnt-a6781681.html.

Inness, S. (Ed.). (2008). *Geek chic: Smart women in popular culture*. Basingstoke: Palgrave Macmillan.

IMDB (Internet Movie Database). Retrieved February 12, 2012, from http://www.imdb.com/.

Ito, M., Davidson, C., Jenkins, H., Lee, C., Eisenberg, M., & Weiss, J. (2008). Foreword. In D. Buckingham (Ed.), *Youth, identity, and digital media* (pp. vii–ix). John D. & Catherine T. MacArthur Foundation Series on Digital Media and Learning. Cambridge, MA: MIT Press.

Jackson, C. (2003). Transitions into higher education: Gendered implications for academic self-concept. *Oxford Review of Education*, 29:3, 331–346.

Jackson, C. (2006). *Lads and ladettes in school: Gender and a fear of failure*. Maidenhead: Open University Press.

Jackson, C., & Nyström, A. S. (2015). 'Smart students get perfect scores in tests without studying much': Why is an effortless achiever identity attractive, and for whom is it possible? *Research Papers in Education*, 30:4, 393–410.

Jagodzinski, J. (2008). *Television and youth culture: Televised paranoia*. Basingstoke: Palgrave Macmillan.

James, A. N. (2009). *Teaching the female brain: How girls learn math and science*. Thousand Oaks, CA: Corwin Press.

Jay, N. (1981). Gender and dichotomy, *Feminist Studies* 7:1, 38–56.

Jenkins, H. (2006). *Convergence culture: Where old and new media collide*. New York: New York University Press.

Jensen, K. (2002a). Media reception: Qualitative traditions. In K. Jensen (Ed.), *A handbook of qualitative communication research* (pp. 156–170). London: Routledge.

Jensen, K. (2002b). The qualitative research process. In K. Jensen (Ed.), *A handbook of qualitative communication research* (pp. 235–253). London: Routledge.

Jesson, D. (2006). Comprehensives. *Education Journal*, 93, 35–55.

Jiwani, Y., Steenbergen, C., & Mitchell, C. (2006). *Girlhood: Redefining the limits.* Montreal: Black Rose Books.

John, W., & Johnson, P. (2000). The pros and cons of data analysis software for qualitative research. *Journal of Nursing Scholarship,* 32:4, 393–397.

Johnson, L. (1993). *The modern girl: Girlhood and growing up.* Buckingham: Open University Press.

Jones, O. (2011). *Chavs: The demonization of the working class.* London: Verso.

Jones, S., & Myhill, D. (2004). 'Troublesome boys' and 'compliant girls': Gender identity and perceptions of achievement and underachievement. *British Journal of Sociology of Education,* 25:5, 547–561.

Jordan-Young, R. M. (2010). *Brain storm: The flaws in the science of sex differences.* Cambridge, MA: Harvard University Press.

Jowett, L. (2005). *Sex and the slayer: A gender studies primer for the Buffy fan.* Middletown, CT: Wesleyan University Press.

Kant, I. (1790). *Observations on the feeling of the beautiful and sublime* (Trans. J. T. Goldthwait, 2003 ed.). Berkeley: University of California Press.

Keaney, E. (2009). *The digital world: A review of the evidence.* The Arts Council, England. Retrieved February 12, 2009, from http://acestage.preloading.co.uk/media/uploads/downloads/evidencereview.pdf.

Kehily, M. J. (2008). Taking centre stage? Girlhood and the contradictions of femininity across three generations. *Girlhood Studies,* 1:2, 51–71.

Kehily, M. J., & Nayak, A. (2008). *Lads, chavs and pram-face girls: Embodiment and emotion in working-class youth cultures.* Paper presented at Emotional Geographies of Education Symposium, Institute of Education, University of London, November 6.

Keller, J. (2015). *Girls' feminist blogging in a postfeminist age.* Abingdon: Routledge.

Kelley, M. (2008). The needs of their genius. *Journal of the Early Republic,* 28, 1–22.

Kellner D. (1999). Aesthetics and popular culture. *Journal of Aesthetics and Art Criticism,* 57:2, 161–175.

Kellner, D. (2004). *Buffy the Vampire Slayer* as spectacular allegory: A diagnostic critique. In S. Steinberg & J. Kincheloe (Eds.), *Kinderculture: The corporate construction of childhood.* Cambridge, MA: Westview Press.

Kelly, D., & Pomerantz, S. (2009). Mean, wild and alienated: Girls and the state of feminism in popular culture. *Girlhood Studies,* 2.1, 1–19.

Kelly, D., Pomerantz, S., & Currie, D. (2006). "No boundaries"? Girls interactive online learning about femininities. *Youth & Society,* 38:1, 3–27.

Kelly, P. (2009). *The risk society and young people: Life @ the intersection of risk, economy and illiberal governmentalities.* Behavioural Studies Working Paper, Series 2. Retrieved May 15, 2011, from http://arts.monash.edu.au/behaviour/working-papers/documents/bhs-working-paper-2009–02-kelly.pdf.

Kendall, G., & Wickham, G. (1999). *Using Foucault's methods.* London: Sage.

Kerr, B. (1997). *Smart girls: A new psychology of girls, women and giftedness.* Scottsdale, AZ: Gifted Psychology Press.

Kerr, B., & Kurpius, S. (1999). Brynhilde's fire: Talent, risk, and betrayal in the lives of gifted girls. *Australasian Journal of Gifted Education,* 7:2, 5–9.

Kerr, C. (1991). Is education really all that guilty? *EdWeek,* 10:23, 30.

Kimble Wrye, H. (2006). Deconstructing the unconscious saboteur: Composing a life with ambition and desire. *International Forum of Psychoanalysis,* 15, 70–80.

Kindlon, D. (2006). *Alpha girls: Understanding the new American girl and how she is changing the world.* New York: Rodale.

Kinnick, K., & Parton, S. (2005). Workplace communication: What the apprentice teaches about communication skills. *Business Communication Quarterly, 68,* 429–456.

Kivy, P. (2001). *The possessor and the possessed: Handel, Mozart, Beethoven and idea of musical genius.* New Haven, CT: Yale University Press.

Koffman, O., & Gill, R. (2013). The revolution will be led by a 12 year old girl: Girl power and the global biopolitics of girlhood. *Feminist Review, 105,* 83–102.

Kohlberg, L. (1963). The development of children's orientations toward a moral order. I. Sequence in the development of moral thought. *Vita Humana, 6,* 11–33.

Kohlberg, L. (1973). *Collected papers on moral development and moral education.* Cambridge: Moral Education and Research Foundation.

Kopald, S. (1924). Where are the women geniuses? In Freda Kirchwey (Ed.), *Our changing morality* (pp. 619–622) New York: Nation.

Kraus, W. (1996). *The self told: The narrative construction of identity in late modernity.* Pfaffenweiler: Centaurus.

Kraus, W. (2006). The narrative negotiation of identity and belonging. *Narrative Inquiry,* 16:1, 103–111.

Krippendorff, K. (1989). On the ethics of constructing communication. In B. Dervin, L. Grossberg, B. O'Keefe, & E. Vartella (Eds.), *Rethinking communication: Paradigm issues* (pp. 66–96). Newbury Park, CA: Sage.

Kristeva, J. (1982). *Powers of horror: An essay on abjection.* New York: Columbia University Press.

Labov, W. (1972). *Sociolinguistic patterns.* Philadelphia: University of Pennsylvania Press.

Lacey, N. (2000). *Narrative and genre. Key concepts in media studies.* New York: St. Martin's Press.

Larsen, P. (2002). Mediated fiction. In K. Jensen (Ed.), *A handbook of qualitative communication research* (pp. 117–137). London: Routledge.

Le Doeuff, M. (2003). *The sex of knowing* (Trans. K. Hamer & L. Code). London: Routledge.

Lee, L. (2008). The impact of young people's Internet use on class boundaries and life trajectories. *Sociology,* 42:137, 137–153.

Lendall, L. (2009). Defining the boundaries: A response to Christine Hine. In A. Markham & N. Baym (Eds.), *Internet enquiry: Conversations about method* (pp. 21–25). London: Sage.

Lenhart, A. (2015). *Teens, social media & technology overview.* Pew Research Centre. Retrieved September 22, 2015, from http://www.pewinternet.org/2015/04/09/teens-social-media-technology-2015/.

Lenhart A., Purcell, K., Smith, A., & Zickuhr, K. (2010). *Social media and mobile Internet use among young adults.* Washington, DC: Pew Internet and American Life Project.

Lenhart, A., Rainie, L., & Lewis, O. (2001). *Teenage life online: The rise of the instant-message generation and the Internet's impact on friendships and family relationships.* Washington, DC: Pew Internet and American Life Project.

Leroux, J. (1998). Follow your dream: Gifted women and the cost of success. *Gifted Educational International,* 13:1, 4–13.

Levin, H., & Kelley, C. (1994). Can education do it alone? In A. H. Halsey, H. Lauder, P. Brown, & A. Wells (Eds.), *Education: Culture, economy, and society* (pp. 240–250) Oxford: Oxford University Press.

Lister, M., Dovey, J., Giddings, S., Grant, I., & Kelly, K. (2009). *New media: A critical introduction* (2nd ed.). London: Routledge.

Litosseliti, L. (2003). *Using focus groups in research*. London: Continuum.

Livingstone, S. (1998). Audience research at the crossroads: The 'implied audience' in media and cultural theory. *European Journal of Cultural Studies*, 1:2, 193–217.

Livingstone, S. (2004). The challenge of changing audiences: Or, what is the audience researcher to do in the age of the Internet? *European Journal of Communication*, 19:1, 75–86.

Livingstone, S. (2007). Strategies of parental regulation in the media rich home. *Computers in Human Behaviour*, 23:2, 920–921.

Livingstone, S. (2008). Taking risky opportunities in youthful content creation: Teenagers' use of social networking sites for intimacy, privacy and self-expression. *New Media & Society*, 10:3, 393–411.

Livingstone, S. (2009). Half a century of television in the lives of our children. *Annals of the American Academy of Political and Social Science*, 62:5, 151–163.

Livingstone, S. (2010). Balancing opportunities and risks in teenagers' use of the Internet: The role of online skills and Internet self-efficacy. *New Media & Society*, 12:2, 309–329.

Livingstone, S., & Helsper, E. (2007). Gradations in digital inclusion: Children, young people and the digital divide. *New Media Society*, 9, 671–696.

Lloyd, G. (1979). The man of reason. *Metaphilosophy*, 10, 18–37.

Loader, B., & Keeble, L. (2004). *Challenging the digital divide? A literature review of community informatics initiatives*. York: Joseph Rowntree Foundation.

Lobe, B., Livingstone, S., Olafsson, K., & Simões, J. (2008). *Best practice research guide: How to research children and online technologies in comparative perspective*. London: EU Kids Online (Deliverable D4.2). Retrieved September 17, 2008, from http://eprints.lse.ac.uk/21658/.

Lomborg, S. (2014). *Social media, social genres: Making sense of the ordinary*: Abingdon: Routledge.

Longinus. (1890). *On the sublime* (Trans. H. L. Havell). London: Macmillan. Project Gutenberg online text. Retrieved April 21, 2010, from http://www.gutenberg.org/files/17957/17957-h/17957-h.htm.

Lotz, A., & Ross, M. (2004). Towards ethical cyberspace audience research: Strategies for using the Internet for television audience studies. *Journal of Broadcasting of Electronic Media*, 48:3, 501–512.

Lotz, R. (1991). *Crime and the American press*. Westport, CT: Praeger.

Lucey, H., Melody, J., & Walkerdine, V. (2003). Uneasy hybrids: Psychosocial aspects of becoming educationally successful for working-class young women. *Gender and Education*, 15:3, 288–299.

Lunsford, A., & Ede, L. (1990). Rhetoric in a new key: Women and collaboration. *Rhetoric Review*, 8:2, 234–241.

Mac An Ghaill, M. (1994). *The making of men: Masculinities, sexualities and schooling*. Buckingham: Open University Press.

Macherey, P. (1978). *A theory of literary production* (Trans. G. Wall). London: Routledge & Kegan Paul.

MacMillan, K. (2005). More than just coding? Evaluating CAQDAS in a discourse analysis of news texts. *FQS: Forum: Qualitative Social Research*, 6:3, 1–18. Retrieved February 17, 2011, from http://www.qualitative-research.net/index.php/fqs/article/view/28/60.

MacMillan, K., & Koenig, T. (2004). The wow factor: Preconceptions and expectations for data analysis software in qualitative research. *Social Science Computer Review*, 22:2, 179–186.

Maguire, E. (2016). Self-branding, hotness, and girlhood in the video blogs of Jenna Marbles. *Biography* 38.1, 72–86. Project MUSE. Retrieved January 19, 2016, from https://muse.jhu.edu/.

Mahony, P. (1985). *Schools for the boys? Co-education reassessed*. London: Hutchinson.

Mahony, P., Epstein, D., Elwood, J., Hey, V., & Maw, J. (Eds.). (1998). *Girls will be girls and boys will be first. Failing boys? Issues in gender and achievement*. Buckingham: Open University Press.

Mailloux, S. (2000). Disciplinary identities: On the rhetorical paths between English and communication studies. *Rhetoric Society Quarterly*, 20, 5–30.

Maker, C. (1996). Identification of gifted minority students: A national problem, needed changes and a promising solution. *Gifted Child Quarterly*, 40, 41–50.

Manago, A., Graham, M., Greenfield, P., & Salimkhan, G. (2008). Self-presentation and gender on MySpace. *Journal of Applied Developmental Psychology*, 29:6, 446–458.

Mann, C., & Stewart, F. (2000). *Internet Communication and Qualitative Research*. London: Sage.

Markham, A. (2005). The politics, ethics, and methods of representation in online ethnography. In N. Denzin & Y. Lincoln (Eds.), *Handbook of Qualitative Research* (3rd ed., pp. 793–820). Thousand Oaks, CA: Sage.

Markham, A., & Baym, N. (2009). *Internet Enquiry: Conversations About Method*. London: Sage.

Martin, B. (1982). Feminism, criticism, and Foucault. *New German Critique*, 27, 3–30.

Marwick, A. (1974). *War and Social Change in the Twentieth Century*. Houndsmill: Macmillan.

Mascheroni, G., Vincent, J., & Jimenez, E. (2015). 'Girls are addicted to likes so they post semi-naked selfies': Peer mediation, normativity and the construction of identity online. *Cyberpsychology: Journal of Psychosocial Research on Cyberspace*, 9:1, DOI: 10.5817/CP2015-1-5.

Maxwell, C., & Aggleton, P. (2014). Agentic practice and privileging orientations among privately educated young women. *Sociological Review* 62:4, 800–820.

Mazzarella, S. (2005). *Girl wide web: Girls, the Internet, and the negotiation of identity*. New York: Peter Lang.

Mazzarella, S., & Pecora, N. (2007). Revisiting girls' studies: Girls creating sites for connection and action. *Journal of Children and Media*, 1:2, 105–125.

McArthur, J. (2009). Digital subculture: A geek meaning of style. *Journal of Communication Inquiry*, 33:1, 58–70.

McAven, E. (2007). 'I think I'm kinda gay': Willow Rosenberg and the absent/present bisexual in *Buffy the Vampire Slayer*. *Slayage* 6.4 [24]; Retrieved February 2, 2011, from http://davidlavery.net/Slayage/PDF/McAvan.pdf.

McCabe, J. (2005). Creating 'quality' audiences for *ER* on channel 4. In M. Hammond & L. Mazdon (Eds.), *The contemporary television series* (pp. 207–223). Edinburgh: Edinburgh University Press.

McDowell, L. (1997). *Capital culture: Gender and work in the city*. Oxford: Blackwell.

McDowell, L. (2012). Post-crisis, post-Ford and post-gender? Youth identities in an era of austerity. *Journal of Youth Studies*, 15:5, 573–590.

McGiveny, V. (1996). *Staying or leaving the course: Non-completion and retention of mature students in further and higher education*. Leicester: National Institute of Adult Continuing Education.

McKinley, E. (1997). *Beverly Hills, 90210: Television, gender, and identity*. Philadelphia: University of Pennsylvania Press.

McLaren, M. (2002). *Feminism, Foucault and embodied subjectivity*. Albany: State University of New York Press.

McLuhan, M. (1964). *Understanding media: The extensions of man*. New York: McGraw Hill.

McNay, L. (1992). *Foucault and feminism*. Cambridge: Polity Press.

McNay, L. (2003). Having it both ways: The incompatibility of narrative identity and communicative ethics in feminist thought. *Theory, Culture and Society*, 20:6, 1–20.

McRobbie, A. (1978). Working class girls and the culture of femininity. In *Centre for Contemporary Cultural Studies: Women take issue* (pp. 96–108). London: Hutchinson.

McRobbie, A. (1991). *Feminism and youth culture*. Basingstoke: Macmillan.

McRobbie, A. (2000). *Feminism and youth culture*. London: Routledge.

McRobbie, A. (2003). *Postmodernism and popular culture*. London: Routledge.

McRobbie, A. (2004). Post-feminism and popular culture. *Feminist Media Studies*, 4.3, 255–264.

McRobbie, A. (2007). Top girls? Young women and the post-feminist sexual contract. *Cultural Studies*, 21:4, 718–737.

McRobbie, A. (2009). *The aftermath of feminism: Gender, culture and social change*. London: Sage.

McRobbie, A. (2011). *Top girls? Young women and the sexual contract*. Lecture for the Harriet Taylor Mill-Institute for Economic and Gender Research at the Berlin School of Economics and Law. April 8. Retrieved January 14, 2012, from http://www.harriet-taylor-mill.de/pdfs/HTMl_Lecture_McRobbie.pdf.

McRobbie, A. (2015). Notes on the perfect: Competitive femininity in neoliberal times. *Australian Feminist Studies*, 30:83, 2–20.

McRobbie, A., & Garber, J. (1976). Girls and subcultures. In S. Hall & T. Jefferson (Eds.), *Resistance through rituals*. London: Hutchinson.

Meehan, E. R. (2002). Gendering the commodity audience: Critical media research, feminism, and political economy. In E. R. Meehan & E. Riordan (Eds.), *Sex & money: Feminism and political economy in the media*. Minneapolis: University of Minnesota Press.

Mendick, H. (2005). A beautiful myth? The gendering of being/doing 'good at maths'. *Gender and Education*, 17:2, 203–219.

Mendick, H., Allen, K., & Harvey, L. (2015). 'We can get everything we want if we try hard': Young people, celebrity, hard work. *British Journal of Educational Studies*, 63:2, 161–178.

Mendick, H., Epstein, D., & Moreau, M. (2008). Mathematical images and identities: Education, entertainment, social justice. Full Research Report ESRC End
of Award Report, RES-000-23-1454. Swindon: Economic and Social Research
Council.

Mendick, H., & Francis, B. (2011). Boffin and geek identities: Abject or privileged?
Gender and Education, 24:1, 15–24.

Mendick, H., & Moreau, M.-P. (2010). Monitoring the presence and representation
of women in SET occupations in UK based online media. Project report. Bradford:
UK Resource Centre for Women in SET.

Merchant, G. (2006). Identity, social networks and online communication. *E-Learning
and Digital Media*, 3:2, 235–244.

Merrick, H. (1997). The readers feminism doesn't see: Feminist fans, critics, and
science fiction. In D. Buckingham (Ed.), *Reading audiences: Young people and the
media* (pp. 48–65). Manchester: Manchester University Press.

Merskin, D. (2007). *Joining forces: Teen girl witches and Internet chat groups*. Paper
presented at the annual meeting of the International Communication Association,
San Francisco, CA. Retrieved October 14, 2010, from http://www.allacademic.
com/meta/p171306_index.html.

Merten, D. E. (1997). The meaning of meanness: Popularity, competition, and conflict among junior high school girls. *Sociology of Education*, 70:3, 175–191.

Michelle, C. (2007). Modes of reception: A consolidated analytical framework.
Communication Review, 10, 181–222.

MidYIS (Middle Years Information System). Retrieved August 7, 2008, from http://
www.cem.org/secondary.

Miller, L. (2000). *The Bronte myth*. London: Jonathon Cape.

Mills, S. (1995). Discontinuity and postcolonial discourse. *ARIEL: A Review of
International English Literature*, 26:3, 73–88.

Mills, S. (1997). *Discourse*. Abingdon: Routledge.

Mills, S. (2003). *Michel Foucault*. Abingdon: Routledge.

Mittell, J. (2003). Television talk shows and cultural hierarchies. *Journal of Popular
Film and Television*, 31:11, 6–46.

Mittell, J. (2004). *Genre and television: From cop shows to cartoons in American
culture*. London: Routledge.

Mizejewski, L. (1993). Picturing the female dick: The *Silence of the Lambs* and *Blue
Steel*. *Journal of Film & Video*, 45:2/3, 6–23.

Moers, E. (1976). *Literary women*. Oxford: Oxford University Press.

Mohamed, S. (2008). Economic policy, globalization and the labour movement:
Changes in the global economy from the golden age to the neoliberal era. Global
Labour University Working Paper No. 1.

Moi, T. (1985). *Sexual textual politics*. Abingdon: Routledge.

Montgomery, D. (2000). *Able underachievers*. London: Whurr.

Montgomery, K. (2008). Youth and digital democracy: Intersections of practice, policy, and the marketplace. In W. Lance Bennett (Ed.), *Civic life online: Learning how
digital media can engage youth* (pp. 25–50.). John D. & Catherine T. MacArthur
Foundation Series on Digital Media and Learning. Cambridge, MA: MIT Press.

Moody, A. (2001). A case-study of the predictive validity and reliability of key stage
2 test results, and teacher assessments, as baseline data for target-setting and
value-added at key stage 3. *Curriculum Journal*, 12:1, 81–101.

Moreau, M.-P., Mendick, H., & Epstein, D. (2010). Constructions of mathematicians in popular culture and learners' narratives: A study of mathematical and nonmathematical subjectivities. *Cambridge Journal of Education*, 40:1, 25–38.

Morley, D. (1992). *Television audiences and cultural studies*. London: Routledge.

Morley, D. (2006). Unanswered questions in audience research. *Communication Review*, 9, 101–121.

Morse, J. (1999). Qualitative generalizability. *Qualitative Health Research*, 9, 5–6.

Moyo, L. (2008). The digital divide: Scarcity, inequality and conflict. In G. Creeber & R. Martin (Eds.), *Digital culture: Understanding new media* (pp. 122–130). Milton Keynes: Open University Press.

Mullan, B. (1997). *Consuming television: Television and its audience*. Oxford: Blackwell.

Murdoch, S. (2009). *How psychology hijacked intelligence*. London: Duckworth Overlook.

Murray, S. (1999). Saving our so-called lives: Girl fandom, adolescent subjectivity and *My So-Called Life*. In M. Kinder (Ed.), *Kids' media culture* (pp. 221–38). Durham, NC: Duke University Press.

Nayak, A. (2006). Displaced masculinities: Chavs, youth and class in the post-industrial city. *Sociology*, 40, 813–831.

Nayak, A., & Kehily, M. (2008). *Gender, youth and culture: Young masculinities and femininities*. Basingstoke: Palgrave Macmillan.

Neall, L. (2002). *Bringing out the best in boys*. Gloucester: Hawthorn Press.

Negra, D. (2009). *What a girl wants? Reclamation of the self in postfeminism*. London: Routledge.

Neihart, M. (1999). The impact of giftedness on psychological well-being. *Roeper Review*, 22:1, 10–17.

Neisser, U., Boodoo, G., Bouchard, T., Boykin, A. W., Brody, N., Ceci, S., Halpern, D., Loehlin, J., Perloff, R., Sternberg, R., & Urbina, S. (1996). Intelligence: Knowns and unknowns. *American Psychologist*, 51, 77–101.

Nespor, J., & Barylske, J. (1991). Narrative discourse and teacher knowledge. *American Educational Research Journal*, 2:8, 805–823.

New York magazine. (2007). Naomi Wolf doesn't watch 'Gossip Girl' but wants to. Interview with Naomi Wolf. Retrieved May 11, 2016, from http://nymag.com/daily/intelligencer/2007/12/naomi_wolf_doesnt_watch_gossip.html.

Nyström, A. S. (2014). Negotiating achievement: Students' gendered and classed constructions of (un)equal ability. In U. Maylor & K. Bhopal (Eds.), *Educational inequalities: Difference and diversity in schools and higher education* (pp. 87–101). London: Routledge.

Oakes, J., & Lipton, M. (1994). Foreword to Sapon-Shavin, M. (1994). *Playing favourites: Gifted education and the disruption of community* (pp. ix–xvi). Albany: State University of New York Press.

O'Connor, C., & Joffe, H. (2013). How has neuroscience affected lay understandings of personhood? A review of the evidence. *Public Understanding of Science*, 22:3, 254–268.

O'Connor, C., & Joffe, H. (2014). Gender on the brain: A case study of science communication in the new media environment. *PloS One*, 9:10, 1–15.

O'Connor, C., Rees, G., & Joffe, H. (2014). Neuroscience in the public sphere. *Neuron*, 74, 220–226.

O'Connor, H., Madge, C., Shaw, R., & Wellens, J. (2008). Internet based interviewing. In N. Fielding, R. M. Lee, & G. Blank (Eds.), *The Sage handbook of online research method* (pp. 271–289). London: Sage.

Ochse, R. (1990). *Before the gates of excellence: The determinants of creative genius.* Cambridge: Cambridge University Press.

Ofcom (Office of Communications). (2007). *The future of children's television programming.* Retrieved May 15, 2016, from http://stakeholders.ofcom.org.uk/binaries/consultations/kidstv/summary/kidstv.pdf.

Ofcom (Office of Communications). (2010). *Children's media literacy in the nations.* Retrieved from http://stakeholders.ofcom.org.uk/market-data-research/other/research-publications/childrens/childrensmedialitsummary/.

Ofcom (Office of Communications). (2011). *UK children's media literacy.* Retrieved from http://stakeholders.ofcom.org.uk/binaries/research/media-literacy/media-lit11/childrens.pdf.

Ofcom (Office of Communications). (2013). *Children and parents: Media use and attitudes report.* Retrieved December 14, 2013, from http://stakeholders.ofcom.org.uk/binaries/research/media-literacy/october-2013/research07Oct2013.pdf.

Ofcom (Office of Communications). (2015). *The communications market (12th annual communications market report).* Retrieved November 12, 2015, from http://stakeholders.ofcom.org.uk/market-data-research/market-data/communications-market-reports/cmr15/.

Ofsted (Office for Standards in Education, Children's Services and Skills). Inspection reports of participating schools. Retrieved December 3, 2010, from http://www.ofsted.gov.uk/.

Ong, A. (2004). *Higher learning: Educational availability and flexible citizenship in global space.* Buckingham: Open University Press.

Osgerby, B. (2004). 'So who's got time for adults!' Femininity, consumption and the development of teen TV – From *Gidget* to *Buffy*. In G. Davis & K. Dickinson Kay (Eds.), *Teen TV: Genre, consumption & identity.* London: British Film Institute.

Ouliette, L. (2002). Victims no more: Postfeminism, television and *Ally McBeal. Communication Review*, 5, 315–335.

Paechter, C. (1998). *Educating the other.* London: Falmer.

Paechter, C. (2013). Young women online: Collaboratively constructing identities. *Pedagogy, Culture & Society*, 21:1, 111–127.

Parke, M., & Wilson, N. (Eds.). (2011). *Theorizing Twilight: Critical essays on what's at stake in a post-vampire world.* Jefferson, NC: McFarlane & Co.

Parsons, T. (1942). Age and sex in the social structure of the United States. *American Sociological Review*, 7, 604–616.

Passmore, S. (2000). Health education unit, Birmingham LA. Quoted in Watson-Smyth, K. (2000). High-flying schools put girls at greater risk of eating disorders. *Independent*, July 6.

Passow, A. (2004). The nature of giftedness and talent. In R. Sternberg (Ed.), *Definitions and conceptions of giftedness* (pp. 1–11). London: Sage.

Paule, M. (2012). Girls, the divine and the prime time. *Feminist Theology*, 20:3, 200–217.

Pearson, R. (2005). The writer/producer in American television. In M. Hammond & L. Mazdon (Eds.), *The contemporary television series* (pp. 11–26). Edinburgh: Edinburgh University Press.

Pearson, R. (2010). Fandom in the digital era. *Popular Communication*, 8, 1–12.

Penman, R., & Turnbull, S. (2007). *Media literacy – Concepts, research and regulatory issues*. Australian Communications and Media Authority. Retrieved March 15, 2010, from http://www.acma.gov.au/webwr/_assets/main/lib310665/media_literacy_report.pdf.

Perakyla, A. (2005). Analysing talk and text. In N. Denzin & Y. Lincoln (Eds.), *The Sage handbook of qualitative research* (3rd ed., pp. 869–886). London: Sage.

Perryman, N. (2008). *Doctor Who* and the convergence of media. *Convergence: The International Journal of Research into New Media Technologies*, 14:1, 21–39.

Peter, J., & Valkenburg, P. (2006). Adolescents' Internet use: Testing the "disappearing digital divide" versus the "emerging digital differentiation" approach. *Poetics*, 34:4/5, 293–305.

Peters, M. (2001). National education policy constructions of the 'knowledge economy': Towards a critique. *Journal of Educational Enquiry*, 2:1, 1–22.

Petersen, K., & Wilson, J. (1976). *Women artists: Recognition and reappraisal from the early middle ages to the twentieth century*. New York: E. P. Dutton.

Pew Research Center. (2015). *Home broadband 2015*. Retrieved May 4, 2011, from http://www.pewinternet.org/2015/12/21/home-broadband-2015/.

Phelan, S. (2007). Messy grand narrative or analytical blind spot? *Comparative European Politics*, 5, 328–338.

Philo, G. (2008). Active audiences and the construction of public knowledge. *Journalism Studies*, 9:4, 535–544.

Pickersgill, M. (2013). The social life of the brain: Neuroscience in society. *Current Sociology* 31:3, 322–340.

Piirto, J. (1991). Why are there so few? (Creative women: Visual artists, mathematicians, musicians). *Roeper Review*, 13:3, 142–147.

Pinar, W., Reynolds, W., Slattery, P., & Taubman, P. (1995). *Understanding curriculum: An introduction to the study of historical and contemporary curriculum discourses*. New York: Peter Lang.

Pipher, M. (1994). *Reviving Ophelia: Saving the selves of adolescent girls*. New York: Ballantine.

Plato. (2008). *Phaedrus* (Trans. B. Jowett). Project Gutenberg edition. Retrieved April 21, 2010, from http://www.gutenberg.org/files/1636/1636-h/1636-h.htm.

Playfair, L. (1855). *British eloquence: Lectures and addresses*. Retrieved November 7, 2009, from http://archive.org/stream/britisheloquenc01aldegoog/britisheloquenc 01aldegoog_djvu.txt.

Plummer, K. (1995). *Telling sexual stories: Power, change and social worlds*. London: Routledge.

Pollock, F. (1976). Empirical research into public opinion. In P. Connerton (Ed.), *Critical sociology* (pp. 24–49). Harmondsworth: Penguin.

Pomerantz, E., Rydell-Altermatt, E., & Saxon, J. (2002). Mental distress and grades: Do girls have the edge over boys at school yet suffer more mental distress? *Journal of Educational Psychology*, 94, 396–404.

Pomerantz, S., & Raby, R. (2011). 'Oh, she's so smart': Girls' complex engagements with post/feminist narratives of academic success. *Gender and Education*, 23:5, 549–564.

Pomerantz, S., & Raby, R. (2015). Reading smart girls: Post-nerds in post-feminist popular culture. In C. Bradford & M. Reimer (Eds.). *Girls, texts, cultures*. Winnipeg: Wilfred Laurier University Press.

Poster, M. (1984). Foucault and the tyranny of Greece. In D. Hoy (Ed.), *Foucault: A critical reader*. Oxford: Blackwell.

Poster, M. (1997). Cyberdemocracy: Internet and the public sphere. In D. Porter (Ed.), *Internet culture* (pp. 201–217). New York: Routledge.

Potter, A. (2012). It's a small world after all: New media constellations and Disney's rising star – the global success of *High School Musical*. *International Journal of Cultural Studies*, 15:2, 117–130.

Potter, J., & Hepburn, A. (2008). Discursive constructionism. In J. Holstein & J. Gubrium (Eds.), *Handbook of constructionist research* (pp. 275–293). New York: Guilford.

Potter, J., & Wetherell, M. (1994). Analyzing discourse. In A. Bryman & R. Burgess (Eds.), *Analyzing qualitative data*. London: Routledge.

Power, S. (2000). Educational pathways into the middle classes. *British Journal of Sociology of Education*, 21:2, 133–145.

Pufall-Jones, E., & Mistry, J. (2010). Navigating across cultures: Narrative constructions of lived experience. *Journal of Ethnographic & Qualitative Research*, 4:3, 151–167.

QCA. (2001). *Working with gifted and talented children: Guidance pack*. Sudbury: QCA.

Quirke, P. (No date). Adult education and the public library in 19th century Wolverhampton. Retrieved June 30, 2010, from http://www.historywebsite.co.uk/.

Raby, R., & Pomerantz, S. (2015). Playing it down/playing it up: Girls' strategic negotiations of academic success. *British Journal of Sociology of Education*, 36:4, 507–525.

Radway, J. (1984). *Reading the romance*. Chapel Hill: University of North Carolina Press.

Radway, J. (2001). *Girls, zines, and the miscellaneous production of subjectivity in an age of unceasing circulation*. Lecture presented for the Center for Interdisciplinary Studies of Writing, Speaker Series No. 18. Retrieved December 15, 2009, from http://www.infoamerica.org/documentos_pdf/radway01.pdf.

Ramazanoglu, C. (1993). *Up against Foucault: Explorations of some tensions between Foucault and feminism*. New York: Taylor & Francis.

Read, B., Francis, B., & Skelton, C. (2011). Gender, popularity and notions of in/authenticity amongst 12-year-old to 13-year-old school girls. *British Journal of Sociology of Education*, 32:2, 169–183.

Reay, D. (2001a). The paradox of contemporary femininities in education: Combining fluidity with fixity. In B. Francis & C. Skelton (Eds.), *Investigating gender: Contemporary perspectives in education* (pp. 152–163). Buckingham: Open University Press.

Reay, D. (2001b). Finding or losing yourself: Working-class relationships to education. *Journal of Education Policy*, 16:4, 333–346.

Reay, D. (2006). The zombie stalking English schools: Social class and educational inequality. *British Journal of Educational Studies*, 54:3, 288–307.

Reay, D. (2008a). Tony Blair, the promotion of the 'active' educational citizen, and middle-class hegemony. *Oxford Review of Education*, 34:6, 639–650.

Reay, D. (2008b). Class, authenticity and the transition to higher education for mature students. *Sociological Review*, 50:3, 398–418.

Reay, D., & Ball, S. (1998). 'Making their minds up': Family dynamics of school choice. *British Educational Research Journal*, 24:4, 431–444.

Reay, D., David, M., & Ball, S. (2005). *Degrees of choice: Social class, race and gender in higher education.* Stoke on Trent: Trentham Books.

Reay, D., & William, D. (1999). 'I'll be a nothing': Structure, agency and the construction of identity through assessment. *British Educational Research Journal,* 25:3, 343–354.

Reis, S. (1998). *Work left undone: Compromises and challenges of talented females.* Mansfield Center, CT: Creative Learning Press.

Reis, S. (2003). Gifted girls, twenty-five years later: Hopes realized and new challenges found. *Roeper Review,* 25, 154–156.

Reissman, C. K. (2001). Analysis of personal narratives. In J. F. Gubrium & J. A. Holstein (Eds.), *Handbook of interviewing* (pp. 695–710). London: Sage.

Renold, E. (2001). 'Square-girls', femininity and the negotiation of academic success in the primary school. *British Educational Research Journal,* 27:5, 577–588.

Renold, E., & Allan, A. (2006). Bright and beautiful: High achieving girls, ambivalent femininities, and the feminization of success in the primary school. *Discourse: Studies in the Cultural Politics of Education,* 27:4, 457–473.

Renold, E., & Ringrose, J. (2008). Regulation and rupture: Mapping tween and teenage girls' resistance to the heterosexual matrix. *Feminist Theory,* 9, 313–338.

Richards, L. (2002). Qualitative computing – A methods revolution? *International Journal of Social Research Methodology,* 5:3, 236–276.

Rimer, S. (2007). 'Supergirl meltdown': For girls, it's be yourself, and be perfect too. *New York Times.* Retrieved April 3, 2009, from http://www.nytimes.com/2007/04/01/education/01girls.html?_r=1&oref=slogin.

Ringrose, J. (2006). A new universal mean girl: Examining the discursive construction and social regulation of a new feminine pathology. *Feminism & Psychology,* 16, 405–424.

Ringrose, J. (2007). Successful girls? Complicating post-feminist, neo-liberal discourses of educational achievement and gender equality. *Gender and Education,* 19:4, 471–489.

Ringrose, J. (2012). *Postfeminist education?* Abingdon: Routledge.

Ringrose, J., Harvey, L., Gill, R., & Livingstone, S. (2013). Teen girls, sexual double standards and 'sexting': Gendered value in digital image exchange. *Feminist Theory,* 14:3.

Ringrose, J., & Walkerdine, V. (2008). Regulating the abject: The TV make-over as site of neo-liberal reinvention toward bourgeois femininity. *Feminist Media Studies,* 8:3, 227–246.

Riordan, E. (2001). Commodified agents and empowered girls: Consuming and producing feminism. *Journal of Communication Enquiry,* 25:3, 279–297.

Roberts, D. (2000). Media and youth: Access, exposure and privatisation. *Journal of Adolescent Health,* 27:2, 8–14.

Roberts, D., Foehr, U., & Rideout, V. (2005). *Generation M: Media in the lives of 8–18 year-olds.* Menlo Park, CA: Kaiser Family Foundation.

Rodriguez, A. (1998). Busting open the meritocracy myth: Rethinking equity and student achievement in science education. *The entity from which ERIC acquires the content, including journal, organization, and conference names, or by means of online submission from the author.Journal of Women and Minorities in Science and Engineering,* 4:2/3, 195–216.

Roeser, R., Galloway, M., Casey-Cannon, S., Watson, C., Keller, L., & Tan, E. (2008). Identity representations in patterns of school achievement and well-being among early adolescent girls: Variable- and person-centered approaches. *Journal of Early Adolescence*, 28, 115–152.

Rose, N. (1996). Power and subjectivity: Critical history and psychology. In C. Graumann & K. Gergen (Eds.), *Historical dimensions of psychological discourse* (pp. 103–124). Cambridge: Cambridge University Press.

Rose, N. (1999). *Governing the soul: The shaping of the private self.* London: Routledge.

Ross, S. (2002). *Super(natural). Women: Female heroes, their friends and their fans.* Unpublished doctoral dissertation, University of Austin, TX. Cited in Lotz, A. D., & Ross, M. (2004). Towards ethical cyberspace audience research: Strategies for using the Internet for television audience studies. *Journal of Broadcasting of Electronic Media*, 48:3, 501–512.

Ross, S. M., & Stein, L. E. (2008). *Teen television: Essays on programming and fandom.* New York: McFarland.

Rosteck, T. (2001). Readers and a cultural rhetorical studies. *Rhetoric Review* 20:1/2, 51–56.

Rousseau, J.-J. (1758). Lettre a M. d'Alembert sur US Spectacles (Trans. M. J. Citron, 1989 ed.). Retrieved November 18, 2009, from UCLA online archive: http://www.archive.org/stream/uclahistoricaljo14univ/uclahistoricaljo14univ_djvu.txt.

Rowling, J. K. (2000). *Harry Potter and the goblet of fire.* London: Bloomsbury.

Rowsell, J., & Pahl, K. (2007). Sedimented identities in texts: Instances of practice. *Reading Research Quarterly*, 42:3, 388–404.

Royster, J. (1989). Contending forces: The struggle of black women for intellectual affirmation. Columbus, OH, March 1. In Lunsford, A. A., & Ede, L. S. (1990). Rhetoric in a new key: Women and collaboration. *Rhetoric Review*, 8:2, 234–241.

Ruo, M., & Toro, M. (2011). *Adolescence and adultescence.* Rome: CISU.

Rustin, N. (2005). Mary Lou Williams plays like a man: Gender, genius and difference in black music discourse. *South Atlantic Quarterly*, 104:3, 445–462.

Sade-Beck, L. (2004). Internet ethnography: Online and offline. *International Journal of Qualitative Methods*, 3, 45–51.

Saltmarsh, S. (2009). Becoming economic subjects: Agency, consumption and popular culture in early childhood. *Discourse*, 30:1, 47–59.

Sammons, P. (1995). Gender, ethnic and socio-economic differences in attainment and progress: A longitudinal analysis of student achievement over 9 years. *British Educational Research Journal*, 21:4, 465–485.

Sandberg, S. (2013). *Lean in: Women work, and the will to lead.* New York: Random House.

Sapon-Shavin, M. (1994). *Playing favourites: Gifted education and the disruption of community.* Albany: State University of New York Press.

SAT scores: Ranking. Retrieved March 3, 2012, from http://www.satscores.us/sat_scores_by_score.asp?score=2300.

Savage, G. (2008). Silencing the everyday experiences of youth? Deconstructing issues of subjectivity and popular/corporate culture in the English classroom. *Discourse: Studies in the Cultural Politics of Education*, 29:1, 51–68.

Savicki, V. (1996). Gender language style and group composition in Internet discussion groups. *Journal of Computer-Mediated Communication*, 2:3. Retrieved May 4, 2011, from http://jcmc.indiana.edu/vol2/issue3/savicki.html on 2.11.2010.

Scardigno, F. (2009). The informal choices of Italian young people: Between increase and erosion of family cultural capital. *Italian Journal of Sociology of Education*, 2, 230–252.

Scheurich, J. (1997). *Research method in the postmodern*. London: Falmer Press.

Schiebinger, L. (1989). *The mind has no sex*. Cambridge: Harvard University Press.

Schlinger, H. (2003). The myth of intelligence. *Psychological Record*, 53, 15–32.

Schober, B., Reimann, R., & Wagner, P. (2004). Is research on gender-specific under-achievement in gifted girls an obsolete topic? New findings on an often discussed issue. *High Ability Studies*, 15, 43–62.

Schofield Clarke, L. (2003). *From angels to aliens: Teenagers, the media, and the supernatural*. Oxford: Oxford University Press.

Schopenhauer, A. (2008). *The world as will and presentation* (Vol. I, Ed. D. Kolakm, Trans. R. Aquila, with D. Carus). Upper Saddle River, NJ: Pearson, Prentice Hall.

Schroder, K., Drotner, K., Kline, S., & Murray, C. (2003). *Researching audiences: A practical guide to methods in media audience analysis*. London: Hodder Arnold Press.

Schuler, P. (1997). Characteristics and perceptions of perfectionism in gifted adolescents in a rural school environment. ETD Collection for University of Connecticut. Retrieved May 4, 2011, from http://digitalcommons.uconn.edu/dissertations/AAI9737431.

Schultz, K. (1999). Identity narratives: Stories from the lives of urban adolescent females. *Urban Review*, 31:1, 79–106.

Scolari, C. (2009). The grammar of hypertelevision: An identikit of convergence-age fiction television (or, how television simulates new interactive media). *Journal of Visual Literacy*, 28:1, 28–49.

Scott, J. (1988). Deconstructing equality-versus-difference: Or, the uses of poststructuralist theory for feminism. *Feminist Studies*, 14:1, 33–51.

Selwyn, N. (2004). Reconsidering political and popular understandings of the digital divide. *New Media & Society*, 6:3, 341–362.

Selwyn, N., & Facer, K. (2007). *Beyond the digital divide: Rethinking digital inclusion for the 21st century*. Bristol: FutureLab. Retrieved February 2, 2011, from http://www.futurelab.org.uk/resources/documents/opening_education/Digital_Divide.pdf.

Seror, J. (2005). Computers and qualitative data analysis: Paper, pens, and highlighters vs. screen, mouse, and keyboard. *TESOL Quarterly*, 39:2, 321–328.

Sfard, A., & Prusak, A. (2005). Telling identities: In search of an analytic tool for investigating learning as a culturally shaped activity. *Educational Researcher*, 34:4, 14–22.

SFR (Statistical First Release). (2007). National statistics first release: Participation rates in higher education: Academic years 1999/2000–2005/2006 (provisional). Retrieved May 4, 2011, from http://www.education.gov.uk/rsgateway/DB/SFR/s000716/SFR10_2007v1.pdf.

Sharkey, A., & Shields, R. (2008). Abject citizenship – Rethinking exclusion and inclusion: Participation, criminality and community at a small town youth centre. *Children's Geographies*, 6:3, 239–256.

Showalter, E. (1982). *A literature of their own*. London: Virago.

Shugart, H., Waggoner, C., & O'Brien Hallstein, D. (2001). Mediating third wave feminism: Appropriation as postmodern media practice. *Critical Studies in Media Communication*, 18, 194–209.

Siapera, E. (2004). From couch potatoes to cybernauts? The expanding notion of the audience in TV web sites. *New Media & Society*, 6:2, 155–172.

Sibielski, R. (2010). 'Nothing hurts the cause more than that': Veronica Mars and the business of the backlash. *Feminist Media Studies*, 10:3, 321–334.

Sim, J. (1998). Collecting and analysing qualitative data: Issues raised by the focus group. *Journal of Advanced Nursing*, 28:2, 345–352.

Simmons, R. (2010). *The curse of the good girl: Raising authentic girls with courage and confidence*. London: Penguin.

Sinanan, J., Graham, C., & Zhong Jie, K. (2014). Crafted assemblage: Young women's 'lifestyle' blogs, consumerism and citizenship in Singapore. *Visual Studies*, 29:2, 201–213.

Singh, A. (2008). *Doctor Who* star Billie Piper in TV mystery. *Daily Telegraph*. Retrieved November 23, 2011, from http://www.telegraph.co.uk/news/celebritynews/2182328/Doctor-Who-star-Billie-Piper-in-TV-mystery.html.

Silverman, D. (2013). *Doing qualitative research*. London: Sage.

Skeggs, B. (1997). *Formations of class and gender: Becoming respectable*. London: Sage.

Skeggs, B. (2005). The making of class and gender through visualizing moral subject formation. *Sociology*, 39, 965–981.

Skeggs, B. (2009). The moral economy of person production: The class relations of self-performance on 'reality' television. *Sociological Review*, 57;4, 626–644.

Skelton, C. (2001). Typical boys? Theorizing masculinity in educational settings. In B. Francis & C. Skelton (Eds.), *Investigating gender: Contemporary perspectives in education* (pp. 164–176). Buckingham: Open University Press.

Skelton, C., & Francis, B. (Eds.). (2003). *Boys and girls in the primary classroom*. Milton Keynes: Open University Press.

Skelton, C., & Francis, B. (2012). The 'Renaissance child': High achievement and gender in late modernity. *International Journal of Inclusive Education*, 16:4, 441–459.

Skelton, C., Francis, B., & Read, B. (2010). Brains before 'beauty'? High achieving girls, school and gender identities. *Educational Studies*, 36:2, 185–194.

Skelton, T. (2001). Girls in the club: Researching working class girls' lives. *Ethics, Place and Environment*, 4:2, 167–173.

Skelton, T., & Valentine, G. (1998). *Cool places: Geographies of youth cultures*. London: Routledge.

Skinner, E. (2004). 'Teenage addiction': Adolescent girls drawing upon popular culture texts as mentors for writing in an after-school writing club. *National Reading Conference Yearbook*, 56, 344–361.

Smithers, A., & Robinson, P. (2012). *Educating the highly able*. Research report for the Sutton Trust. Retrieved July 16, 2012, from http://www.suttontrust.com/research/educating-the-highly-able/.

Smythe, D. W. (1994). Communications: Blindspot of Western Marxism. In T. Guback (Ed.), *Counterclockwise: Perspectives on communication* (pp. 263–291). Boulder, CO: Westview Press.

Soyland, A., & Kendall, G. (1997). Abusing Foucault: Methodology, critique and subversion. *History and Philosophy of Psychology*, 9–17.

Spelman, E. (1990). *Inessential woman*. Boston: Beacon Press.

Spencer, J. (1986). *The rise of the woman novelist from Aphra Benn to Jane Austen*. Oxford: Basil Blackwell.

Spender, D. (1981). Education: The patriarchal paradigm and the response to feminism. In D. Spender (Ed.), *Men's studies modified: The impact of feminism on the academic disciplines* (pp. 155–175). New York: Teachers College Press.

Spender, D. (1986). *Mothers of the novel*. London: Pandora.

Spicer, A. (2002). *Film noir*. Essex: Pearson.

Spieler, S. (2012). Stephenie Meyer's *Twilight* series and the 'post(-)ing' of feminism. *As/Peers: Emerging Voices in American Studies*, 5, 119–144. Retrieved April 12, 2012, from http://www.aspeers.com/2012/spieler?fulltext.

Spiggle, S. (1998). Creating the frame and the narrative: From text to hypertext. In B. Stern (Ed.), *Representing consumers: Voices, views, and visions* (pp. 156–189). London: Routledge.

Stables, A., Murakami, K., McIntosh, S., & Martin, S. (2014). Conceptions of effort among students, teachers and parents within an English secondary school. *Research Papers in Education*, 29:5, 626–648.

Stacey, J. (1988). Can there be a feminist ethnography? *Women's Studies International Forum*, 11, 21–27.

Stadler, G. (1999). Louisa May Alcott's queer geniuses. *American Literature*, 71:4, 657–677.

Stamatkis, E., Hillsdon, M., Mishra, G., Hamer, M., & Marmot, M. (2009). Television viewing and other screen-based entertainment in relation to multiple socioeconomic status indicators and area deprivation: The Scottish Health Survey 2003. *Journal of Epidemiology and Community Health*, 63:9, 734–740.

Steemers, J. (2004). Europe as a television market. In J. Sinclair & G. Turner (Eds.), *Contemporary world television* (pp. 35–38). London: British Film Institute.

Steger, M. B., & James, P. (2013). Levels of subjective globalization: Ideologies, imaginaries, ontologies. *Perspectives on Global Development and Technology*, 12:1–2, 23.

Steier, F. (1995). *Research and reflexivity*. London: Sage.

Steinke, J., Applegate, B., Lapinski, M., Ryan, L., & Long, M. (2012). Gender differences in adolescents' wishful identification with scientist characters on television. *Science Communication*, 34:2, 163–199.

Stern, S. (2002). Virtually speaking: Girls' self-disclosure on the WWW. *Women's Studies in Communication*, 25:2, 223–253.

Stern, S. (2004a). Expressions of identity online: Prominent features and gender differences in adolescents' World Wide Web home pages. *Journal of Broadcasting & Electronic Media*, 48, 218–243.

Stern, S. (2004b). Studying adolescents online: A consideration of ethical issues. In E. Buchanan (Ed.), *Readings in virtual research ethics: Issues and controversies* (pp. 274–287). Hershey, PA: Idea Group.

Stern, S. (2008). Producing sites, exploring identities: Youth online authorship. In D. Buckingham (Ed.), *Youth, identity, and digital media* (pp. 95–118). John D. & Catherine T. MacArthur Foundation Series on Digital Media and Learning. Cambridge, MA: MIT Press.

Sternberg, R. (1988). Abilities are forms of developing expertise. *Educational Researcher*, 27:3, 11–20.

Sternberg, R. (2004). *Definitions and conceptions of giftedness*. Thousand Oaks, CA: Corwin Press.

Sternberg, R., & Davidson, J. E. (2005). *Conceptions of giftedness*. Cambridge: Cambridge University Press.

Stiver, I. (1982). Work inhibitions in women. In A. Kaplan & J. Jordan (Eds.), *Women's growth in connection: Writings from the Stone Center* (pp. 223–236). New York: Guilford Press.

Stollery, M. (2002). Eisenstein, Shub and the gender of the author as producer. *Film History*, 14:1, 87–99.

Stone, A. R. (1996). *The war of desire and technology at the close of the mechanical age*. Cambridge, MA: MIT Press.

Strinati, D. (1995). *Introduction to theories of popular culture*. London: Routledge.

Subrah-manyam, K., Greenfield, P., & Tynes, B. (2004). Constructing sexuality and identity in an online teen chat room. *Applied Developmental Psychology*, 25, 651–666.

Suler, J. (2004). The online disinhibition effect. *Cyberpsychology & Behavior*, 7:3.

Summers, S. (2010). 'Twilight is so anti-feminist that I want to cry': *Twilight* fans finding and defining feminism on the World Wide Web. *Computers & Composition*, 27:4, 315–323.

Sutherland Harris, A., & Nochlin, L. (1976). *Women artists, 1550–1950*. New York: Knopf.

Sydie, R. (1989). Humanism, patronage and the question of women's artistic genius in the Italian Renaissance. *Journal of Historical Sociology*, 2:3, 175–205.

Taesler, P., & Janneck, M. (2010). Emoticons and impression formation: The impact of emoticon use on the perception of online communication partners. *Gruppendynamik und Organisationsberatung*, 41:4, 375–384.

Tally, P. (2005). Re-imagining girlhood: Hollywood and the tween girl film market. In C. Mitchell & J. Reid-Walsh (Eds.), *Seven going on seventeen: Tween studies in the culture of girlhood* (pp. 311–329). New York: Peter Lang.

Tamboukou, M. (1999). Writing genealogies: An exploration of Foucault's strategies for doing research. *Discourse: Studies in the Cultural Politics of Education*, 20:2, 201–217.

Taylor, D., & Vintges, K. (2004). *Feminism and the final Foucault*. Urbana: University of Illinois Press.

Taylor, M. (2005). University gender gap widens as women increase their lead. *Guardian*, January 27. Retrieved May 4, 2011, from http://www.guardian.co.uk/uk/2005/jan/27/highereducation.students.

Terman, L. (1926). *Genetic studies of genius*. Palo Alto, CA: Stanford University Press.

Terman L., & Oden, M. (1951). The Stanford studies of the gifted. In P. Witty (Ed.), *The gifted child*. New York: Heath.

thinkbroadband.com. (2011). Estimated speeds in the UK. Map retrieved February 12, 2011, from http://maps.thinkbroadband.com/#!lat=55.37805099893188&lng=-3.435972999999992&zoom=6&type=terrain&estimated-speeds.

Thomas, A. (2006). 'MSN was the next big thing after Beanie Babies': Children's virtual experiences as an interface to their identities and their everyday lives. *E-Learning*, 3:2, 126–142.

Thomas, N., Mulligan M., & Wiramihardja, L. (2000). *How European teens consume media: Understanding the impact of the media meltdown on 12- to 17-year-olds*. Forrester Research.com, December 4, 2009. Retrieved May 19, 2015, from https://www.forrester.com/report/How+European+Teens+Consume+Media/-/E-RES53763.

Thrupp, M. (2001). School-level education policy under New Labour and New Zealand Labour: A comparative update. *British Journal of Educational Studies*, 49:2, 187–212.

Thrupp, M. (2002). Education policy and social change. *British Journal of Sociology of Education*, 23:2, 321–332.

Tierney, W. (2002). Getting real: Representing reality. *International Journal of Qualitative Studies in Education*, 15:4, 385–398.

Tinkler, P., & Jackson, C. (2014). The past in the present: Historicizing contemporary debates in gender and education. *Gender and Education*, 26:1, 70–86Tomas, M., & Gengnagel, V. (2011). *Enabling sovereignty? The ethical limits of hegemony.* Paper presented at the 6th Interpretative Policy Analysis Conference, Cardiff, June 23–25. Retrieved February 12, 2012, from http://www.ipa-2011.cardiff.ac.uk/wp-content/uploads/file_uploads/16/16-Marttila%20&%20Gengnagel.pdf.

Tomlinson, S. (2003). New Labour and education. *Children and Society*, 17:3, 195–204.

Tomlinson, S. (2008). Gifted, talented and high ability: Selection for education in a one-dimensional world. *Oxford Review of Education*, 34:1, 59–74.

Tonelli, G. (1966). Kant's early theory of genius (1770–1779). *Journal of the History of Philosophy*, 4:3, 209–202.

Trudgill, P. (2001). *Sociolinguistics: An introduction to language and society.* London: Penguin.

Turkle, S. (1994). Constructions and reconstructions of self in virtual reality: Playing in MUDs. *Mind, Culture, and Activity*, 1:3, 158–167.

Turkle, S. (1995). *Life on the screen: Identity in the age of the Internet.* New York: Simon & Schuster.

UCAS statistical services. Retrieved October 6, 2012, from http://www.ucas.com/about_us/stat_services/stats_online/data_tables/gender.

Valdivia, A., & Bettivia, R. (1999). A guided tour through one adolescent girl's culture. In S. Mazzarella & N. Pecora (Eds.), *Growing up girls: Popular culture and the construction of identity* (pp. 159–174). New York: Peter Lang.

Valkenburg, P., & Buijzen, M. (2003). Children, computer games and the Internet. *Netherlands Journal of Social Sciences*, 39:1, 23–34.

Valkenburg, P., & Peter, J. (2007). Preadolescents' and adolescents' online communication and their closeness to friends. *Developmental Psychology*, 43:2, 267–277.

Valkenburg, P., Schouten, A., & Peter, J. (2005). Adolescents' identity experiments on the Internet. *New Media & Society*, 7:3, 83–402.

Van Damme, E., & Van Bauwel, S. (2010). 'I don't wanna be anything other than me': A case study on gender representations of teenagers in American teen drama series *One Tree Hill*. *Interactions: Studies in Communication & Culture*, 2:1, 17–33.

Van Damme, E., & Van Bauwel, S. (2012). Sex as spectacle: An overview of gender and sexual scripts in teen series popular with Flemish teenagers. *Journal of Children and Media.* ifirst article retrieved May 12, 2012, from http://www.tandfonline.com/doi/abs/10.1080/17482798.2012.673499.

Vanderkam, L. (2008). Blazing a trail for women in math: Moon Duchin. *Scientific American*, 6. Retrieved March 30, 2010, from http://www.scientificamerican.com/article.cfm?id=blazing-a-trail-for-women&sc=rss.

van Deursen, A., & van Dijk, J. (2011). Internet skills and the digital divide. *New Media & Society*, 13:6, 893–911.

van Dijck, J. (2005). Users like you? Theorizing agency in user-generated content. *Media, Culture & Society* 31:1, 41–58.

van Dijk, J., & Hacker, K. (2003). The digital divide as a complex and dynamic phenomenon. *Information Society*, 19, 315–326.

Vaughn, S., Schumm, J., & Sinagub, J. (1996). *Focus group interviews in psychology and education*. London: Sage.

Walberg, H., Rasher, S., & Hase, K. (1978). IQ correlates with high eminence. *Gifted Child Quarterly*, 22:2, 196–200.

Walker, A. (1976). Saving the life that is your own: The importance of models in the artist's life. In H. Arnett Ervin (Ed.), *African American literary criticism, 1773 to 2000* (pp. 155–161). New York: Twayne.

Walker, L., & Logan, A. (2009). *Using digital technologies to promote inclusive practices in education*. Bristol: Future Lab. Retrieved February 2, 2011, from http://www.futurelab.org.uk/resources/documents/handbooks/digital_inclusion_handbook.pdf.

Walker, R. (1995). *To be real: Telling the truth and changing the face of feminism*. New York: Anchor.

Walkerdine, V. (1988). *The mastery of reason: Cognitive development and the production of rationality*. London: Routledge.

Walkerdine, V. (1989). *Counting girls out*. London: Virago.

Walkerdine, V. (1990). *Schoolgirl fictions*. New York: Verso.

Walkerdine, V. (1993). Daddy's gonna buy you a dream to cling to (and mummy's gonna love you just as much as she can). In D. Buckingham (Ed.), *Reading audiences: Young people and the media* (pp. 74–88). Manchester: Manchester University Press.

Walkerdine, V. (1996). Subjectivity and social class: New directions for feminist psychology. *Feminism and Psychology*, 6:3, 355–360.

Walkerdine, V. (2003). Reclassifying upward mobility: Femininity and the neo-liberal subject. *Gender and Education*, 15:3, 237–248.

Walkerdine, V., Lucey, H., & Melody, J. (2001). *Growing up girl: Psycho-social explorations of gender and class*. Basingstoke: Palgrave Macmillan.

Warf, B., & Grimes, J. (1997). Cyberspace and geographical space. *Geographical Review*, 87:2, 259–274.

Wartella, E., & Mazzarella, S. (1990). An historical comparison of children's use of time and media: 1920s to 1980s. In R. Butsch (Ed.), *For fun and profit: The transformation of leisure into consumption* (pp. 173–194). Philadelphia: Temple.

Wartella, E., & Robb, M. (2008). Historical and recurring concerns about children's use of the mass media. In S. Calvert & B. Wilson (Eds.), *The handbook of children, media and development*. Oxford: Blackwell.

Weber, K. (2010). Exploding sexual binaries in *Buffy* and *Angel*. In E. Waggoner (Ed.), *Sexual rhetoric in the works of Joss Whedon: New essays* (pp. 248–262). London: McFarland & Co.

Webster, J., & Ksiazek, T. (2012). The dynamics of audience fragmentation: Public attention in an age of digital media. *Journal of Communication*, 62:1, 39–56.

Wee, V. (2008). Teen television and the WB television network. In S. Ross & L. Stein (Eds.), *Teen television: Essays on programming and fandom* (pp. 43–60). Jefferson, NC: McFarland.

Weedon, C. (1987). *Feminist practice and poststructuralism*. New York: Basil Blackwell.

Weiner, G., & Arnot, M. (1987). *Gender and the politics of schooling*. London: Hutchinson.

Weisberg, R. (1986). *Creativity: Genius and other myths*. New York: W. H. Freeman.

West, A., Pennell, H., & West, R. (2000). New Labour and school-based education in England: Changing the system of funding? *British Educational Research Journal*, 26:4, 523–536.

Whelahan, I. (2000). *Overloaded: Popular culture and the future of feminism.* London: Women's Press.

White, J. (2006). *Intelligence, destiny and education: The ideological roots of intelligence testing.* London: Routledge.

White, M., & Schwoch, J. (2006). *Questions of method in cultural studies.* Oxford: Blackwell.

Whiteman, N. (2012). *Undoing ethics: Rethinking practice in online research.* New York: Springer.

Wilcox, R. (1999). There will never be a 'very special' *Buffy*: *Buffy* and the monsters of teen life. *Journal of Popular Film and Television*, 27:2, 16–23.

Wilkinson, H., & Howard, M., with Gregory, S., Hayes, H., & Young, R. (1997). *Tomorrow's women.* London: Demos.

Wilkinson, S. (1999). Focus groups: A feminist method. *Psychology of Women Quarterly (Special Issue on Innovative Methods in Feminist Research, Part 2)*, 23:2, 221–244.

Willett, R. (2008a). Consumer citizens online: Structure, agency and gender in online participation. In D. Buckingham (Ed.), *Youth, identity and digital media.* John D. & Catherine T. MacArthur Foundation Series on Digital Media and Learning. Cambridge, MA: MIT Press.

Willett, R. (2008b). 'What you wear tells a lot about you': Girls dress up online. *Gender and Education*, 20:5, 421–434.

Willis, P. (1977). *Learning to labour.* Aldershot: Gower.

Willmott, P. (1969). *Adolescent boys of East London.* Harmondsworth: Penguin.

Wilson, V. (1997). Focus groups: A useful qualitative method for educational research? *British Educational Research Journal*, 23:2, 209–224.

Winstanley, C. (2004). *Too clever by half.* Stoke: Trentham Books.

Witty, P. (1951). *The gifted child.* New York: Heath.

Wolfenstein, M., & Leites, N. (1950). *Movies, a psychological study.* Glencoe, IL: Free Press.

Wollstonecraft, M. (1792). *A vindication of the rights of woman* (Ed. Miriam Brody, 1992 ed.). London: Penguin.

Woods, C. (1996). Gender differences in moral development and acquisition: A review of Kohlberg's and Gilligan's models of justice and care. *Social Behavior & Personality: An International Journal*, 24:4, 375–384.

Wrye, H. (2006). Deconstructing the unconscious saboteur: Composing a life with ambition and desire. *International Forum of Psychoanalysis*, 15:2, 70–80.

Youdell, D. (2004). Engineering school markets, constituting schools and subjectivating students: The bureaucratic, institutional and classroom dimensions of educational triage. *Journal of Education Policy*, 19:4, 407–431.

Young, E. (1759). *Conjectures on original composition.* Retrieved April 21, 2011, from Representative Poetry Online: https://tspace.library.utoronto.ca/html/1807/4350/displayprose7146.html?prosenum=16.

Zaslow, E. (2009). *Feminism, Inc. coming of age in girl power media culture.* New York: Palgrave Macmillan.

Ziegler, A., & Heller, K. A. (1997). Attribution retraining for self-related cognitions among women. *Gifted and Talented International*, 12, 36–41.

Zilsel, E. (2003). The social origins of modern science. In D. Raven, W. Krohn, & R. Cohen (Eds.), *Boston studies in the philosophy of science*. Dordrecht, Netherlands: Kluwer Academic.

Filmography

8 Simple Rules (2002–2005). Television series. Creator: Tracy Gamble. USA: Shady Acres Entertainment; Touchstone Television.

90210 (2008–2012). Creators: Gabe Sachs, Jeff Judah, Darren Star, & Rob Thomas. USA: Sachs/Judah Productions; CBS Productions.

Absolutely Fabulous (1992–2012). Television series. Creators: Jennifer Saunders & Dawn French. UK: French & Saunders Productions; BBC.

Big Brother (2000–2012). Creator: John de Mol, Endemol, NL. UK: Channel 4 Television Corporation.

Bones (2005–2012). Television series. Creator: Hart Hanson. USA: 20th Century Fox Television.

Buffy the Vampire Slayer (1997–2003). Television series. Creator: Joss Whedon. USA: Mutant Enemy Productions.

Charmed (1998–2006). Television series. Creator: Constance M. Burge. USA: Spelling Television; Warner Bros. Television.

CSI (2000–2012). Television series. Creators: Ann Donahue & Anthony E. Zuiker. USA: CBS Productions.

Dark Angel (2000–2002). Television series. Creators: James Cameron & Charles H. Eglee. USA: 20th Century Fox Television.

Dawson's Creek (1998–2003). Television series. Creator: Kevin Williamson. USA: Outerbank Entertainment, Columbia TriStar Television; Procter & Gamble Productions.

Dead Like Me (2003–2004). Television series. Creator: Bryan Fuller. USA: John Masius Productions; MGM Television.

Doctor Who (2005–2012) (Revived format). Television series. Original creator: Sydney Newman, C. E. Webber, & Donald Wilson. Writer: Russell T. Davis. UK: BBC.

Dora the Explorer (2000–2006). Cartoon. Creators: Chris Gifford, Valerie Walsh, & Eric Weiner. USA: Nickelodeon.

ER (1994–2009). Television series. Creator: Michael Crichton. USA: Warner Bros. Television.

Freaks and Geeks (1999–2000). Television series. Creator: Paul Feiger. USA: Dreamworks Television.

Friends (1994–2004). Television series. Creators: David Crane & Marta Kauffman. USA: Warner Bros. Television.

Gilmore Girls (2000–). Television series. Creator: Amy Sherman. USA: Warner Bros. Television.

Glee (2009–2012). Television series. Creators: Ian Brennan, Ryan Murphy, & Brad Falchuk. USA: 20th Century Fox Television.

Gossip Girl (2007–). Television series. Creators: Josh Schwartz & Stephanie Savage. USA: Warner Bros. Television.

Grey's Anatomy (2005–). Television series. Creator: Sondra Rhimes. USA: Shonda-Land, in association with the Mark Gordon Company & ABC Studios.

Harry Potter and the Goblet of Fire (2005). Film. Dir. Mike Newell. USA: Warner Bros.

High School Musical (2006). Film. Dir. Kenny Ortega. USA: Walt Disney Pictures.

House (2004–2012). Television series. Creator: David Shore. USA: Heel & Toe Films; Shore Z Productions; Bad Hat Harry Productions (all); NBC Universal Television Studio (2004–2007); Universal Media Studios (2007–2011); Universal Television (2004, 2011–2012).

Joan of Arcadia (2004–2005). Television series. Creator: Barbara Hall. USA: Barbara Hall Productions, CBS Productions, & Sony Pictures Television.

Legally Blonde (2001). Film. Dir. Robert Luketic. USA: MGM Studios.

Lizzie McGuire (2001–2004). Television series. Creator: Terri Minsky. USA: Stan Rogow Productions, Disney Enterprises.

Lizzie McGuire: The Movie (2003). Film: Dir. Jim Fall. USA: Walt Disney Pictures.

Malcolm in the Middle (2000–2006). Creator: Linwood Boomer. USA: 20th Century Fox Television.

Mean Girls (2004). Film. Dir. Mark Waters. USA: Paramount Pictures.

My So-Called Life (1994–1995). Television series. Creator: Winnie Holzman. USA: ABC Productions.

The OC (2003–2007). Television series. Creator: Josh Schwartz. USA: Wonderland Sound and Vision; Warner Bros. Television: College Hill Pictures, Inc.

One Tree Hill (2003–2012). Television series. Creator: Mark Schwahn. USA: Warner Bros. Television.

Pretty Little Liars (2010–). Television series. Creator: I. Marlene King. USA: Warner Bros. Television.

Scrubs (2001–2010). Television series. Creator: Bill Lawrence. USA: ABC Studios.

Tru Calling (2003–2005). Television series. Creator: Jon Harmon Feldman. USA: 20th Century Fox Television.

Twilight (2008). Film. Dir. Catherine Hardwicke. USA: Summit Entertainment.

Ugly Betty (2006–2010). Television series. Creator: Frenando Gaitan. USA: ABC Studios.

The Vampire Diaries (2009–). Television series. Developers: Kevin Williamson & Julie Plec. USA: Warner Bros. Television.

Veronica Mars (2004–2007). Television series. Creator: Rob Thomas. USA: Warner Bros. Television, Silver Pictures Television, Stu Segall Productions, Inc., & Rob Thomas Productions.

Wonderfalls (2004–2005). Television series. Creators: Todd Holland, Bryan Fuller, & Tim Minnear. USA/Canada: Walking Bud Productions; C.O.R.E.; Regency Television & 20th Century Fox Television.

Image Addresses

- Ugly Betty: http://3awohr3pyl7xwmh8k3b6e5sb.wpengine.netdna-cdn.com/wp-content/uploads/2015/07/ugly_betty-1024x819.jpg (1024 × 819)
- Lizzie McGuire: http://lizziemcguire.wikia.com/wiki/Lizzie_McGuire_(soundtrack) (892 × 900)
- Legally Blonde: http://dcl.vg.to/files/5n0h2ipfqjjk83895nqp.jpg (3246 × 2160)
- 90210: http://www.sidereel.com/posts/101897-news-90210-scoops-for-season-3 (1265 × 2048)

- Harry Potter's Hermione: http://www.themarysue.com/psychology-of-inspirational-women-hermione-granger/ (1383 × 2100)
- The OC: http://www.dvdca.com/download/9434–1/349OC_Season_3_.jpg (1841 × 2144)
- Veronica Mars: http://www.mike.sk/covers/Veronica.Mars-Season.1.jpg (1703 × 2171)

Index

For Product Safety Concerns and Information please contact our EU
representative GPSR@taylorandfrancis.com
Taylor & Francis Verlag GmbH, Kaufingerstraße 24, 80331 München, Germany